# TRANSFORMERS ™

# Matrix Quest

Simon    Furman
José     Delbo
Geoff    Senior
Dwayne   Turner

TITAN    BOOKS

TRANSFORMERS™: MATRIX QUEST
ISBN 1 84023 471 7
*DIAMOND EXCLUSIVE EDITION*
*ISBN 1 84023 507 1*

Published by Titan Books,
a division of Titan Publishing Group Ltd.
144 Southwark St
London SE1 0UP
UK

This book collects issues #63-68 of *Transformers*
(vol 1), originally published in single-issue form
by Marvel Comics, USA.

A CIP catalogue record for this title is available
from the British Library.

First paperback edition: June 2002
10 9 8 7 6 5 4 3 2 1
*Diamond exclusive edition: July 2002*
*10 9 8 7 6 5 4 3 2 1*

Printed in Italy.

Also available from Titan Books:

Transformers: All Fall Down (ISBN: 1 84023 300 1)
Transformers: End of the Road (ISBN: 1 84023 372 9)
Transformers: Primal Scream (ISBN: 1 84023 401 6)

What did you think of this book? We love to hear
from our readers. Please email us at:
readerfeedback@titanemail.com or write to us at the
above address.

Paperback cover art and computer effects by Andrew
Wildman.

*Diamond exclusive cover art by Pat Lee.*

# PULLING IT ALL TOGETHER

It can't have escaped your attention that these books have appeared in somewhat the wrong order. In strict chronology, *Primal Scream* comes first, then this volume, and then *All Fall Down* and finally *End of the Road*. Collectively, my whole run on the US *Transformers* comic, issues #59 through #80, the entire Unicron saga. So why, you ask, didn't Titan just start with *Primal Scream*? Well, that would be my fault, I'm afraid.

When I first took the idea of collecting *Transformers* to Titan, neither I — nor they — were exactly sure if and how it would take off. I knew there was an audience out there still and I didn't doubt the books would sell, but I was realistic enough to acknowledge that it might not be enough in the final analysis to sustain an ongoing series. So, I began with the end, the chunk of issues on which I'd collaborated with Andrew Wildman (and Geoff Senior), a reasonably self-contained bit of story and the run I am most proud of.

But, of course, it did take off, and how! The collections have been an unqualified success, both in terms of sales and fan reaction. The standard editions, Botcon exclusive, Diamond exclusive editions… it seems you just can't get enough of this stuff. So, of course, we went back, to the start of my run, and filled in the missing chunk. It's only when I see it again, like this, collected and polished, that I realise just how much it's really all one big epic, not divisible at all, a rolling story that just gathers pace and scale. So, for the sake of continuity and my peace of mind, all I ask is that you rearrange the books slightly on your shelf, place *Primal Scream* and *Matrix Quest* first.

So where do we go from here? Well, to Generation 2, of course. *Transformers: Dark Designs* and *Transformers: Rage in Heaven* collect the entirety of the 12-issue series. And then there are the UK collections, *Target: 2006* and the like. And beyond that… well, let's just say we might have to go back again, right to the beginning this time.

I think it's safe to say it's a series now.

Simon Furman, London, 2002

# MELDING UNIVERSES

When Larry Ditillio and I first began working on *Beast Wars: Transformers* we had no intention of involving ourselves with the entire *Transformers* universe. There was just too much of it, for one thing. And besides, we thought, who cares? The kids who watched the original series have outgrown it by now, and the comic books are a completely different medium. We were just going to create our own little bubble of a series which would be a CGI sci-fi show, and it would just happen to have transforming robots in it. No one would really care if it matched up to anything else that had ever been done with the *Transformers* product line.

Hah.

To their credit, Hasbro tried to warn us. They told us there was a huge and rabid fan base out there that cared *deeply* about all things TF. They told us about the alt.toys.transformers newsgroup and the large number of fan web sites. "Yeah, yeah," we said. "This is gonna be a different Optimus and a different Megatron and it won't matter."

Again, hah.

So we started the series. I wrote the pilot myself — it was finished and aired way before the rest of the series was launched. In it, I started with two spaceships crashing on a deserted planet, because we had to get the characters there somehow. And, just as an afterthought, I mentioned a "Great War."

Oh, what that all started.

Larry was the first to call me. "You'd better check out that *Transformers* newsgroup," he said. "They're going nuts."

The Internet was still fairly new to me, but I managed to find the alt.toys.transformers newsgroup. From it, I learned that my mention of a "Great War" was already being interpreted as the war between the Autobots and the Decepticons. I was more aghast, however, to learn that I had unintentionally plagiarized the beginning of "More Than Meets The Eye," which I had never seen.

Now, I'm a firm believer in the adage "talent borrows, genius steals" — but when I swipe great work, I prefer to do it *intentionally*. And it was also very apparent to me that I had a *lot* of research to do. Fast. Because here was a bunch of people who *cared*.

So Larry and I lurked on the newsgroups and corresponded with fans like Ben Yee. We were sent tapes, we bought comic books. And we learned as fast as we could. It was fun. By tying into the whole TF universe, we were able to give our stories a richness and depth that we never could have dreamed of otherwise.

But the greatest surprise was yet to come.

In one episode we needed to have Rhinox say something like "God help us all." But using the word "God" in that context is forbidden in Children's Television (lest someone take offense) and in any case it didn't sound TF enough. So we did a quick browse through the newsgroup, found someone using the word "Primus" and figured that would do. We dropped it into the script and sent it off for production.

And oh, what THAT started.

When the show aired, the newsgroup practically exploded. *PRIMUS!* This, we swiftly learned, was never in the TV canon. Primus was the invention of one Simon Furman, who wrote many of the comics. We had now tied the TV continuity with the comic continuity and opened a whole new dimension for the series. Frankly, Larry and I were stunned. But we went with it — and as a result, we ended up meeting Simon Furman himself, who not only became a friend but a reliable writing associate. And we've continued to work together on various projects ever since.

Over the years, I've worked on a lot of series. But *Beast Wars: Transformers* was by far the most exciting and the most fun — mainly for the intensely committed audience it (and the whole TF universe) engendered. I'm glad to see that in some form or another the TF canon will be carried on — there's a million stories left to tell.

And with the speed Simon works, he'll probably be telling about half of them.

I'm glad they're in good hands.

Bob Forward, Los Angeles, 2002

Check out http://www.bobforward.com and http://www.skyjammers.tv

# WHO'S WHO IN THE

OPTIMUS PRIME (AUTOBOT) — The most noble and dedicated of all the Autobots, holder of the Creation Matrix, the sacred life-force of the Transformers. Transforms into a truck/trailer, with mobile command base.

MEGATRON (DECEPTICON) — Megatron is the ultimate enemy of all free-thinking lifeforms. Cold, calculating and utterly remorseless, he cares only about his quest for ultimate power. Transforms into a gun of vast destructive force.

GRIMLOCK (DINOBOT) — Leader of the Dinobots (Swoop, Snarl, Slag and Sludge), allied, more or less, to the Autobots. Brash, stubborn and headstrong, Grimlock is nevertheless fiercely protective of those under his command. Transforms into a Tyrannosaurus Rex.

SCORPONOK (DECEPTICON) — Part Transformer, part alien humanoid, Scorponok is a binary-bonded being known as a Headmaster. As leaders fell by the wayside, he seized control of the Decepticons. But his dual nature may be his undoing. Transforms into a giant scorpion.

RATCHET (AUTOBOT) — Dedicated to the preservation of life, Ratchet is a healer first and foremost, a warrior only by necessity. His skill in the surgery is matched only by his courage and capacity for self-sacrifice. Transforms into an ambulance.

STARSCREAM (DECEPTICON) — Megatron's second-in-command… when he isn't conniving and stabbing him in the back. Treacherous, self-serving and, ultimately, cowardly, Starscream is always looking after #1. Transforms into a hypersonic jet.

# TRANSFORMERS UNIVERSE

JAZZ (AUTOBOT) — Right-hand man to Optimus Prime, Jazz's ease with Earthen culture and environments makes him indispensible. Jazz takes on the most dangerous missions, but however tough the scrape, he never loses his cool. Transforms into a racing car.

BLUDGEON (DECEPTICON) — Master of Metallikato, the forbidden Cybertronian dark martial art, Bludgeon is a stone-killer. Mirroring his Pretender nature, he wears two faces, the obedient servant masking ruthless, single-minded ambition. Transforms into a tank.

GOLDBUG/BUMBLEBEE (AUTOBOT) — Once he was Bumblebee, the cute, wise-cracking "little brother", but a brush with death, and his recreation as Goldbug, leave him serious and assertive in his new role as Autobot Espionage Director. Transforms into a VW Beetle.

THUNDERWING (DECEPTICON) — Supremely confident, utterly ruthless and immensely powerful, Thunderwing was created to command. War is a science and his strategy is an evolving equation, based on discipline, observation and guile. Transforms into a flying gunship.

NIGHTBEAT (AUTOBOT) — Tough, no-nonsense, hard-working, not afraid to break the rules, Nightbeat's ultimate quest is for the truth, his detective's logic centre never happier than when it's untangling a mystery. Transforms into a super-charged sports car.

GALVATRON (DECEPTICON) — In one or more possible futures, Galvatron is Megatron re-born. Crafted by the planet-devouring Unicron to serve as his herald, Galvatron is awesomely powerful and utterly insane. Transforms into a cannon.

# WAR WITHOUT END!

**C**ybertron: a distant metal planet populated by robots able to transform their bodies into vehicles, beast forms and cutting edge technological hardware. A world of harmony dedicated to universal peace.

Until civil war tore it apart!

The evil Decepticons, a renegade splinter faction dedicated only to conquest and evil. Their agenda was straightforward: enslave Cybertron and transform it into a colossal war-world, with which to devastate the galaxy. Led by the malevolent Megatron, they struck without warning, tearing apart the intellectual idyll.

But under the command of the noble and dauntless Optimus Prime the other Transformers rallied and fought back. They dubbed themselves Autobots, and strove to uphold the ideals of their god-like progenitor Primus, whose dream of universal peace had been passed down the generations like a torch.

The conflict raged for countless millennia, Cybertron shook under the devastating Decepticon assault and the universe held its breath. Then, in an audacious attempt to tip the balance of power, the Ark — a giant spacecraft — was launched. On board were Optimus Prime and a hand-picked crew of Autobots, their mission to secure a supply of energon. Rich in power, the fuel of choice for Transformers, energon was the key to winning the war.

But Megatron was ready, waiting. The Ark was ambushed in deep space, and boarded by Decepticon warriors. To prevent the Ark falling into Megatron's clutches, Prime locked the giant ship on a collision course with a nearby planet, where it crashed with devastating force. All aboard suffered a complete systems shutdown.

The Autobots and Decepticons awoke millions of years later, restored and recreated by the Ark's computer. Their secondary modes had been adapted to blend in with what the computer assumed — logically — were the local lifeforms. The war began anew...

... on Earth.

# LOST IN SPACE

*Much has changed for the Autobots and Decepticons since they came to Earth. The battle lines have shifted, and many key players have either fallen or been changed beyond recognition.*

When Optimus Prime is killed by his arch enemy Megatron, the seeds of future destruction are unwittingly sown. Unaware that Prime's entire personality was downloaded into a computer game before his 'death', the grieving Autobots prepare a ceremonial funeral in which their former leader's mortal remains are sent hurtling out into deep space. Along with Prime's body, nestling in a secret chest cavity, goes the Creation Matrix, the sacred lifeforce of the Transformer race and the essence of their creator, Primus.

Time passes, and eventually – on a distant planet called Nebulos – Optimus Prime is restored to life… in a new body. He is now a Powermaster: Transformer and Nebulan combined in a symbiotic relationship. But Prime realises that the Matrix is lost. Despite his new power, he feels empty and diminished without it. Prime hopes its power will not be needed in the many battles looming on the horizon.

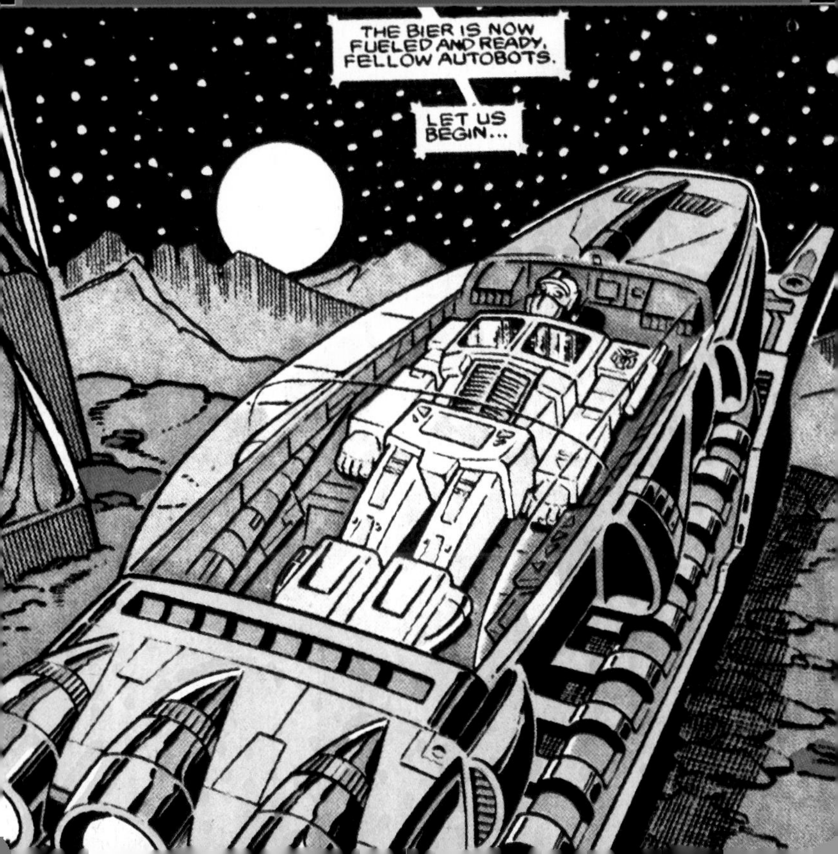
THE BIER IS NOW FUELED AND READY, FELLOW AUTOBOTS.
LET US BEGIN...

RICOCHET PROVES
THAN ENOUGH...
BAM!

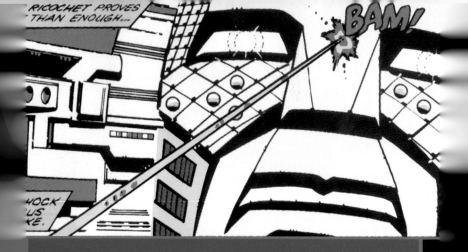

The first major conflict involves Starscream, Megatron's traitorous lieutenant. Though Megatron is gone, presumed dead, Starscream remains as self-serving as ever. In order to usurp current Decepticon leader, Ratbat, he claims the power of Underbase, and turns on Autobot and Decepticon alike. Though he is defeated, the casualties on both sides are high. The loss of the Matrix is again keenly felt.

But worse is yet to come, and the return of Megatron heralds the dawning of true darkness. Starscream is recreated as a Pretender, a Transformer within an armoured outer shell, and Ratchet is killed, he and Megatron caught in a devastating blast. Then, deep beneath Cybertron, Pretender Autobots Grimlock, Bumblebee and Jazz (restored by Ratchet in the climactic battle with Megatron) discover their creator Primus in complete systems shutdown. They are warned that his awakening will alert Unicron, the chaos-bringer, who will destroy Cybertron. Thunderwing, Decepticon commander on Cybertron, despatches his Mayhem Attack Squad to deal with Grimlock and the others, and the resultant battle shocks Primus awake. His scream reaches Unicron, who immediately sets course for Cybertron.

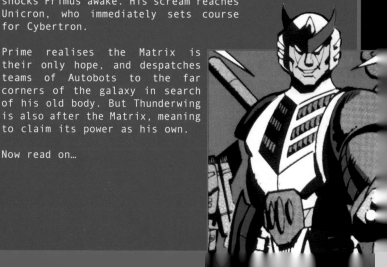

Prime realises the Matrix is their only hope, and despatches teams of Autobots to the far corners of the galaxy in search of his old body. But Thunderwing is also after the Matrix, meaning to claim its power as his own.

Now read on…

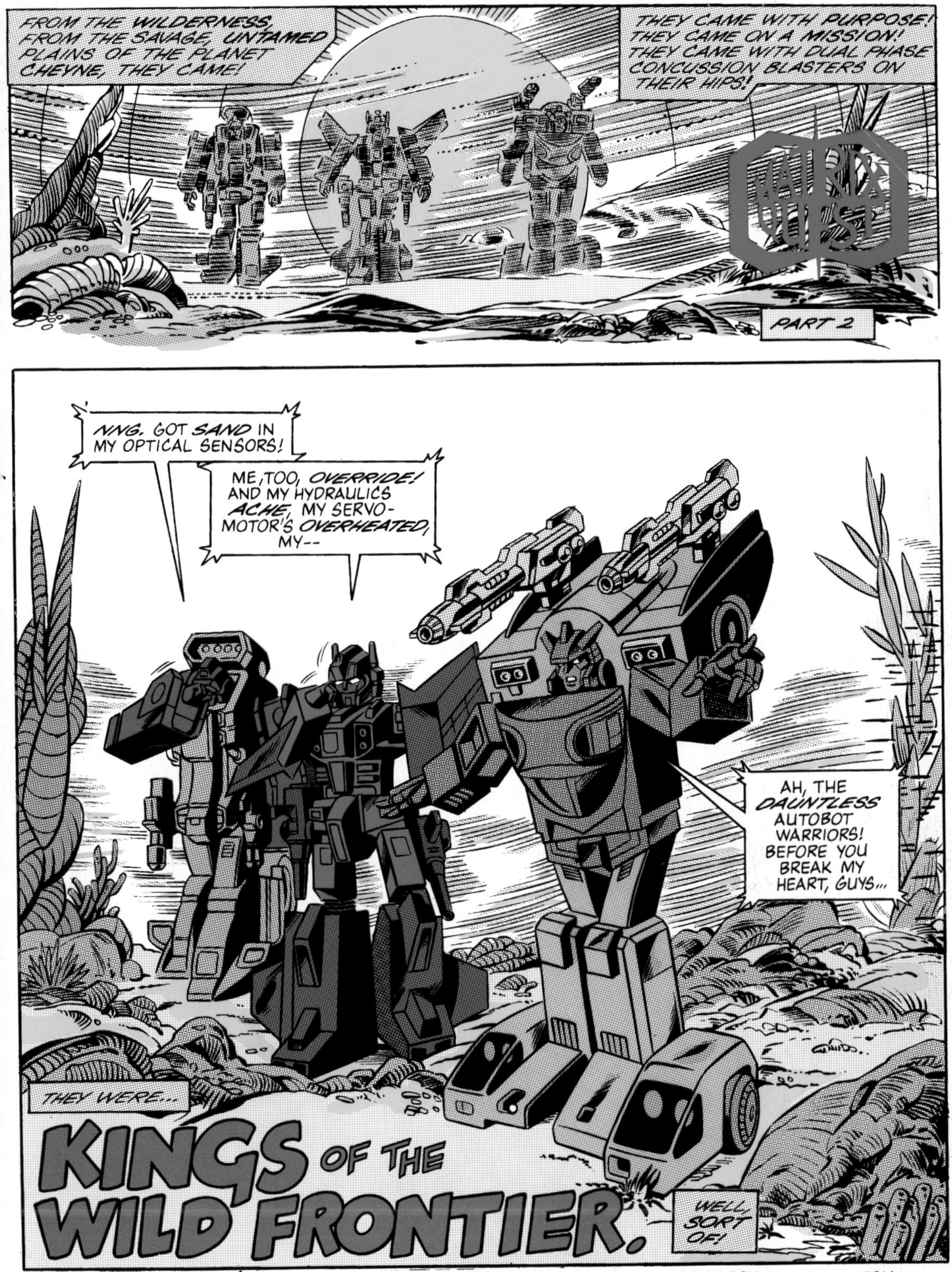
FROM THE WILDERNESS, FROM THE SAVAGE, UNTAMED PLAINS OF THE PLANET CHEYNE, THEY CAME!
THEY CAME WITH PURPOSE! THEY CAME ON A MISSION! THEY CAME WITH DUAL PHASE CONCUSSION BLASTERS ON THEIR HIPS!
MATRIX QUEST
PART 2
NNG. GOT SAND IN MY OPTICAL SENSORS!
ME, TOO, OVERRIDE! AND MY HYDRAULICS ACHE, MY SERVO-MOTOR'S OVERHEATED, MY--
AH, THE DAUNTLESS AUTOBOT WARRIORS! BEFORE YOU BREAK MY HEART, GUYS...
THEY WERE...
KINGS OF THE WILD FRONTIER.
WELL, SORT OF!

SIMON FURMAN *WRITER* | JOSÉ DELBO *PENCILER* | DAVE HUNT *INKER* | JIM MASSARA *LETTERER* | NEL YOMTOV *COLORIST* | DON DALEY *EDITOR* | TOM DeFALCO *TRIGGER*

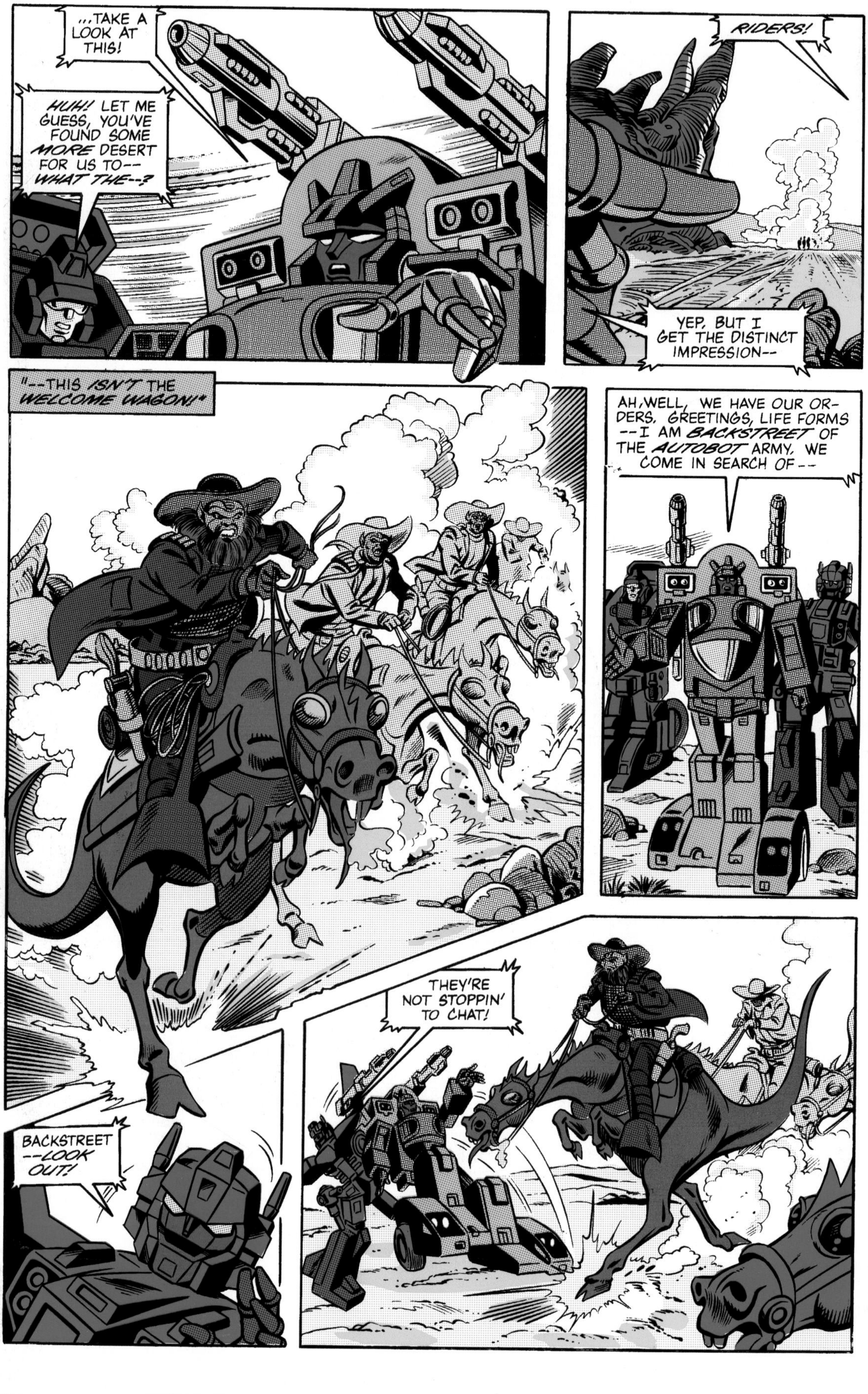
...TAKE A LOOK AT THIS!
HUH! LET ME GUESS, YOU'VE FOUND SOME MORE DESERT FOR US TO-- WHAT THE--?
RIDERS!
YEP, BUT I GET THE DISTINCT IMPRESSION--
"--THIS ISN'T THE WELCOME WAGON!"
AH, WELL, WE HAVE OUR ORDERS. GREETINGS, LIFE FORMS --I AM BACKSTREET OF THE AUTOBOT ARMY. WE COME IN SEARCH OF--
BACKSTREET --LOOK OUT!
THEY'RE NOT STOPPIN' TO CHAT!

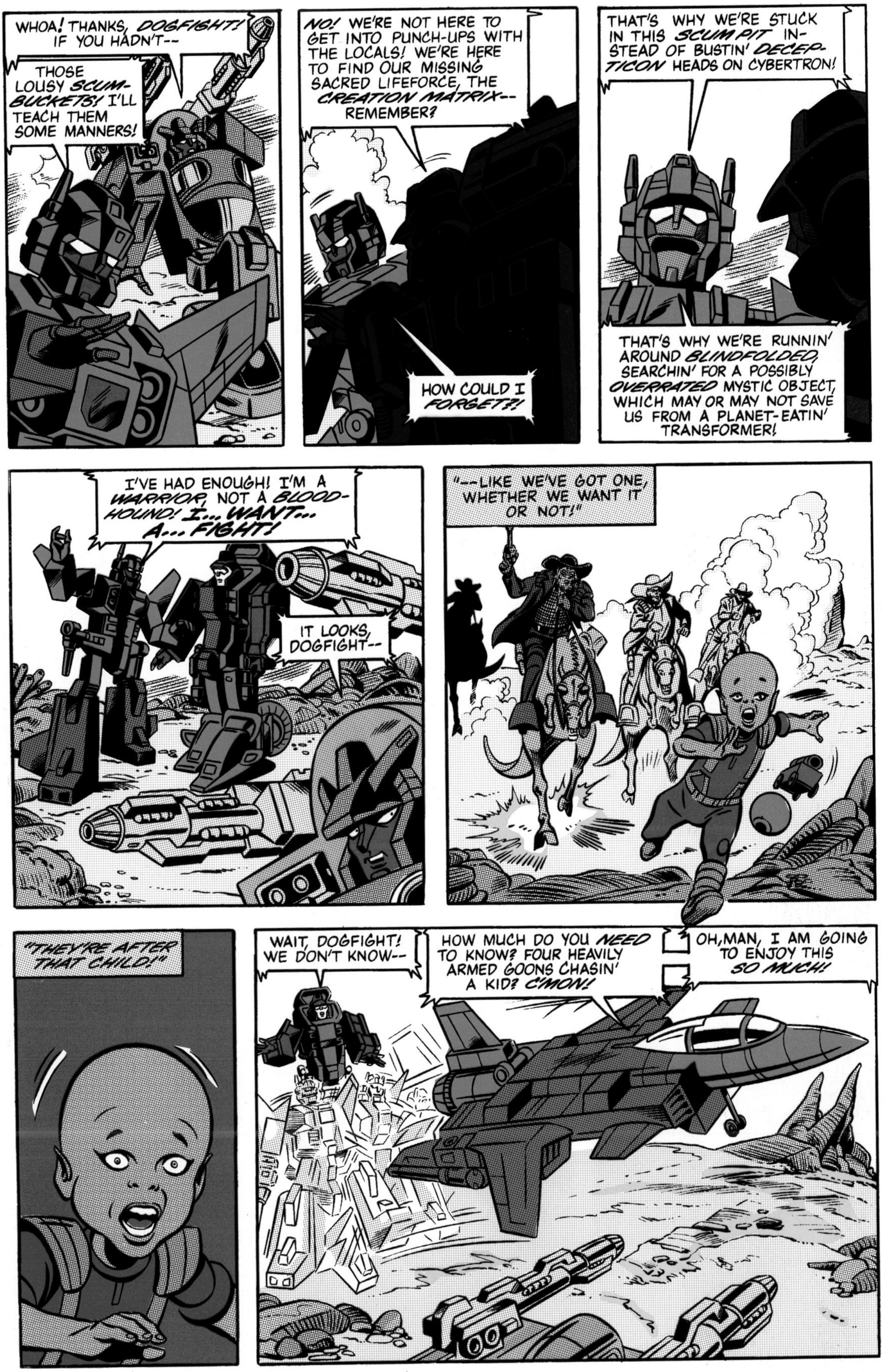
WHOA! THANKS, DOGFIGHT! IF YOU HADN'T--
THOSE LOUSY SCUM-BUCKETS! I'LL TEACH THEM SOME MANNERS!
NO! WE'RE NOT HERE TO GET INTO PUNCH-UPS WITH THE LOCALS! WE'RE HERE TO FIND OUR MISSING SACRED LIFEFORCE, THE CREATION MATRIX-- REMEMBER?
HOW COULD I FORGET?!
THAT'S WHY WE'RE STUCK IN THIS SCUM PIT IN-STEAD OF BUSTIN' DECEP-TICON HEADS ON CYBERTRON!
THAT'S WHY WE'RE RUNNIN' AROUND BLINDFOLDED, SEARCHIN' FOR A POSSIBLY OVERRATED MYSTIC OBJECT, WHICH MAY OR MAY NOT SAVE US FROM A PLANET-EATIN' TRANSFORMER!
I'VE HAD ENOUGH! I'M A WARRIOR, NOT A BLOOD-HOUND! I... WANT... A... FIGHT!
IT LOOKS, DOGFIGHT--
"--LIKE WE'VE GOT ONE, WHETHER WE WANT IT OR NOT!"
"THEY'RE AFTER THAT CHILD!"
WAIT, DOGFIGHT! WE DON'T KNOW--
HOW MUCH DO YOU NEED TO KNOW? FOUR HEAVILY ARMED GOONS CHASIN' A KID? C'MON!
OH, MAN, I AM GOING TO ENJOY THIS SO MUCH!

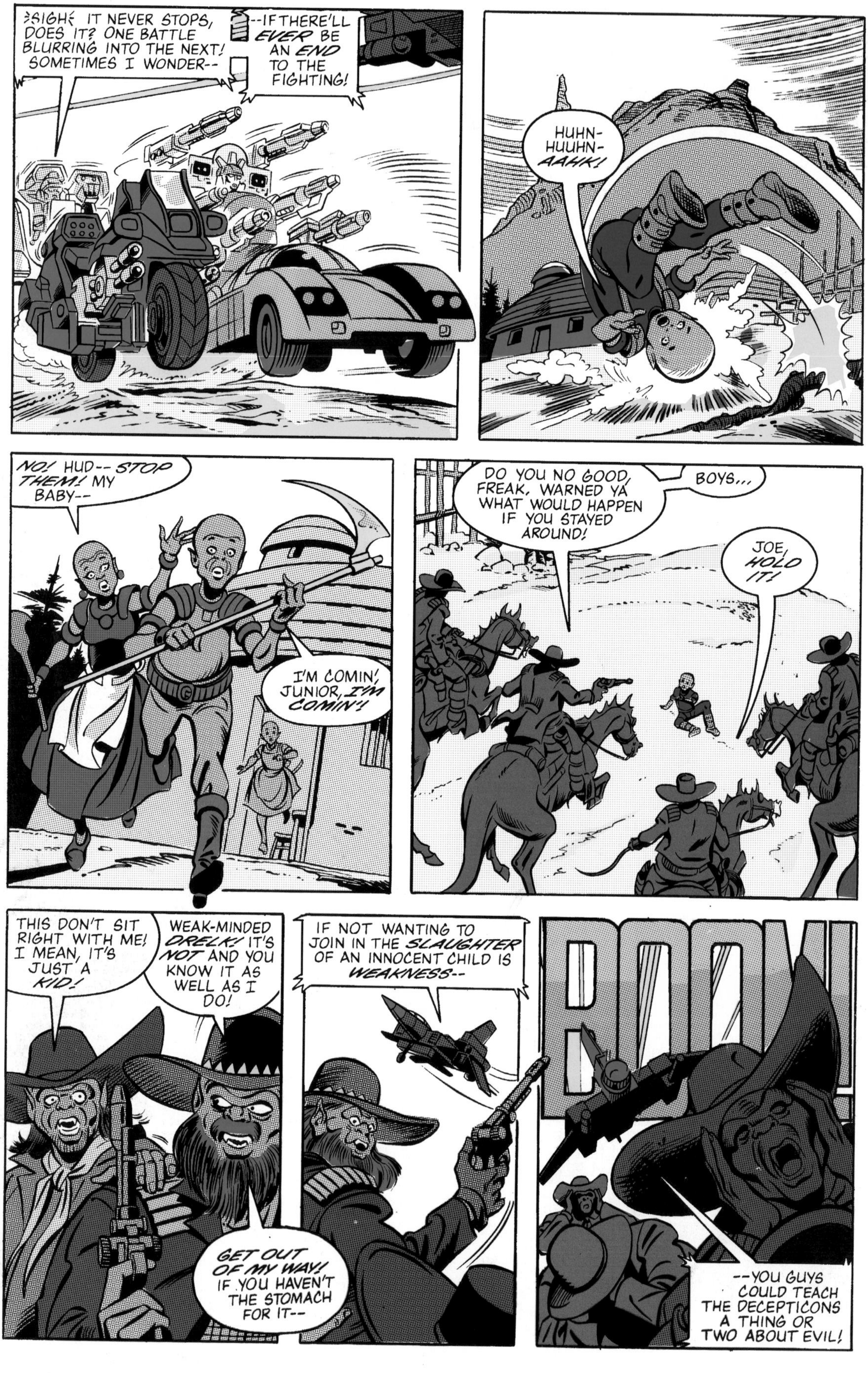

*SIGH* IT NEVER STOPS, DOES IT? ONE BATTLE BLURRING INTO THE NEXT! SOMETIMES I WONDER--
--IF THERE'LL EVER BE AN END TO THE FIGHTING!
HUHN-HUUHN-AAHK!
NO! HUD-- STOP THEM! MY BABY--
I'M COMIN', JUNIOR, I'M COMIN'!
DO YOU NO GOOD, FREAK. WARNED YA WHAT WOULD HAPPEN IF YOU STAYED AROUND!
BOYS...
JOE, HOLD IT!
THIS DON'T SIT RIGHT WITH ME! I MEAN, IT'S JUST A KID!
WEAK-MINDED DRELK! IT'S NOT AND YOU KNOW IT AS WELL AS I DO!
GET OUT OF MY WAY! IF YOU HAVEN'T THE STOMACH FOR IT--
IF NOT WANTING TO JOIN IN THE SLAUGHTER OF AN INNOCENT CHILD IS WEAKNESS--
BOOM!
--YOU GUYS COULD TEACH THE DECEPTICONS A THING OR TWO ABOUT EVIL!

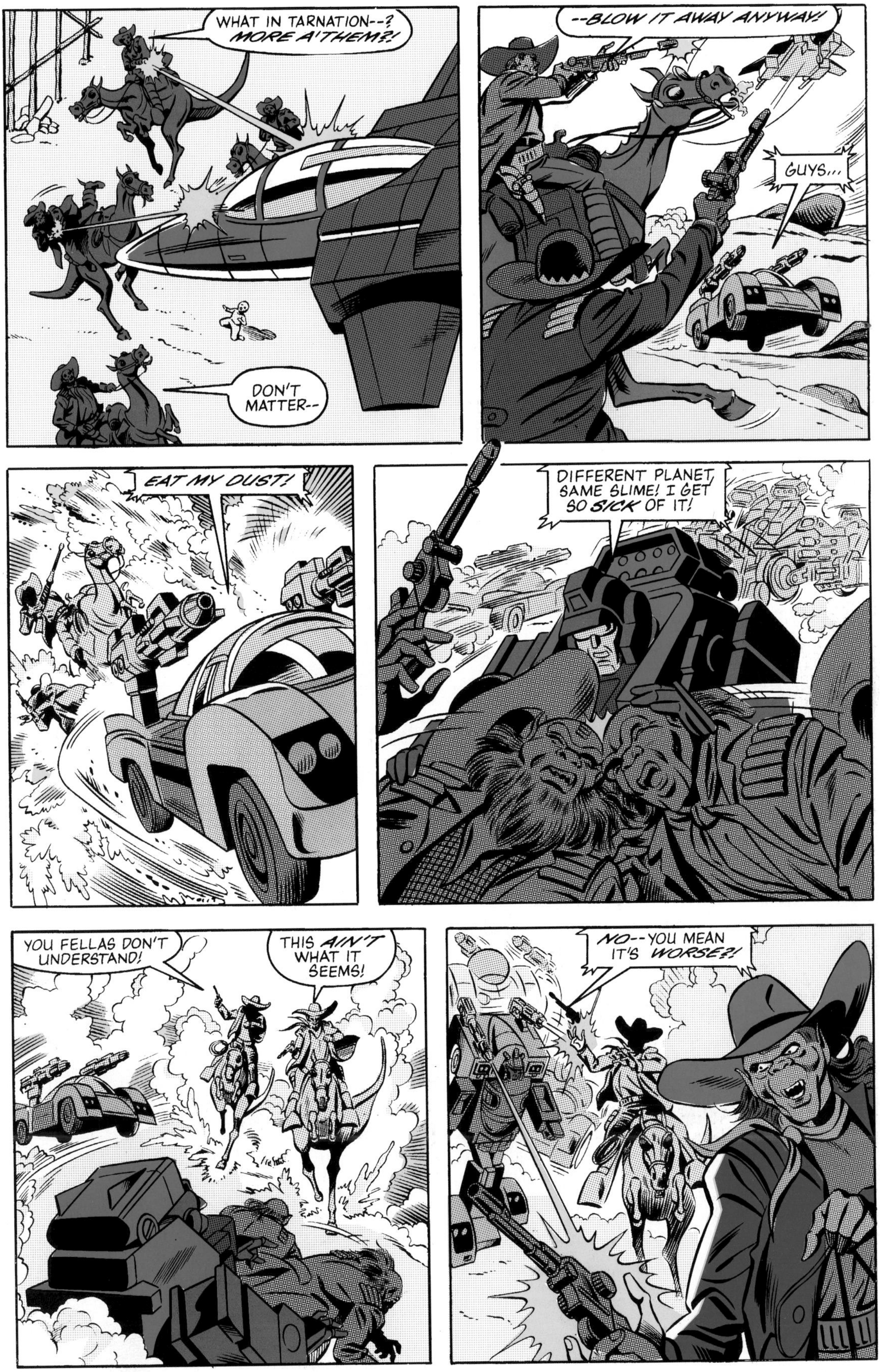
WHAT IN TARNATION--? MORE A'THEM?!
DON'T MATTER--
--BLOW IT AWAY ANYWAY!
GUYS...
EAT MY DUST!
DIFFERENT PLANET, SAME SLIME! I GET SO SICK OF IT!
YOU FELLAS DON'T UNDERSTAND!
THIS AIN'T WHAT IT SEEMS!
NO--YOU MEAN IT'S WORSE?!

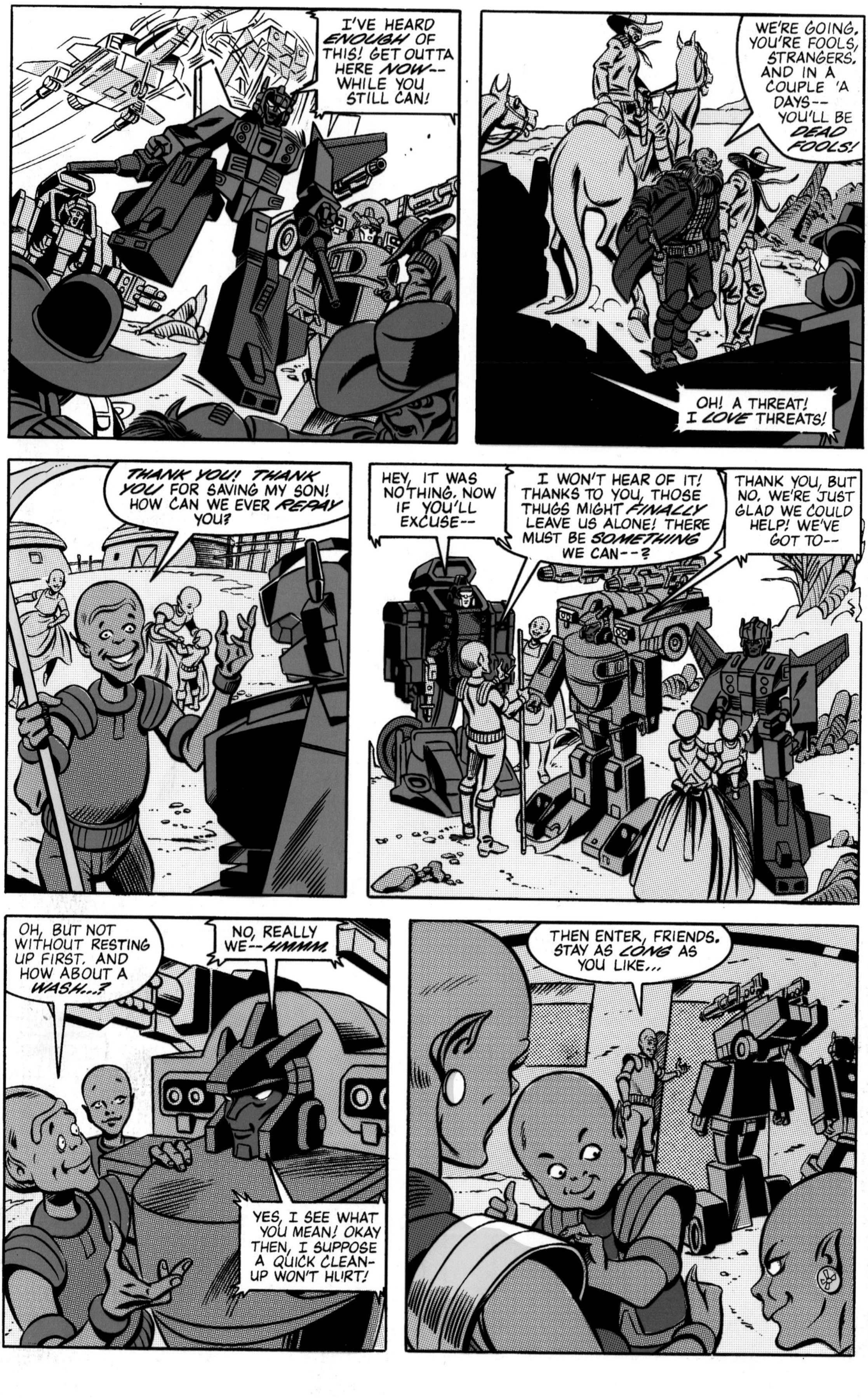
I'VE HEARD ENOUGH OF THIS! GET OUTTA HERE NOW-- WHILE YOU STILL CAN!
WE'RE GOING, YOU'RE FOOLS, STRANGERS. AND IN A COUPLE 'A DAYS-- YOU'LL BE DEAD FOOLS!
OH! A THREAT! I LOVE THREATS!
THANK YOU! THANK YOU FOR SAVING MY SON! HOW CAN WE EVER REPAY YOU?
HEY, IT WAS NOTHING. NOW IF YOU'LL EXCUSE--
I WON'T HEAR OF IT! THANKS TO YOU, THOSE THUGS MIGHT FINALLY LEAVE US ALONE! THERE MUST BE SOMETHING WE CAN--?
THANK YOU, BUT NO, WE'RE JUST GLAD WE COULD HELP! WE'VE GOT TO--
OH, BUT NOT WITHOUT RESTING UP FIRST. AND HOW ABOUT A WASH...?
NO, REALLY WE--HMMMM.
YES, I SEE WHAT YOU MEAN! OKAY THEN, I SUPPOSE A QUICK CLEAN-UP WON'T HURT!
THEN ENTER, FRIENDS. STAY AS LONG AS YOU LIKE...

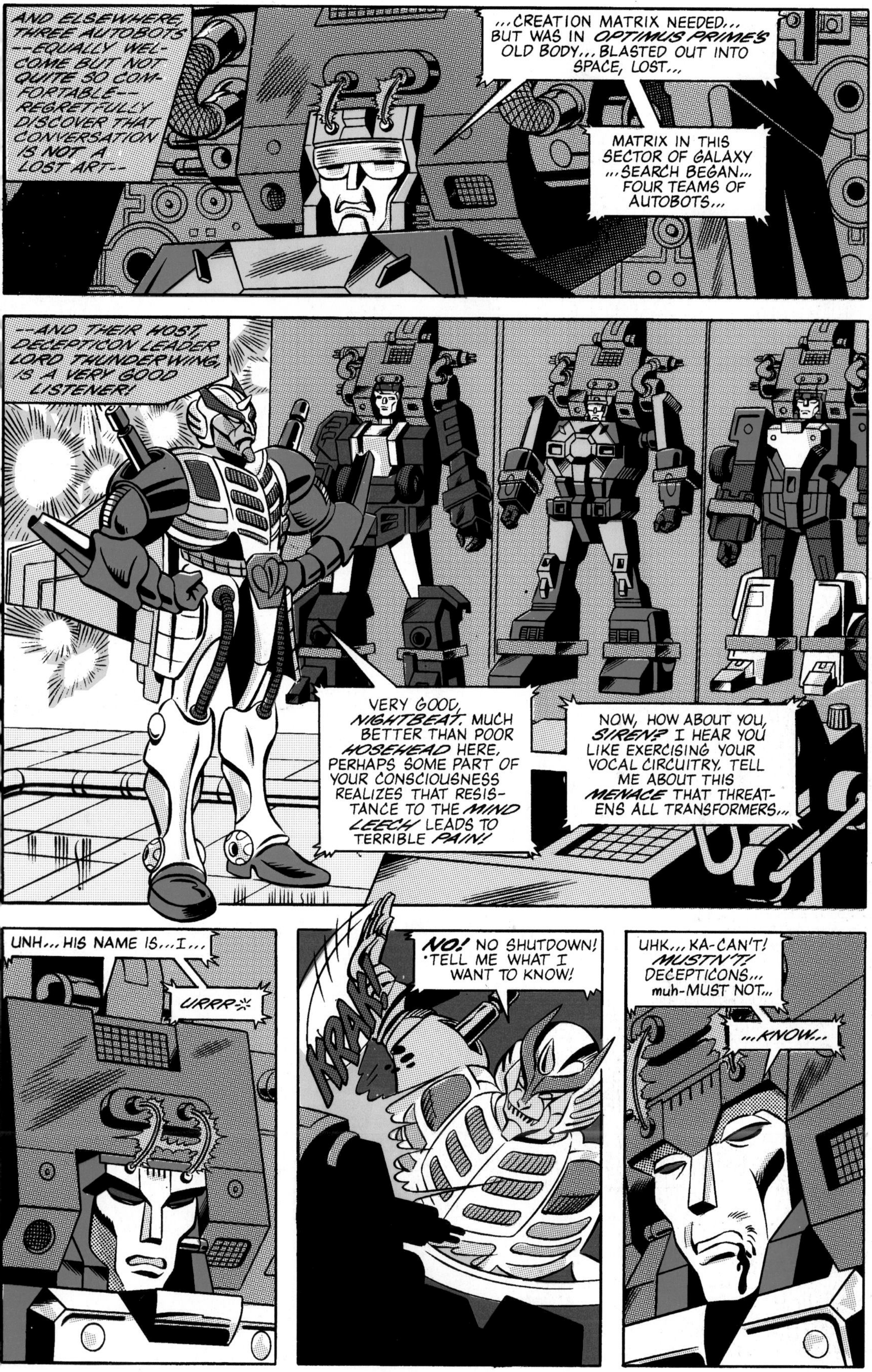
AND ELSEWHERE, THREE AUTOBOTS --EQUALLY WELCOME BUT NOT QUITE SO COMFORTABLE-- REGRETFULLY DISCOVER THAT CONVERSATION IS NOT A LOST ART--
...CREATION MATRIX NEEDED... BUT WAS IN OPTIMUS PRIME'S OLD BODY... BLASTED OUT INTO SPACE, LOST...
MATRIX IN THIS SECTOR OF GALAXY ...SEARCH BEGAN... FOUR TEAMS OF AUTOBOTS...
--AND THEIR HOST, DECEPTICON LEADER LORD THUNDERWING, IS A VERY GOOD LISTENER!
VERY GOOD, NIGHTBEAT. MUCH BETTER THAN POOR HOSEHEAD HERE. PERHAPS SOME PART OF YOUR CONSCIOUSNESS REALIZES THAT RESISTANCE TO THE MIND LEECH LEADS TO TERRIBLE PAIN!
NOW, HOW ABOUT YOU, SIREN? I HEAR YOU LIKE EXERCISING YOUR VOCAL CIRCUITRY. TELL ME ABOUT THIS MENACE THAT THREATENS ALL TRANSFORMERS...
UNH... HIS NAME IS... I...
URRR
NO! NO SHUTDOWN! TELL ME WHAT I WANT TO KNOW!
KRAK!
UHK... KA-CAN'T! MUSTN'T! DECEPTICONS... muh-MUST NOT...
...KNOW...

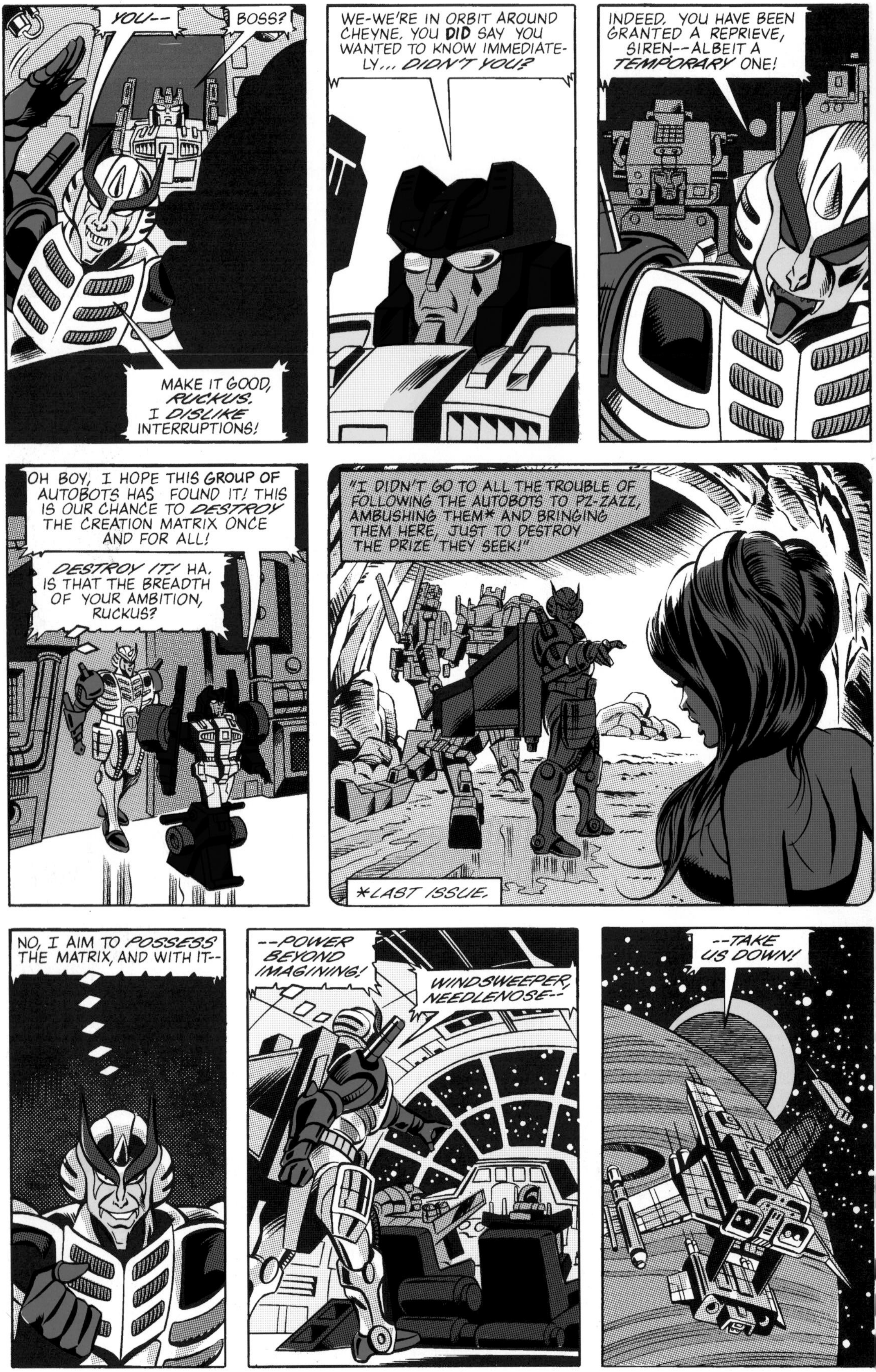

YOU--
BOSS?
MAKE IT GOOD, RUCKUS. I DISLIKE INTERRUPTIONS!
WE-WE'RE IN ORBIT AROUND CHEYNE. YOU DID SAY YOU WANTED TO KNOW IMMEDIATELY... DIDN'T YOU?
INDEED. YOU HAVE BEEN GRANTED A REPRIEVE, SIREN--ALBEIT A TEMPORARY ONE!
OH BOY, I HOPE THIS GROUP OF AUTOBOTS HAS FOUND IT! THIS IS OUR CHANCE TO DESTROY THE CREATION MATRIX ONCE AND FOR ALL!
DESTROY IT! HA. IS THAT THE BREADTH OF YOUR AMBITION, RUCKUS?
"I DIDN'T GO TO ALL THE TROUBLE OF FOLLOWING THE AUTOBOTS TO PZ-ZAZZ, AMBUSHING THEM* AND BRINGING THEM HERE, JUST TO DESTROY THE PRIZE THEY SEEK!"
*LAST ISSUE.
NO, I AIM TO POSSESS THE MATRIX, AND WITH IT--
--POWER BEYOND IMAGINING!
WINDSWEEPER, NEEDLENOSE--
--TAKE US DOWN!

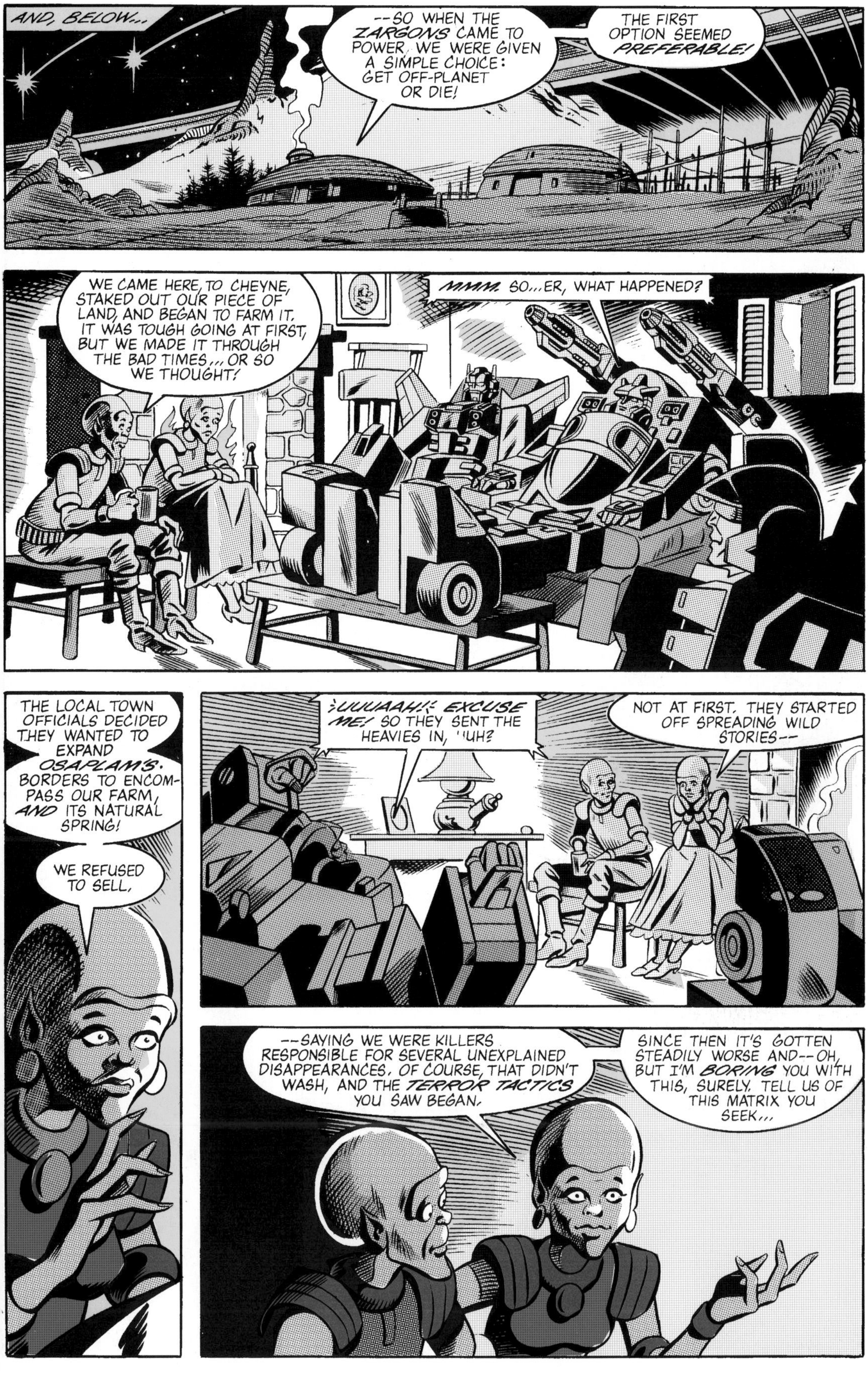
AND, BELOW...
--SO WHEN THE ZARGONS CAME TO POWER, WE WERE GIVEN A SIMPLE CHOICE: GET OFF-PLANET OR DIE!
THE FIRST OPTION SEEMED PREFERABLE!
WE CAME HERE, TO CHEYNE, STAKED OUT OUR PIECE OF LAND, AND BEGAN TO FARM IT. IT WAS TOUGH GOING AT FIRST, BUT WE MADE IT THROUGH THE BAD TIMES... OR SO WE THOUGHT!
MMMM. SO... ER, WHAT HAPPENED?
THE LOCAL TOWN OFFICIALS DECIDED THEY WANTED TO EXPAND OSAPLAM'S BORDERS TO ENCOMPASS OUR FARM, AND ITS NATURAL SPRING!
WE REFUSED TO SELL,
¡UUUAAH!¡ EXCUSE ME! SO THEY SENT THE HEAVIES IN, 'UH?
NOT AT FIRST. THEY STARTED OFF SPREADING WILD STORIES--
--SAYING WE WERE KILLERS RESPONSIBLE FOR SEVERAL UNEXPLAINED DISAPPEARANCES. OF COURSE, THAT DIDN'T WASH, AND THE TERROR TACTICS YOU SAW BEGAN.
SINCE THEN IT'S GOTTEN STEADILY WORSE AND--OH, BUT I'M BORING YOU WITH THIS, SURELY. TELL US OF THIS MATRIX YOU SEEK...

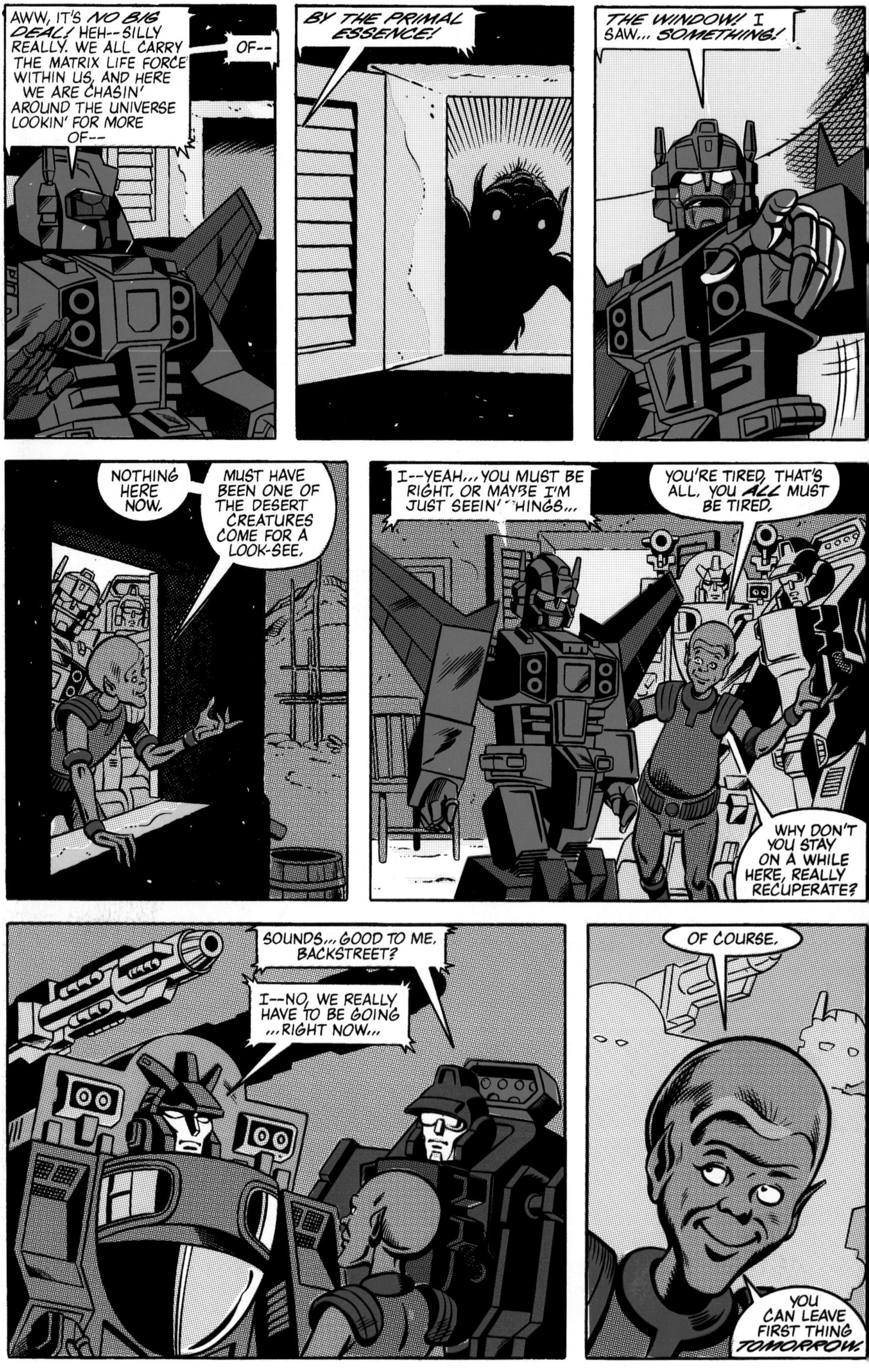

AWW, IT'S NO BIG DEAL! HEH--SILLY REALLY. WE ALL CARRY THE MATRIX LIFE FORCE WITHIN US, AND HERE WE ARE CHASIN' AROUND THE UNIVERSE LOOKIN' FOR MORE OF--
OF--
BY THE PRIMAL ESSENCE!
THE WINDOW! I SAW... SOMETHING!
NOTHING HERE NOW.
MUST HAVE BEEN ONE OF THE DESERT CREATURES COME FOR A LOOK-SEE.
I--YEAH... YOU MUST BE RIGHT. OR MAYBE I'M JUST SEEIN' THINGS...
YOU'RE TIRED, THAT'S ALL. YOU ALL MUST BE TIRED.
WHY DON'T YOU STAY ON A WHILE HERE, REALLY RECUPERATE?
SOUNDS... GOOD TO ME. BACKSTREET?
I--NO, WE REALLY HAVE TO BE GOING ...RIGHT NOW...
OF COURSE.
YOU CAN LEAVE FIRST THING TOMORROW.

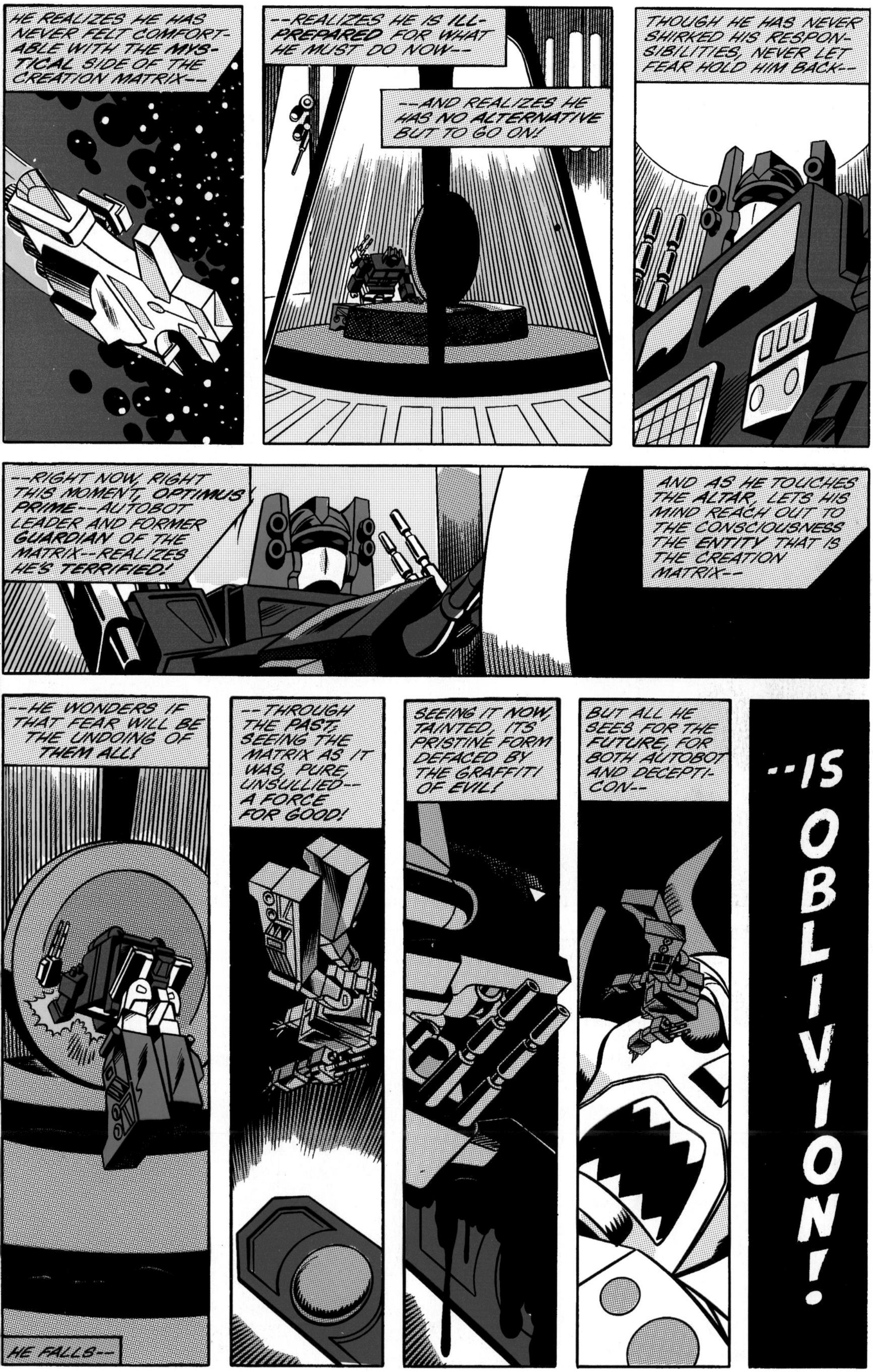
HE REALIZES HE HAS NEVER FELT COMFORTABLE WITH THE MYSTICAL SIDE OF THE CREATION MATRIX--
--REALIZES HE IS ILL-PREPARED FOR WHAT HE MUST DO NOW--
--AND REALIZES HE HAS NO ALTERNATIVE BUT TO GO ON!
THOUGH HE HAS NEVER SHIRKED HIS RESPONSIBILITIES, NEVER LET FEAR HOLD HIM BACK--
--RIGHT NOW, RIGHT THIS MOMENT, OPTIMUS PRIME--AUTOBOT LEADER AND FORMER GUARDIAN OF THE MATRIX--REALIZES HE'S TERRIFIED!
AND AS HE TOUCHES THE ALTAR, LETS HIS MIND REACH OUT TO THE CONSCIOUSNESS THE ENTITY THAT IS THE CREATION MATRIX--
--HE WONDERS IF THAT FEAR WILL BE THE UNDOING OF THEM ALL!
HE FALLS--
--THROUGH THE PAST, SEEING THE MATRIX AS IT WAS, PURE, UNSULLIED--A FORCE FOR GOOD!
SEEING IT NOW, TAINTED, ITS PRISTINE FORM DEFACED BY THE GRAFFITI OF EVIL!
BUT ALL HE SEES FOR THE FUTURE, FOR BOTH AUTOBOT AND DECEPTICON--
--IS OBLIVION!

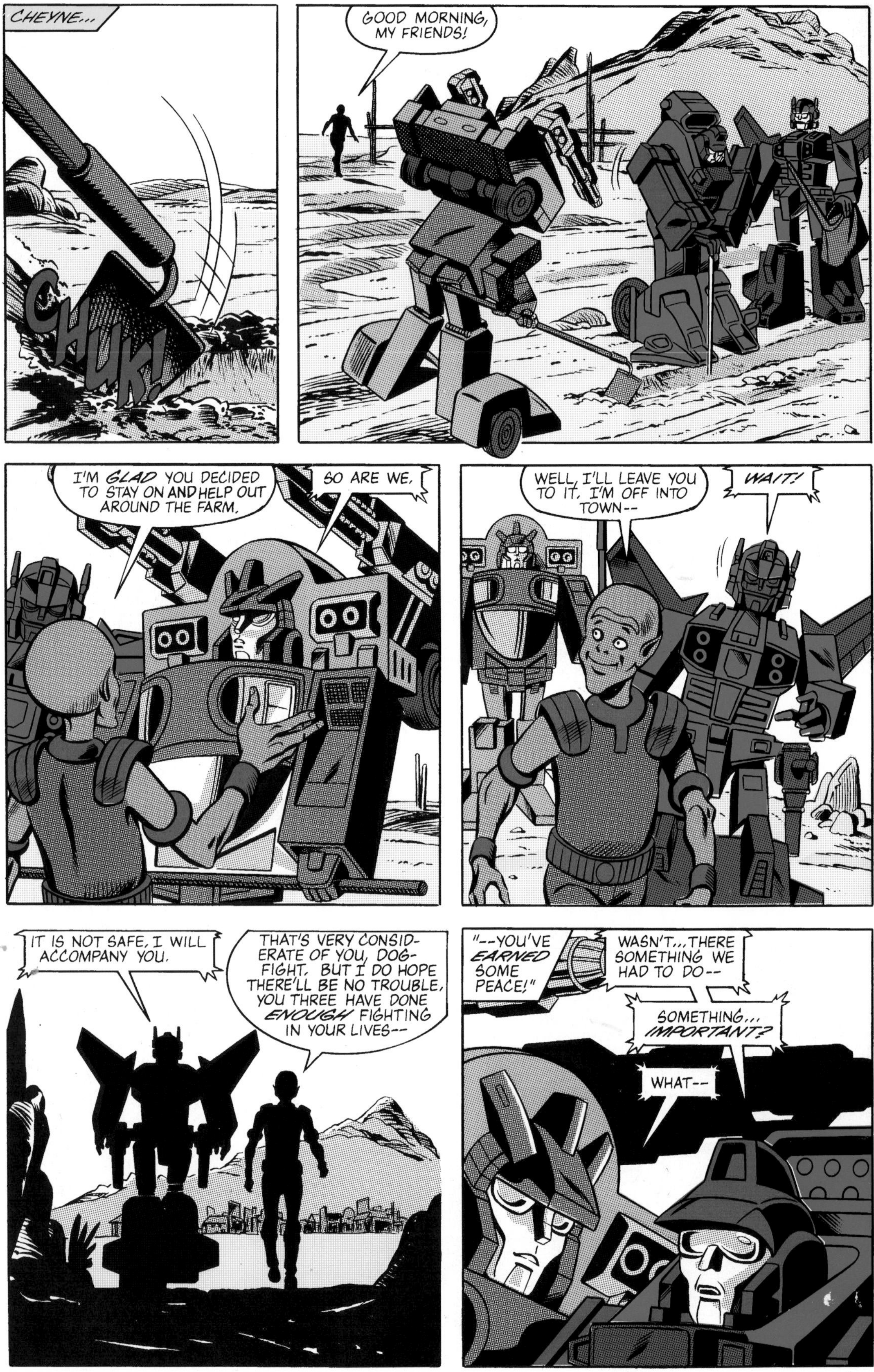
CHEYNE...
CHUK!
GOOD MORNING, MY FRIENDS!
I'M GLAD YOU DECIDED TO STAY ON AND HELP OUT AROUND THE FARM.
SO ARE WE.
WELL, I'LL LEAVE YOU TO IT. I'M OFF INTO TOWN--
WAIT!
IT IS NOT SAFE. I WILL ACCOMPANY YOU.
THAT'S VERY CONSIDERATE OF YOU, DOG-FIGHT. BUT I DO HOPE THERE'LL BE NO TROUBLE. YOU THREE HAVE DONE ENOUGH FIGHTING IN YOUR LIVES--
"--YOU'VE EARNED SOME PEACE!"
WASN'T... THERE SOMETHING WE HAD TO DO--
SOMETHING... IMPORTANT?
WHAT--

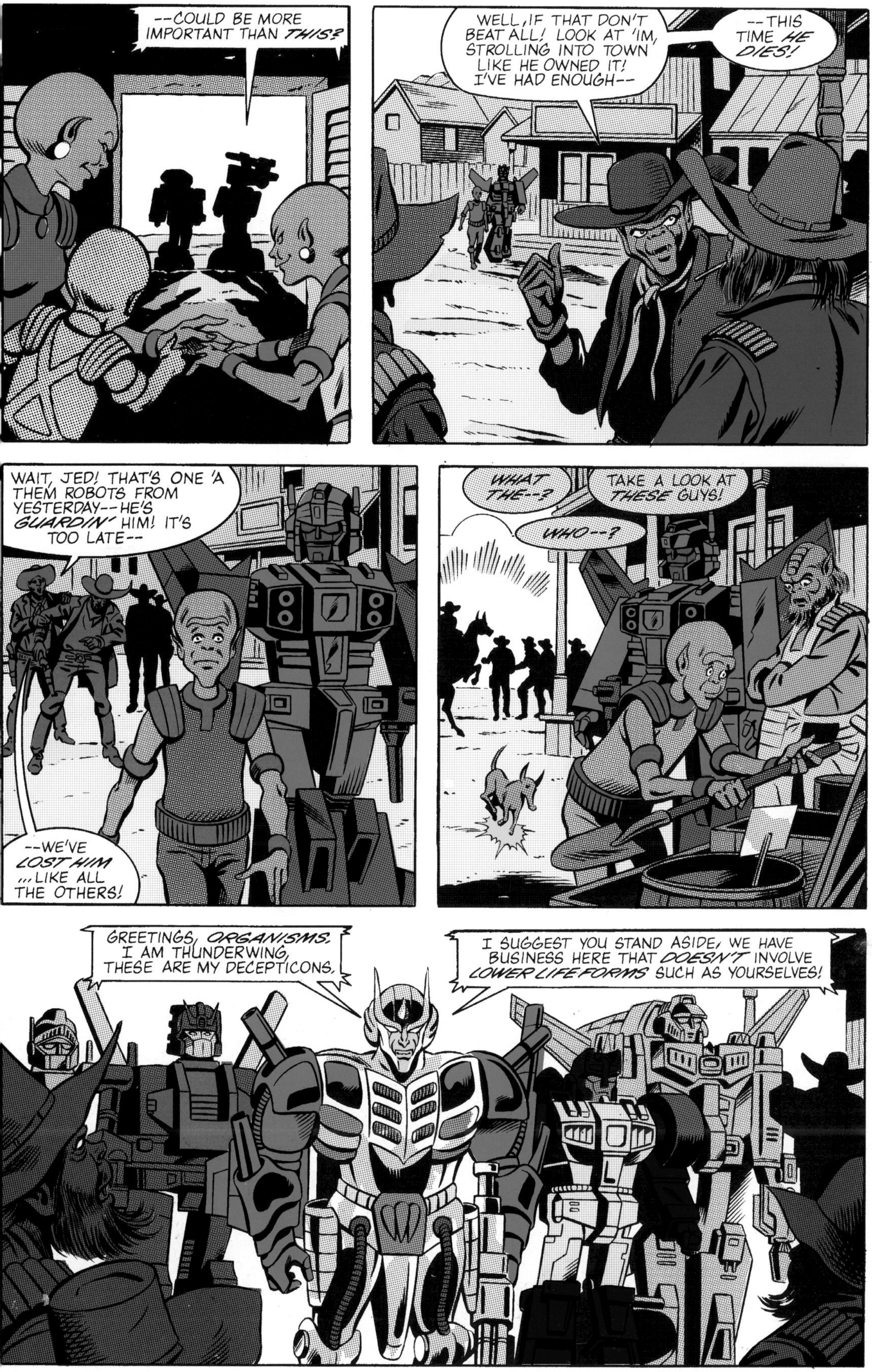
--COULD BE MORE IMPORTANT THAN *THIS?*
WELL, IF THAT DON'T BEAT ALL! LOOK AT 'IM, STROLLING INTO TOWN LIKE HE OWNED IT! I'VE HAD ENOUGH--
--THIS TIME *HE DIES!*
WAIT, JED! THAT'S ONE 'A THEM ROBOTS FROM YESTERDAY--HE'S *GUARDIN'* HIM! IT'S TOO LATE--
--WE'VE *LOST HIM* ...LIKE ALL THE OTHERS!
*WHAT THE--?*
TAKE A LOOK AT *THESE* GUYS!
*WHO--?*
GREETINGS, *ORGANISMS.* I AM THUNDERWING, THESE ARE MY DECEPTICONS,
I SUGGEST YOU STAND ASIDE, WE HAVE BUSINESS HERE THAT *DOESN'T* INVOLVE *LOWER LIFE FORMS* SUCH AS YOURSELVES!

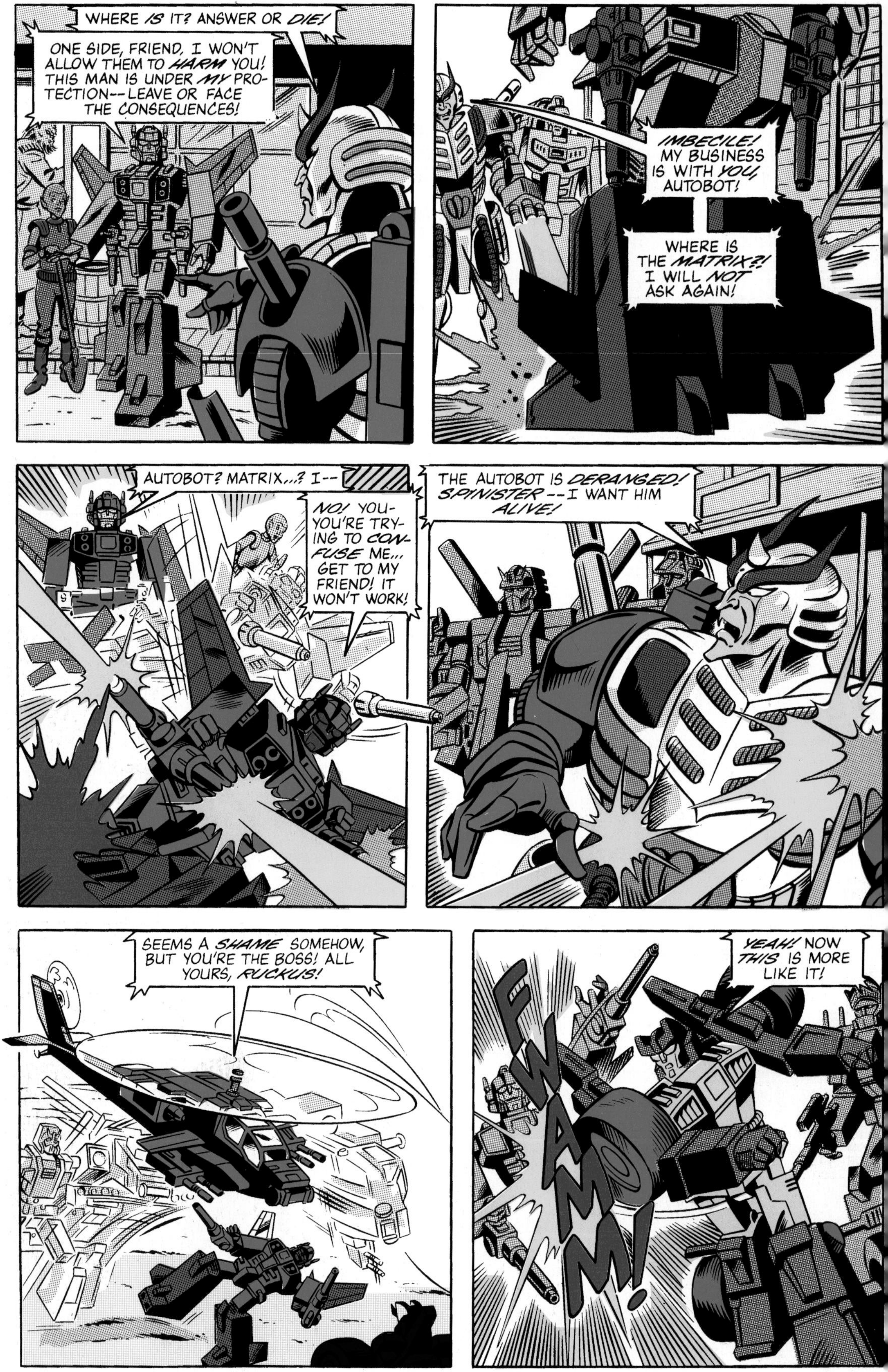
WHERE IS IT? ANSWER OR DIE!
ONE SIDE, FRIEND, I WON'T ALLOW THEM TO HARM YOU! THIS MAN IS UNDER MY PROTECTION--LEAVE OR FACE THE CONSEQUENCES!
IMBECILE! MY BUSINESS IS WITH YOU, AUTOBOT!
WHERE IS THE MATRIX?! I WILL NOT ASK AGAIN!
AUTOBOT? MATRIX...? I--
NO! YOU-YOU'RE TRYING TO CONFUSE ME... GET TO MY FRIEND! IT WON'T WORK!
THE AUTOBOT IS DERANGED! SPINISTER--I WANT HIM ALIVE!
SEEMS A SHAME SOMEHOW, BUT YOU'RE THE BOSS! ALL YOURS, RUCKUS!
YEAH! NOW THIS IS MORE LIKE IT!
FWAMM!

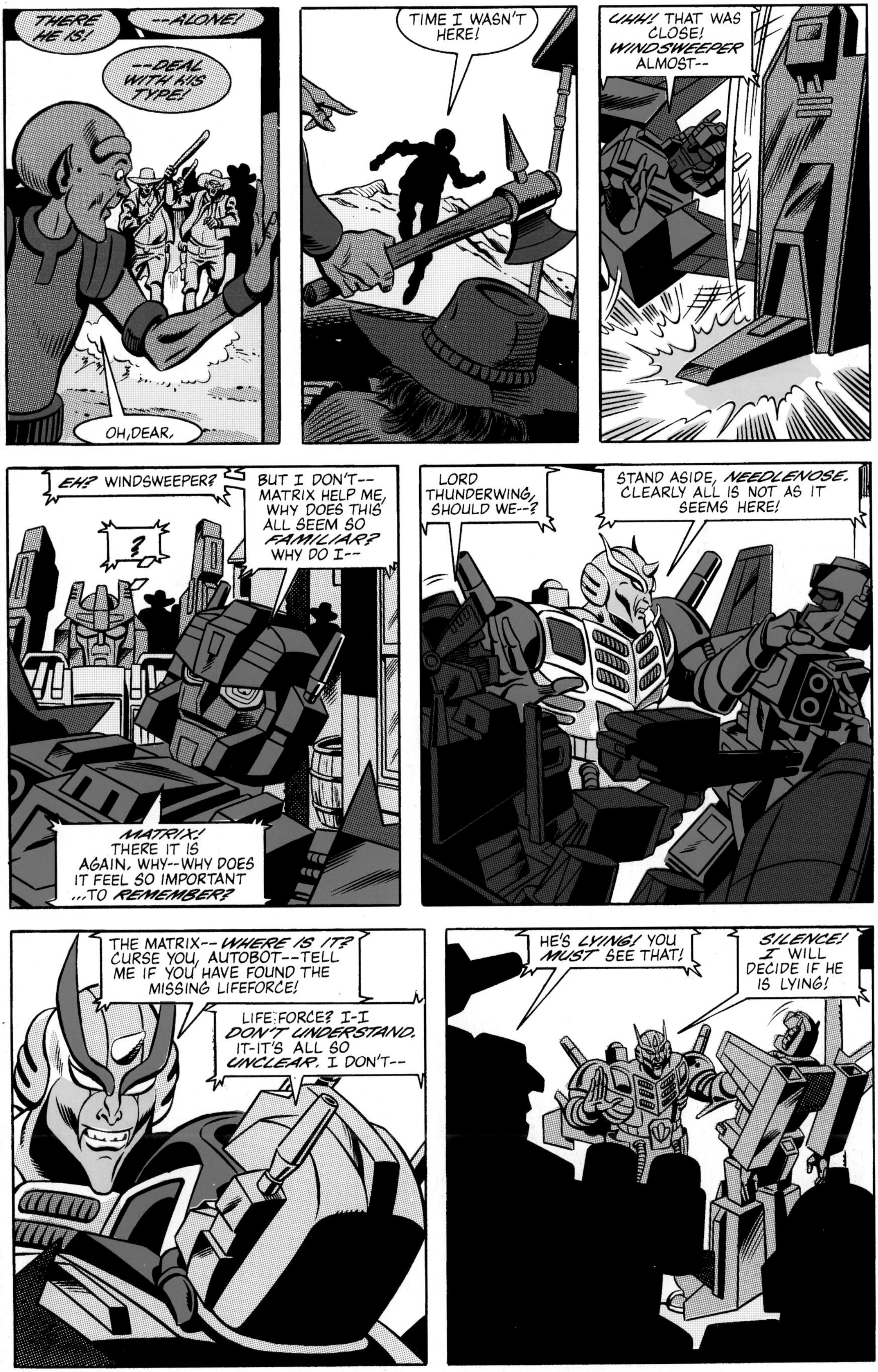

THERE HE IS!
--ALONE!
--DEAL WITH HIS TYPE!
OH, DEAR.
TIME I WASN'T HERE!
UHH! THAT WAS CLOSE! WINDSWEEPER ALMOST--
EH? WINDSWEEPER?
?
BUT I DON'T-- MATRIX HELP ME, WHY DOES THIS ALL SEEM SO FAMILIAR? WHY DO I--
MATRIX! THERE IT IS AGAIN. WHY--WHY DOES IT FEEL SO IMPORTANT ...TO REMEMBER?
LORD THUNDERWING, SHOULD WE--?
STAND ASIDE, NEEDLENOSE. CLEARLY ALL IS NOT AS IT SEEMS HERE!
THE MATRIX--WHERE IS IT? CURSE YOU, AUTOBOT--TELL ME IF YOU HAVE FOUND THE MISSING LIFEFORCE!
LIFE:FORCE? I-I DON'T UNDERSTAND. IT-IT'S ALL SO UNCLEAR. I DON'T--
HE'S LYING! YOU MUST SEE THAT!
SILENCE! I WILL DECIDE IF HE IS LYING!

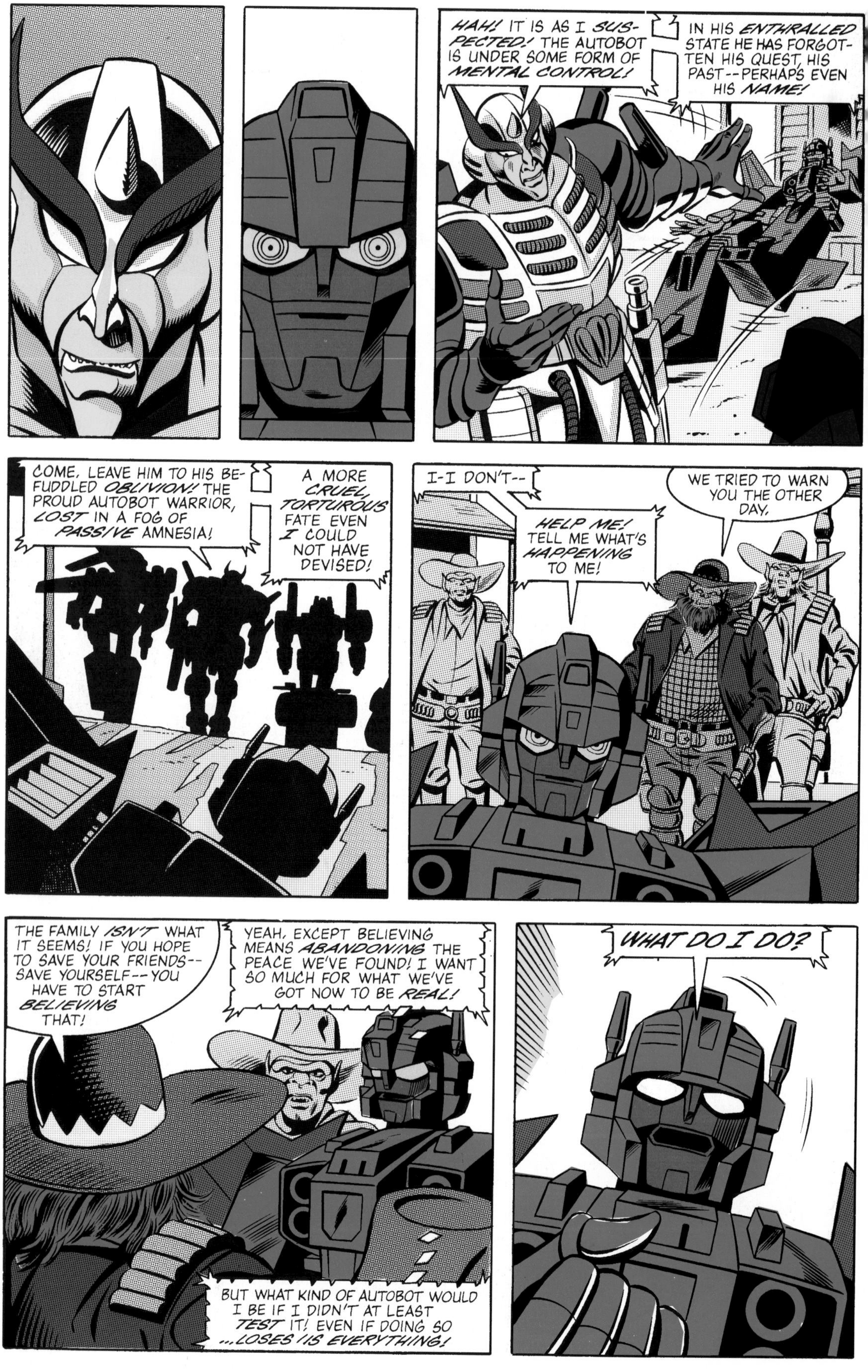
HAH! IT IS AS I SUSPECTED! THE AUTOBOT IS UNDER SOME FORM OF MENTAL CONTROL!
IN HIS ENTHRALLED STATE HE HAS FORGOTTEN HIS QUEST, HIS PAST--PERHAPS EVEN HIS NAME!
COME. LEAVE HIM TO HIS BEFUDDLED OBLIVION! THE PROUD AUTOBOT WARRIOR, LOST IN A FOG OF PASSIVE AMNESIA!
A MORE CRUEL, TORTUROUS FATE EVEN I COULD NOT HAVE DEVISED!
I-I DON'T--
HELP ME! TELL ME WHAT'S HAPPENING TO ME!
WE TRIED TO WARN YOU THE OTHER DAY.
THE FAMILY ISN'T WHAT IT SEEMS! IF YOU HOPE TO SAVE YOUR FRIENDS--SAVE YOURSELF--YOU HAVE TO START BELIEVING THAT!
YEAH, EXCEPT BELIEVING MEANS ABANDONING THE PEACE WE'VE FOUND! I WANT SO MUCH FOR WHAT WE'VE GOT NOW TO BE REAL!
BUT WHAT KIND OF AUTOBOT WOULD I BE IF I DIDN'T AT LEAST TEST IT! EVEN IF DOING SO ...LOSES US EVERYTHING!
WHAT DO I DO?

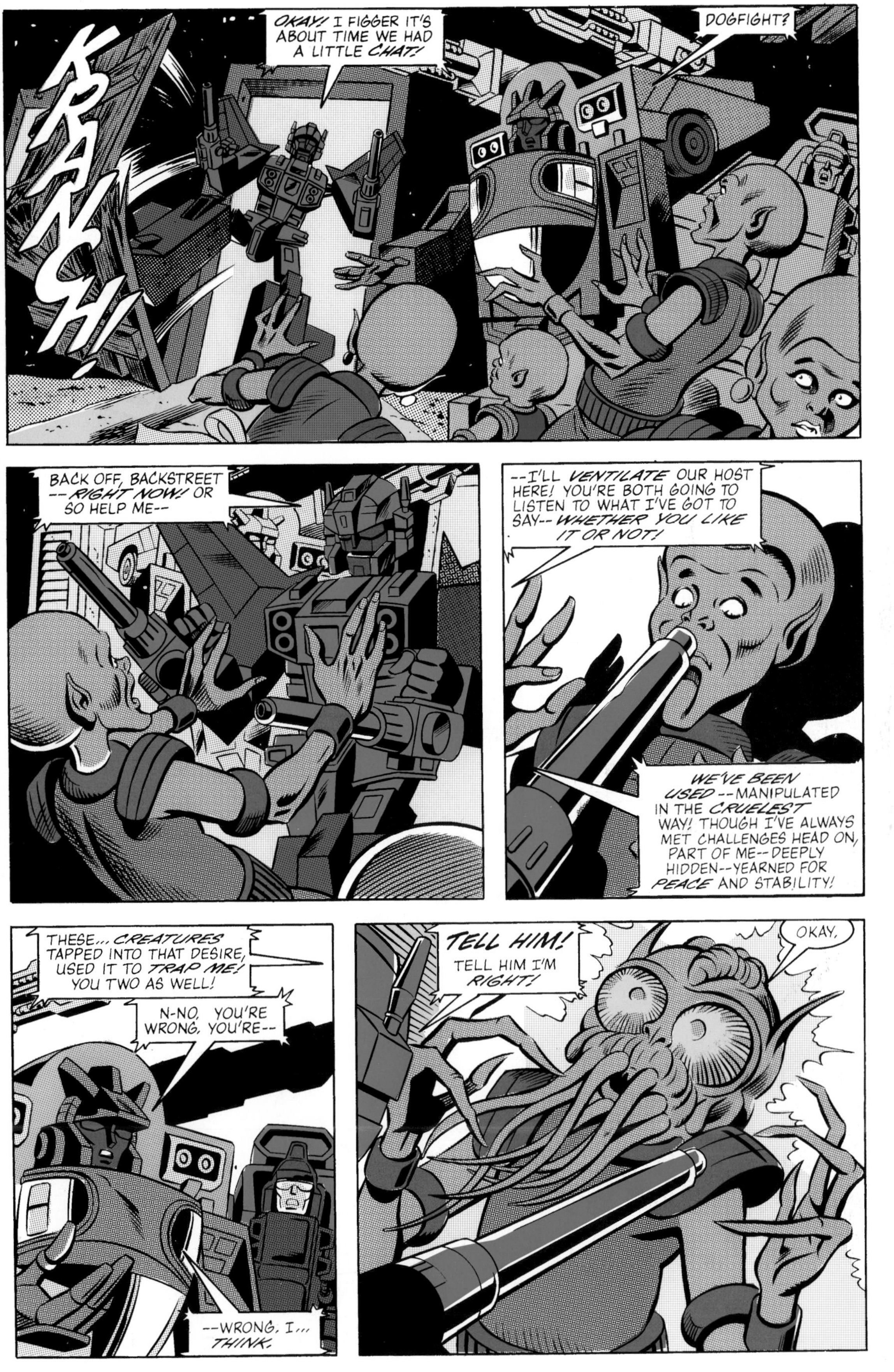
KRANCH!
OKAY! I FIGGER IT'S ABOUT TIME WE HAD A LITTLE CHAT!
DOGFIGHT?
BACK OFF, BACKSTREET --RIGHT NOW! OR SO HELP ME--
--I'LL VENTILATE OUR HOST HERE! YOU'RE BOTH GOING TO LISTEN TO WHAT I'VE GOT TO SAY-- WHETHER YOU LIKE IT OR NOT!
WE'VE BEEN USED --MANIPULATED IN THE CRUELEST WAY! THOUGH I'VE ALWAYS MET CHALLENGES HEAD ON, PART OF ME--DEEPLY HIDDEN--YEARNED FOR PEACE AND STABILITY!
THESE... CREATURES TAPPED INTO THAT DESIRE, USED IT TO TRAP ME! YOU TWO AS WELL!
N-NO, YOU'RE WRONG, YOU'RE--
--WRONG, I... THINK.
TELL HIM! TELL HIM I'M RIGHT!
OKAY,

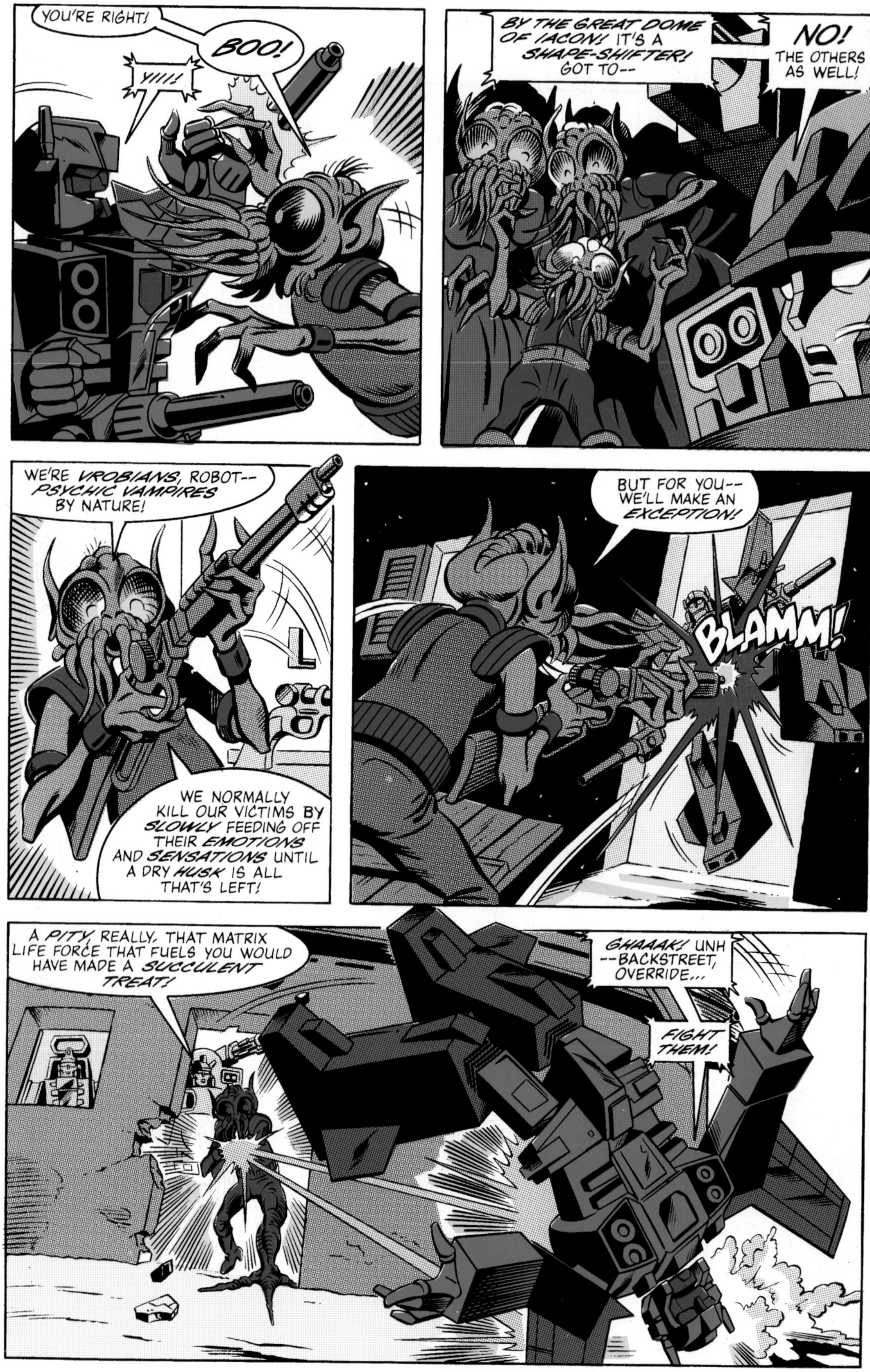

YOU'RE RIGHT!
BOO!
YIII!
BY THE GREAT DOME OF IACON! IT'S A SHAPE-SHIFTER! GOT TO--
NO! THE OTHERS AS WELL!
WE'RE VROBIANS, ROBOT-- PSYCHIC VAMPIRES BY NATURE!
WE NORMALLY KILL OUR VICTIMS BY SLOWLY FEEDING OFF THEIR EMOTIONS AND SENSATIONS UNTIL A DRY HUSK IS ALL THAT'S LEFT!
BUT FOR YOU-- WE'LL MAKE AN EXCEPTION!
BLAMM!
A PITY, REALLY, THAT MATRIX LIFE FORCE THAT FUELS YOU WOULD HAVE MADE A SUCCULENT TREAT!
GHAAAK! UNH --BACKSTREET, OVERRIDE...
FIGHT THEM!

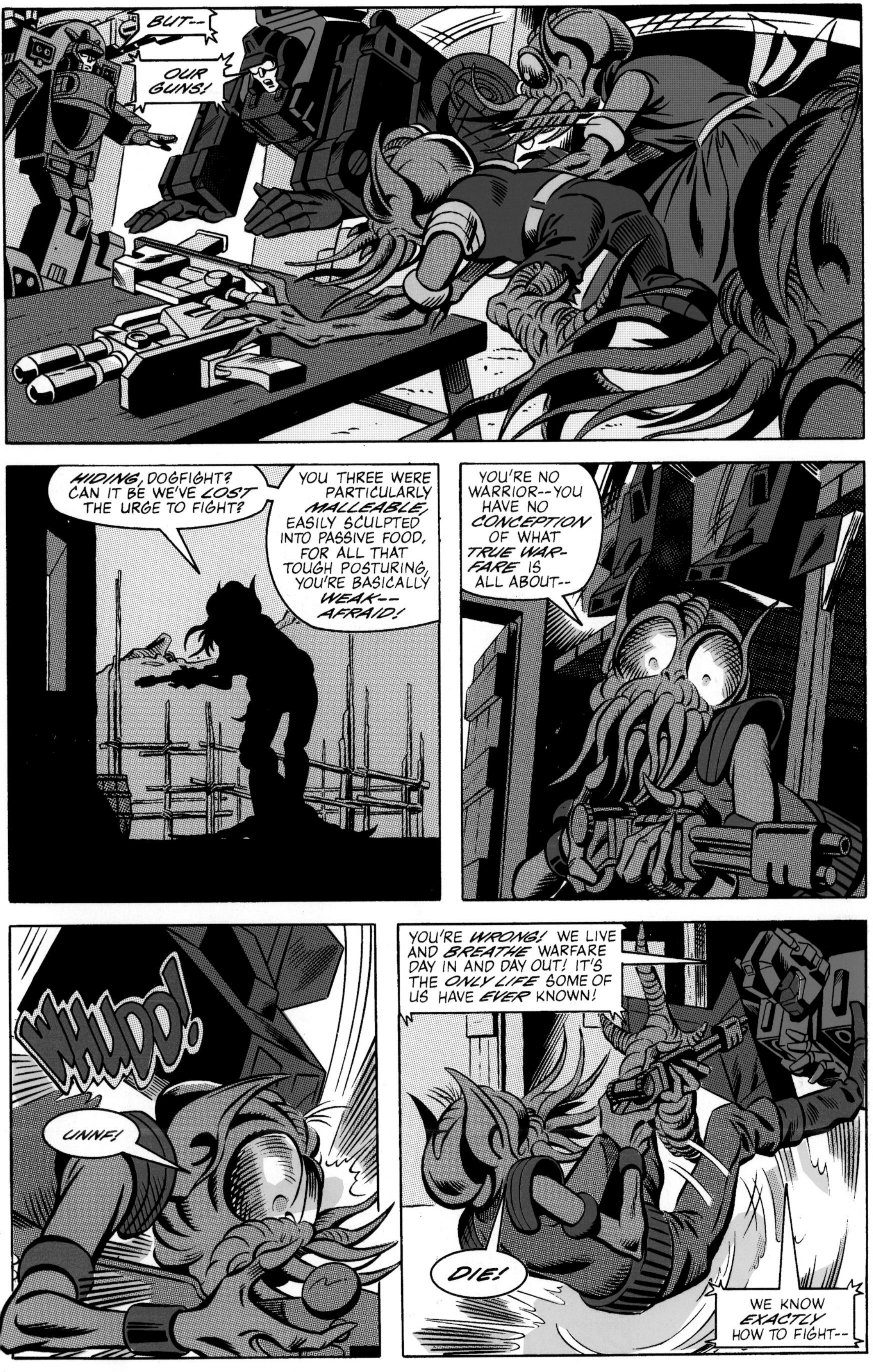
BUT--
OUR GUNS!
HIDING, DOGFIGHT? CAN IT BE WE'VE LOST THE URGE TO FIGHT?
YOU THREE WERE PARTICULARLY MALLEABLE, EASILY SCULPTED INTO PASSIVE FOOD. FOR ALL THAT TOUGH POSTURING, YOU'RE BASICALLY WEAK--AFRAID!
YOU'RE NO WARRIOR--YOU HAVE NO CONCEPTION OF WHAT TRUE WARFARE IS ALL ABOUT--
WHUDD!
UNNF!
YOU'RE WRONG! WE LIVE AND BREATHE WARFARE DAY IN AND DAY OUT! IT'S THE ONLY LIFE SOME OF US HAVE EVER KNOWN!
DIE!
WE KNOW EXACTLY HOW TO FIGHT--

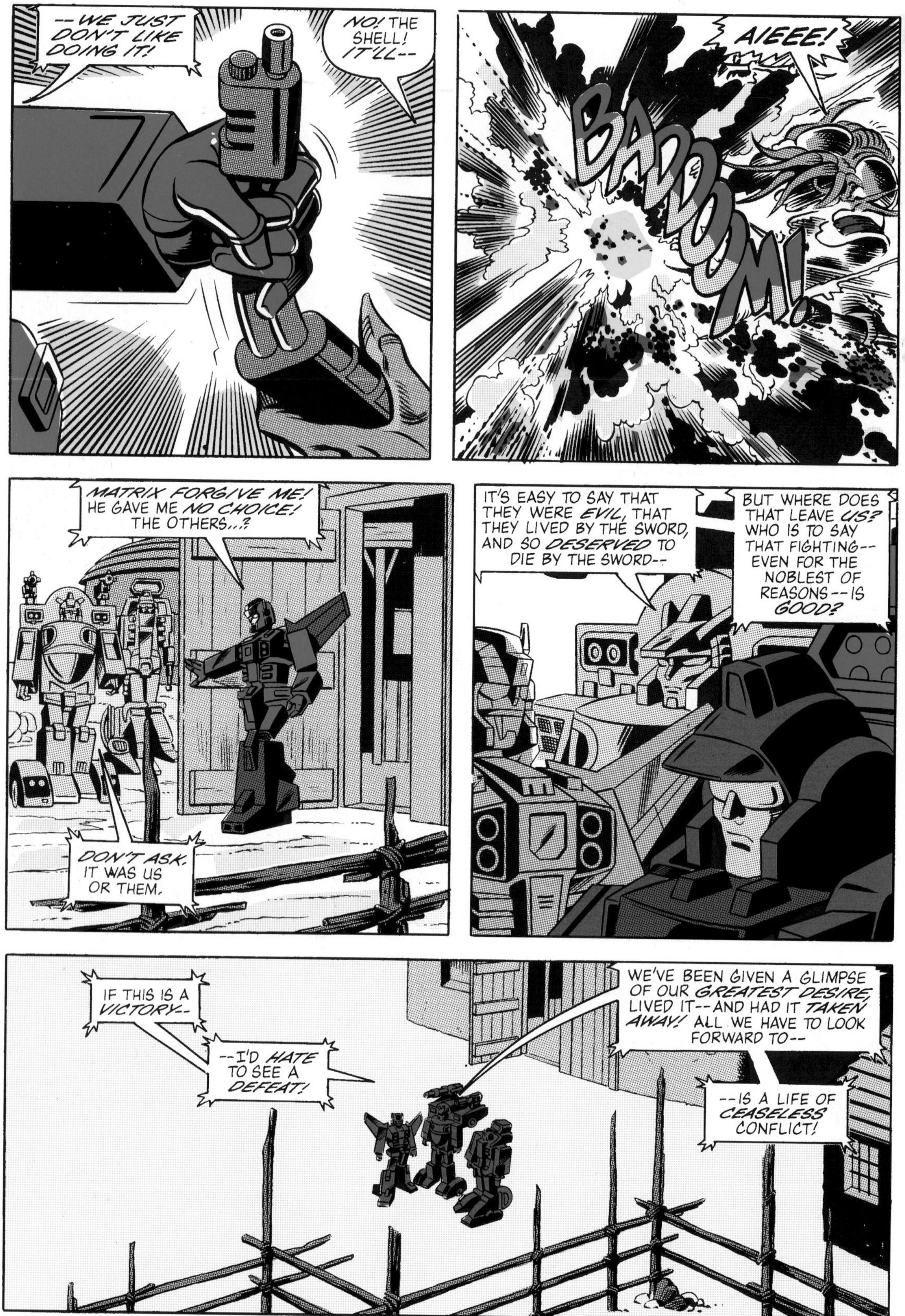

--WE JUST DON'T LIKE DOING IT!
NO! THE SHELL! IT'LL--
AIEEE!
BADOOM!
MATRIX FORGIVE ME! HE GAVE ME NO CHOICE! THE OTHERS...?
DON'T ASK. IT WAS US OR THEM.
IT'S EASY TO SAY THAT THEY WERE EVIL, THAT THEY LIVED BY THE SWORD, AND SO DESERVED TO DIE BY THE SWORD--
BUT WHERE DOES THAT LEAVE US? WHO IS TO SAY THAT FIGHTING-- EVEN FOR THE NOBLEST OF REASONS--IS GOOD?
IF THIS IS A VICTORY--
--I'D HATE TO SEE A DEFEAT!
WE'VE BEEN GIVEN A GLIMPSE OF OUR GREATEST DESIRE, LIVED IT--AND HAD IT TAKEN AWAY! ALL WE HAVE TO LOOK FORWARD TO--
--IS A LIFE OF CEASELESS CONFLICT!


**NEXT ISSUE** CONTINUING THE SEARCH FOR THE MATRIX, *DOUBLEHEADER*, *LONGTOOTH*, AND *PINCHER* VOYAGE TO AN OCEANIC WORLD AND FIND THEMSELVES PITTED AGAINST THE LAST OF THE TECHNO-ORGANIC WHALES, BUT WHAT STARTED AS A QUEST SOON BECOMES A **DEADLY OBSESSION!** IN THIRTY DAYS!

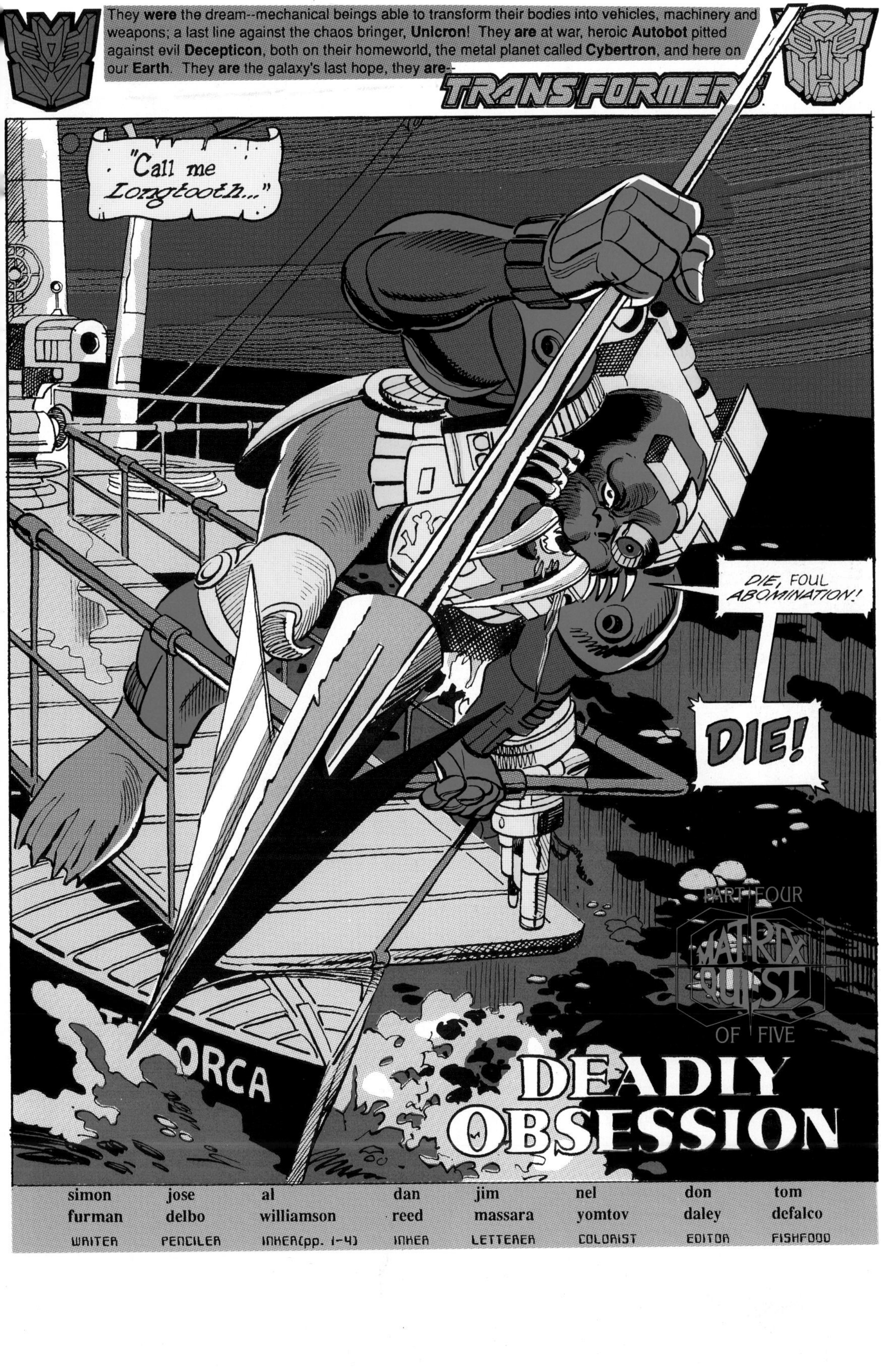
They were the dream--mechanical beings able to transform their bodies into vehicles, machinery and weapons; a last line against the chaos bringer, Unicron! They are at war, heroic Autobot pitted against evil Decepticon, both on their homeworld, the metal planet called Cybertron, and here on our Earth. They are the galaxy's last hope, they are--
TRANSFORMERS
"Call me Longtooth..."
DIE, FOUL ABOMINATION!
DIE!
ORCA
PART FOUR
MATRIX QUEST
OF FIVE
DEADLY OBSESSION
simon furman WRITER
jose delbo PENCILER
al williamson INKER(pp. 1-4)
dan reed INKER
jim massara LETTERER
nel yomtov COLORIST
don daley EDITOR
tom defalco FISHFOOD

YOU'VE GIVEN ME FAIR CHASE, MONSTER, BUT THE PURSUIT IS ALMOST OVER--

"'Twas the sixth day of my voyage through the churning seas of *Pequod* that the *beast* was sighted..."

--AND *VENGEANCE* IS MINE! YOU HEAR ME? *MINE!*

HAH! MOCK ME IF YOU WILL-- *GNNN!*

*UNH,* BUT I HAVE SWORN THAT FOR THE PAIN AND SUFFERING YOU HAVE BROUGHT TO ME AND OTHER SEAFARERS--

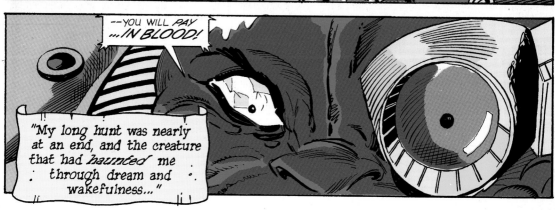

--YOU WILL *PAY* ...*IN BLOOD!*

"My long hunt was nearly at an end, and the creature that had *haunted* me through dream and wakefulness..."

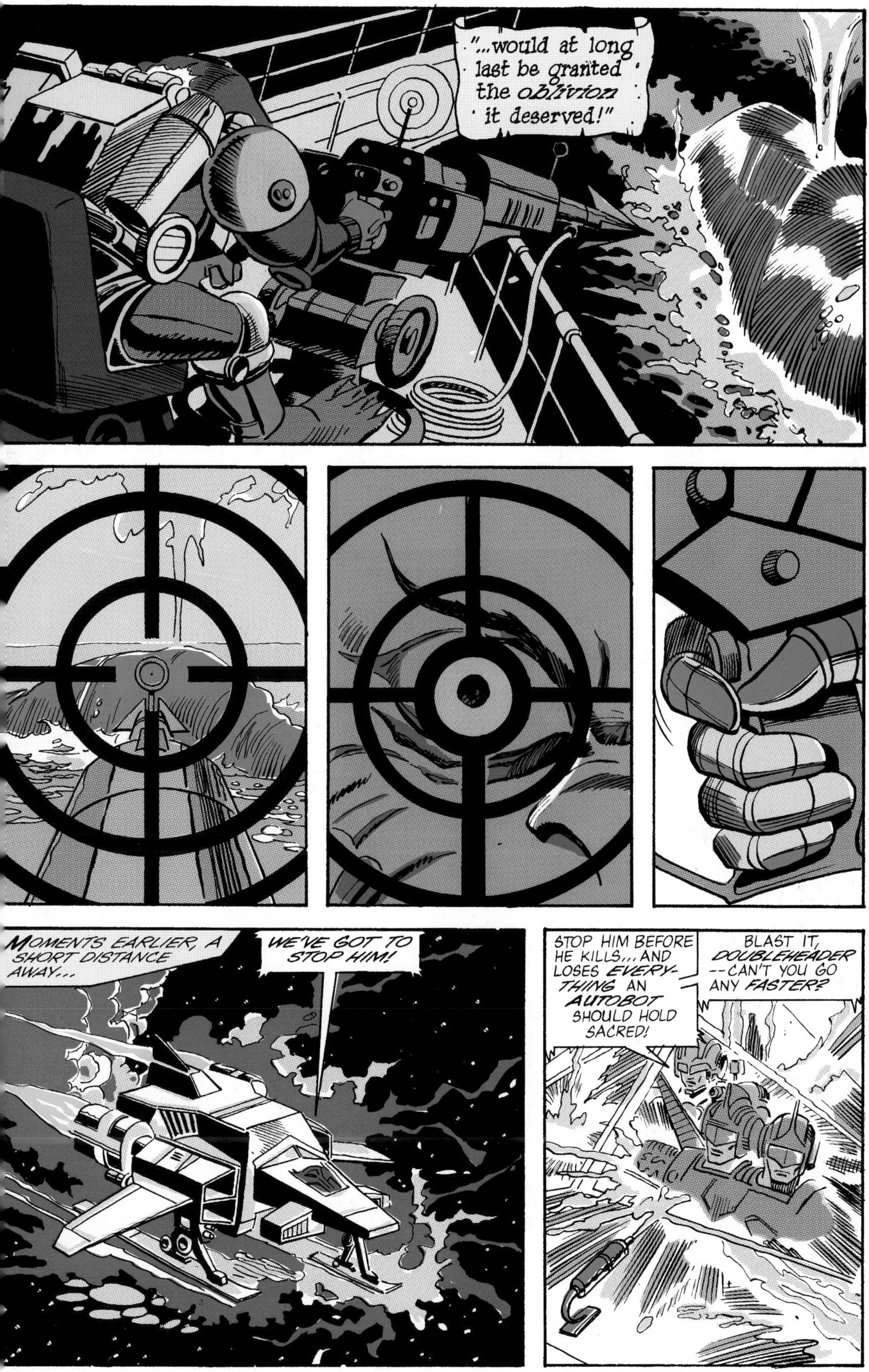
"...would at long last be granted the oblivion it deserved!"
MOMENTS EARLIER, A SHORT DISTANCE AWAY...
WE'VE GOT TO STOP HIM!
STOP HIM BEFORE HE KILLS... AND LOSES EVERY-THING AN AUTOBOT SHOULD HOLD SACRED!
BLAST IT, DOUBLEHEADER --CAN'T YOU GO ANY FASTER?

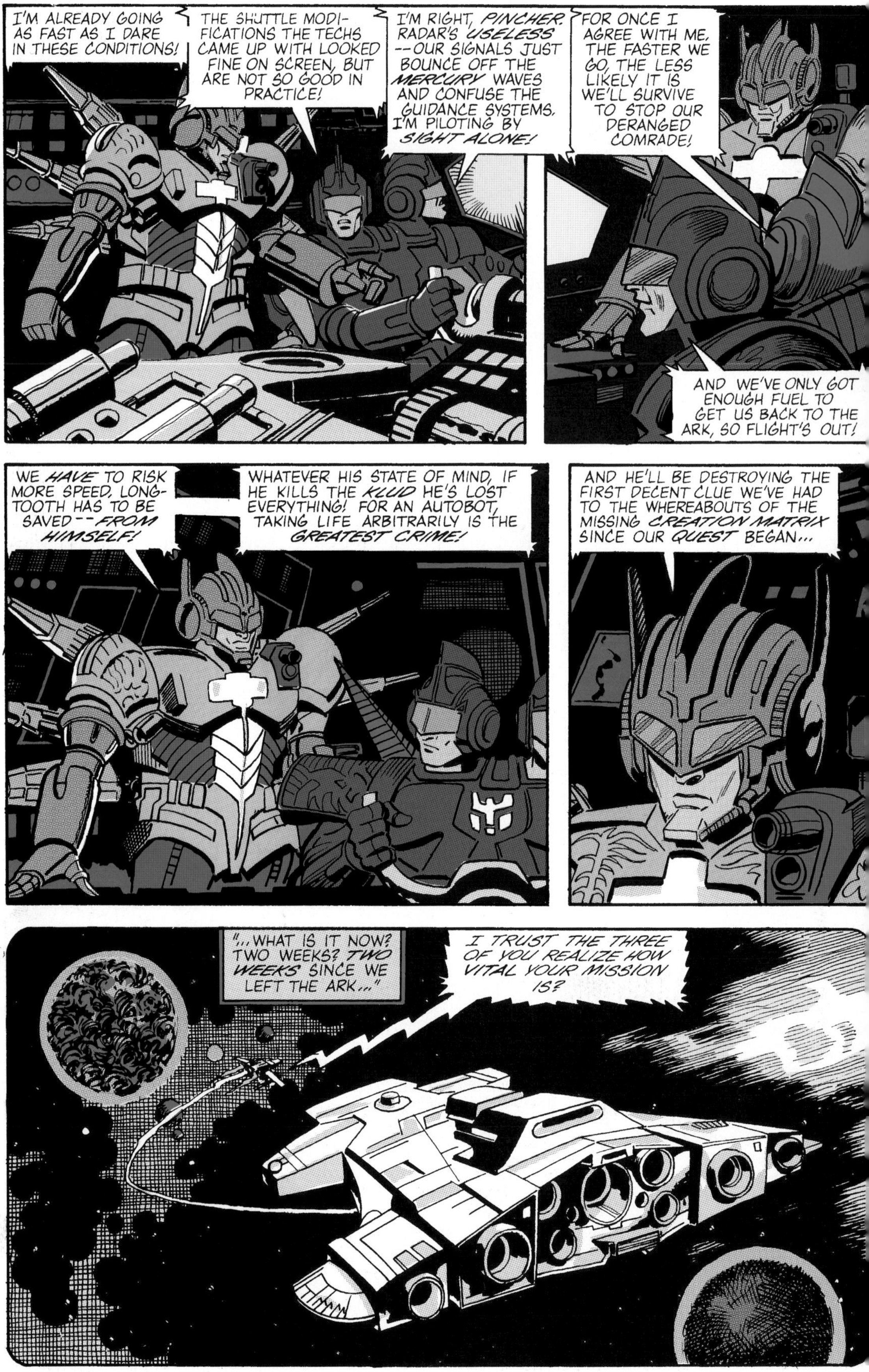
I'M ALREADY GOING AS FAST AS I DARE IN THESE CONDITIONS!
THE SHUTTLE MODIFICATIONS THE TECHS CAME UP WITH LOOKED FINE ON SCREEN, BUT ARE NOT SO GOOD IN PRACTICE!
I'M RIGHT, PINCHER. RADAR'S USELESS --OUR SIGNALS JUST BOUNCE OFF THE MERCURY WAVES AND CONFUSE THE GUIDANCE SYSTEMS. I'M PILOTING BY SIGHT ALONE!
FOR ONCE I AGREE WITH ME. THE FASTER WE GO, THE LESS LIKELY IT IS WE'LL SURVIVE TO STOP OUR DERANGED COMRADE!
AND WE'VE ONLY GOT ENOUGH FUEL TO GET US BACK TO THE ARK, SO FLIGHT'S OUT!
WE HAVE TO RISK MORE SPEED. LONGTOOTH HAS TO BE SAVED--FROM HIMSELF!
WHATEVER HIS STATE OF MIND, IF HE KILLS THE KLUD HE'S LOST EVERYTHING! FOR AN AUTOBOT, TAKING LIFE ARBITRARILY IS THE GREATEST CRIME!
AND HE'LL BE DESTROYING THE FIRST DECENT CLUE WE'VE HAD TO THE WHEREABOUTS OF THE MISSING CREATION MATRIX SINCE OUR QUEST BEGAN...
"...WHAT IS IT NOW? TWO WEEKS? TWO WEEKS SINCE WE LEFT THE ARK..."
I TRUST THE THREE OF YOU REALIZE HOW VITAL YOUR MISSION IS?

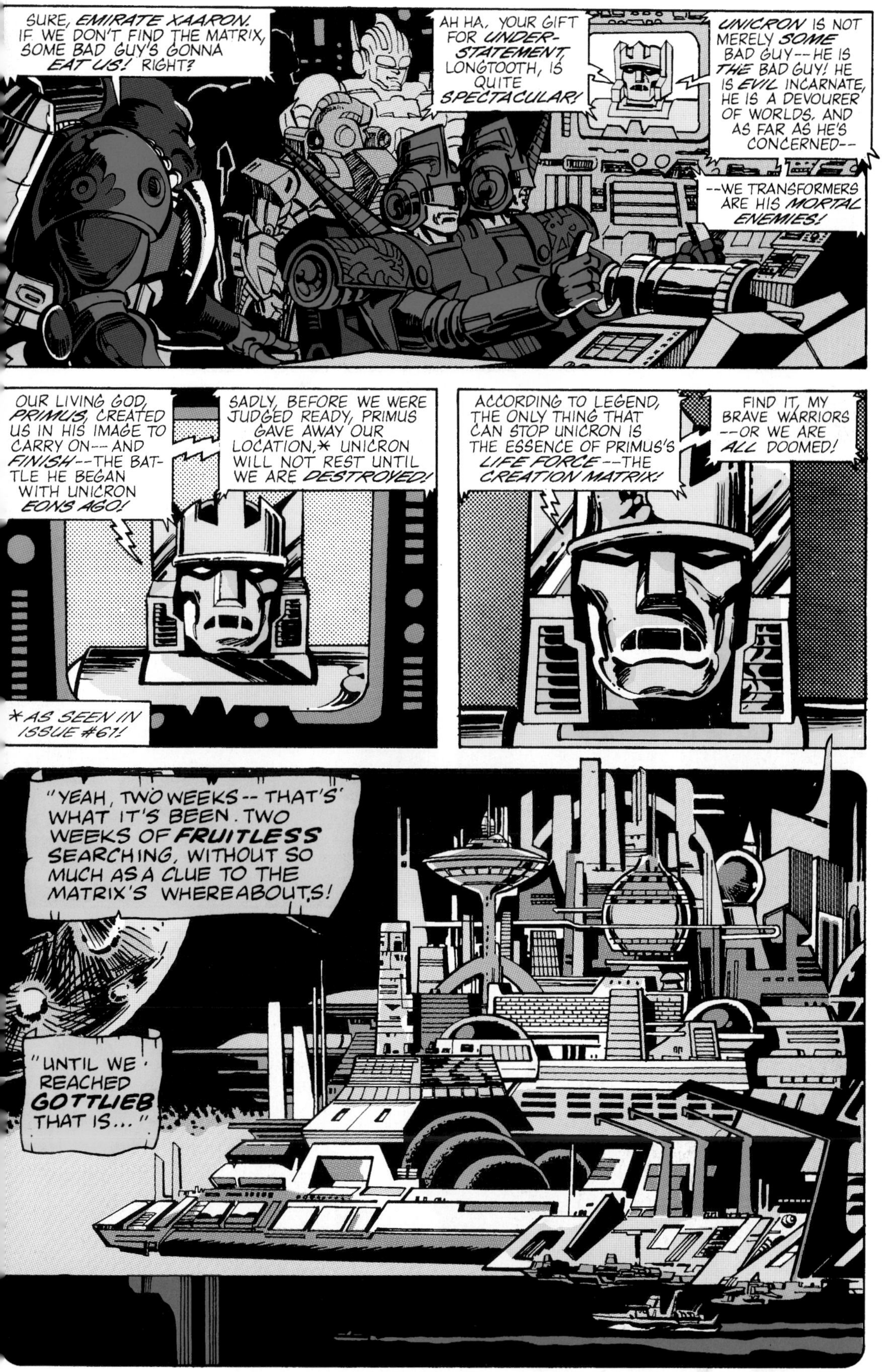
SURE, EMIRATE XAARON. IF WE DON'T FIND THE MATRIX, SOME BAD GUY'S GONNA EAT US! RIGHT?
AH HA, YOUR GIFT FOR UNDERSTATEMENT, LONGTOOTH, IS QUITE SPECTACULAR!
UNICRON IS NOT MERELY SOME BAD GUY--HE IS THE BAD GUY! HE IS EVIL INCARNATE, HE IS A DEVOURER OF WORLDS. AND AS FAR AS HE'S CONCERNED--
--WE TRANSFORMERS ARE HIS MORTAL ENEMIES!
OUR LIVING GOD, PRIMUS, CREATED US IN HIS IMAGE TO CARRY ON--AND FINISH--THE BATTLE HE BEGAN WITH UNICRON EONS AGO!
SADLY, BEFORE WE WERE JUDGED READY, PRIMUS GAVE AWAY OUR LOCATION,* UNICRON WILL NOT REST UNTIL WE ARE DESTROYED!
*AS SEEN IN ISSUE #61!
ACCORDING TO LEGEND, THE ONLY THING THAT CAN STOP UNICRON IS THE ESSENCE OF PRIMUS'S LIFE FORCE--THE CREATION MATRIX!
FIND IT, MY BRAVE WARRIORS --OR WE ARE ALL DOOMED!
"YEAH, TWO WEEKS--THAT'S WHAT IT'S BEEN. TWO WEEKS OF FRUITLESS SEARCHING, WITHOUT SO MUCH AS A CLUE TO THE MATRIX'S WHEREABOUTS!
"UNTIL WE REACHED GOTTLIEB THAT IS..."

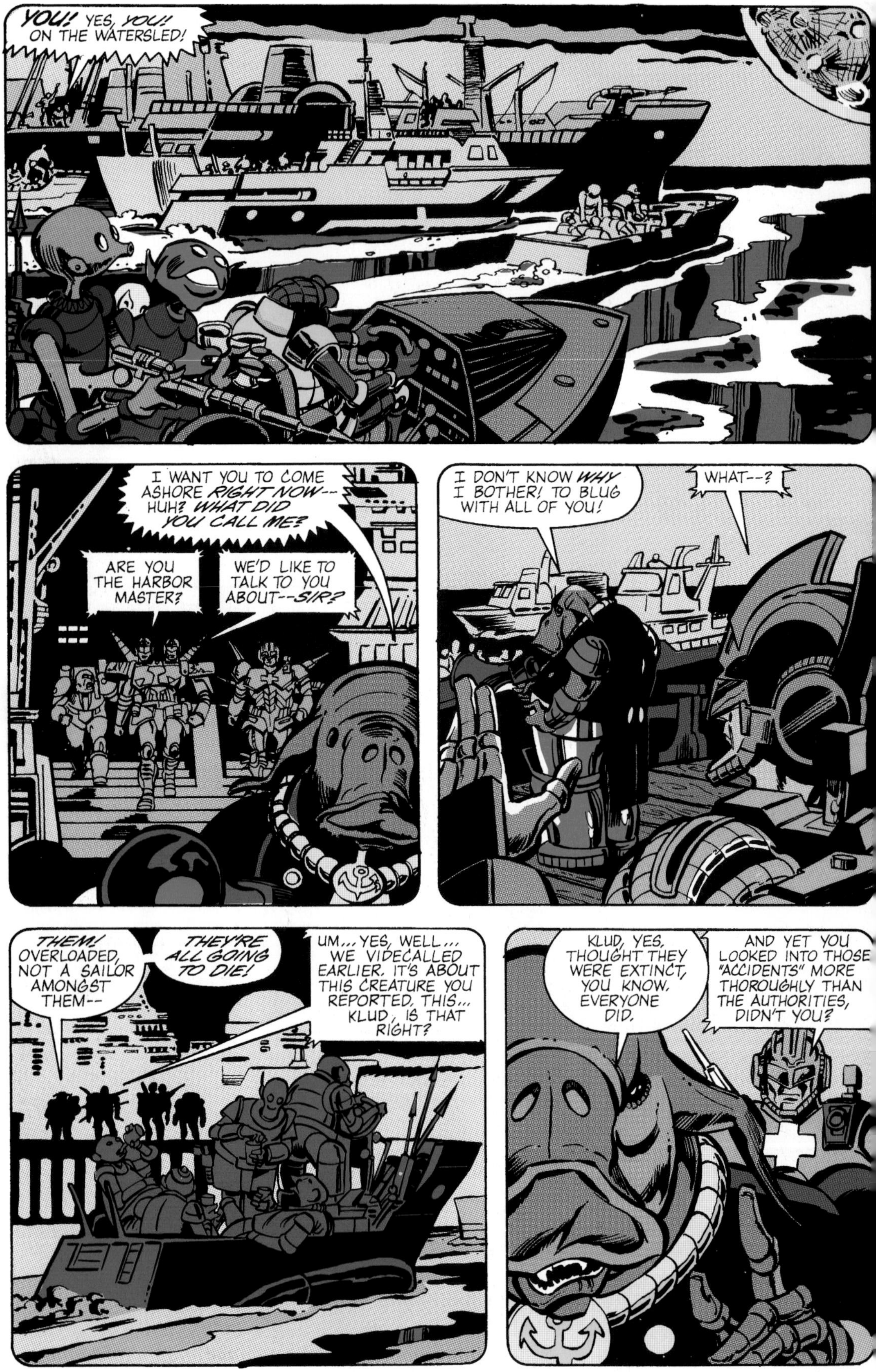
YOU! YES, YOU! ON THE WATERSLED!
I WANT YOU TO COME ASHORE RIGHT NOW-- HUH? WHAT DID YOU CALL ME?
ARE YOU THE HARBOR MASTER?
WE'D LIKE TO TALK TO YOU ABOUT--SIR?
I DON'T KNOW WHY I BOTHER! TO BLUG WITH ALL OF YOU!
WHAT--?
THEM! OVERLOADED, NOT A SAILOR AMONGST THEM--
THEY'RE ALL GOING TO DIE!
UM... YES, WELL... WE VIDECALLED EARLIER. IT'S ABOUT THIS CREATURE YOU REPORTED. THIS... KLUD, IS THAT RIGHT?
KLUD, YES, THOUGHT THEY WERE EXTINCT, YOU KNOW. EVERYONE DID.
AND YET YOU LOOKED INTO THOSE "ACCIDENTS" MORE THOROUGHLY THAN THE AUTHORITIES, DIDN'T YOU?

YEAH, I KNOW A *WHITEWASH* JOB WHEN I SEE ONE! BAD FOR THE HOLIDAY TRADE TO HAVE -- *HOLD IT!*

YOU FROM THE *TOURIST OFFICE?*

NO-- *NO!* JUST... *INTERESTED.*

HRM, OKAY. JUST CHECKIN'. SINCE I CALLED THEM ALL LIARS, I'VE BEEN EX- PECTING A *VISIT.* KNOW WHAT I MEAN? PEOPLE HAVE "DISAPPEARED" FOR LESS!

ANYWAY, AFTER A THIRD CRAFT DIDN'T MAKE IT BACK HERE, I DE- CIDED TO INVESTIGATE. I MEAN, IT'S NOT LIKE WE DON'T HAVE THE ODD ACCIDENT--

--BUT *THREE* IN AS MANY GUHKS?! *NO WAY!*

"WHEN THE WRECKAGE OF THE LAST ONE WAS WASHED UP, I DID ME SOME CHECKIN'...."

*THIS WAS NO BOATING ACCIDENT!*

13

THE HULL HAD *TEETH MARKS* IN IT-- AND THE ONLY THING WITH A BITE RADIUS OF THAT SIZE WAS A *KLUD!*

'COURSE, ONCE THE LOCAL VIDS GOT HOLD OF THE "BACK FROM THE DEAD" STORY, THERE WAS NO WAY THEY COULD HUSH IT UP, AND--

HOLD IT.

*YOU!* YES, *YOU!* I WANT YOU TO COME ASHORE--

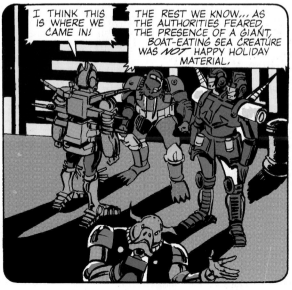

I THINK THIS IS WHERE WE CAME IN!

THE REST WE KNOW.... AS THE AUTHORITIES FEARED, THE PRESENCE OF A GIANT, BOAT-EATING SEA CREATURE WAS *NOT* HAPPY HOLIDAY MATERIAL.

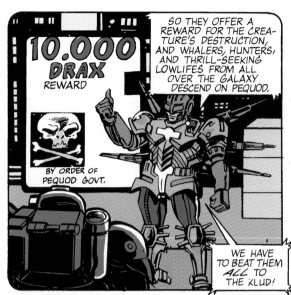

**10,000 DRAX** REWARD

BY ORDER OF PEQUOD GOVT.

SO THEY OFFER A REWARD FOR THE CREATURE'S DESTRUCTION, AND WHALERS, HUNTERS, AND THRILL-SEEKING LOWLIFES FROM ALL OVER THE GALAXY DESCEND ON PEQUOD.

WE HAVE TO BEAT THEM *ALL* TO THE KLUD!

**WHAT?!** XAARON TELLS US *NOT* TO GET INVOLVED WITH LOCAL AFFAIRS, AND HERE WE ARE LOOKING TO *SLAUGHTER* A CREATURE WHICH MAY OR MAY NOT BE A MENACE AND CLAIM THE REWARD?

WELL, *COUNT ME OUT!*

YOU DON'T UNDERSTAND

XAARON ALSO TOLD US

TO LOOK FOR INCIDENTS

OF MIRACULOUS *RESURRECTIONS*

THAT COULD BE

THE MATRIX AT WORK!

HUUUH!

YOU WERE RIGHT, OF COURSE, WE JUST DIDN'T KNOW HOW *BADLY* THINGS WOULD TURN OUT!

LONGTOOTH MAY NOT BE IN CONTROL OF HIS MENTAL FACILITIES RIGHT NOW, BUT HE'S STILL A *ROGUE* AUTOBOT!

FASTER, DOUBLEHEADER, BEFORE WE RUN OUT OF OPTIONS! WE HAVE TO--

STOP HIM! *NOW!*

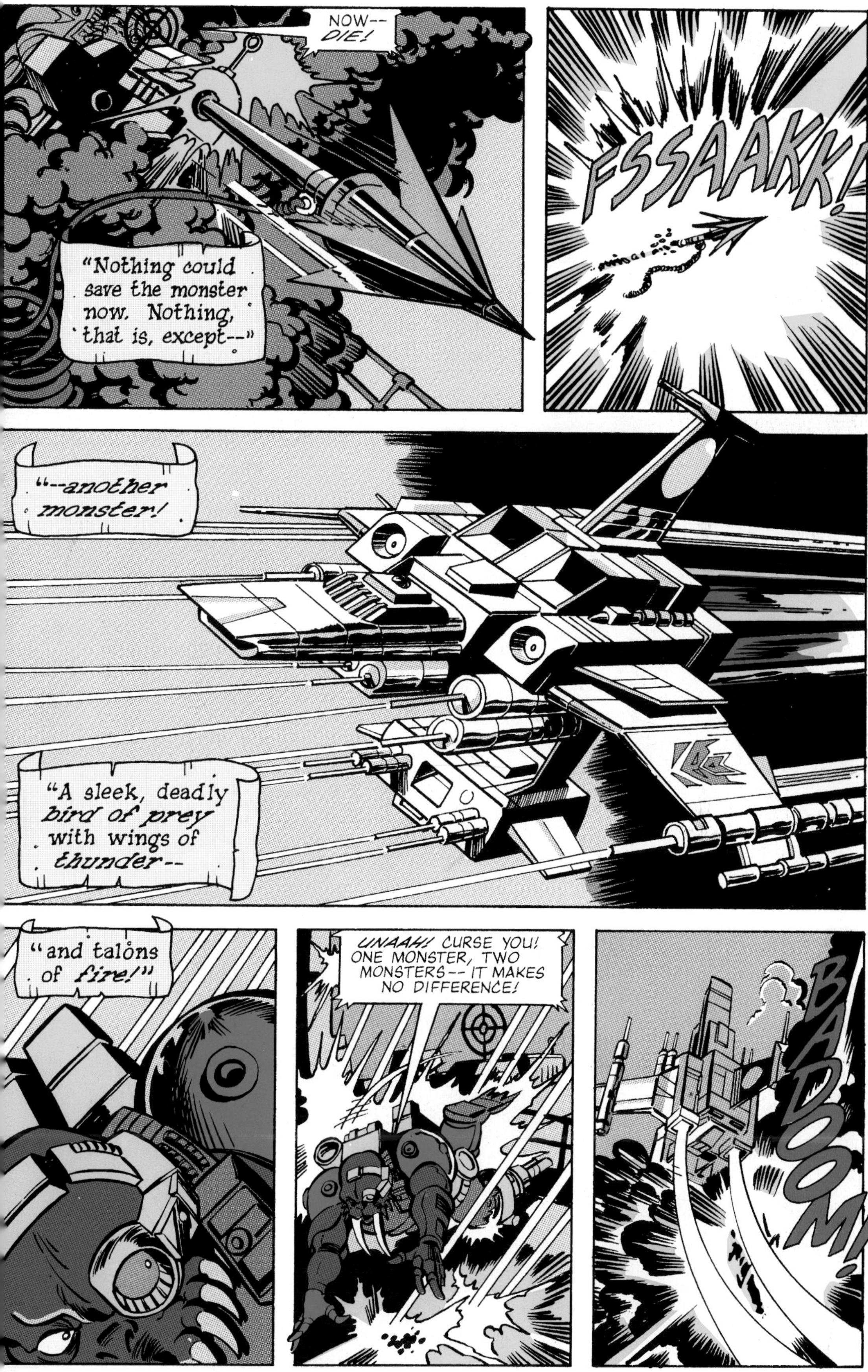
NOW-- DIE!
"Nothing could save the monster now. Nothing, that is, except--"
FSSAAKK!
"--another monster!
"A sleek, deadly bird of prey with wings of thunder--
"and talons of fire!"
UNAAH! CURSE YOU! ONE MONSTER, TWO MONSTERS-- IT MAKES NO DIFFERENCE!
BADOOOM!

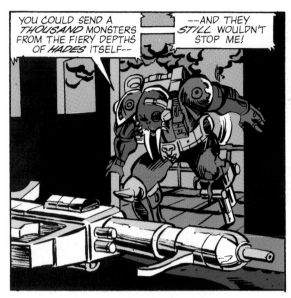

YOU COULD SEND A *THOUSAND* MONSTERS FROM THE FIERY DEPTHS OF *HADES* ITSELF--

--AND THEY *STILL* WOULDN'T STOP ME!

DID WE GET HIM?

I'M NOT SURE, *WINDSWEEPER*, *NEEDLENOSE*--BRING US AROUND FOR ANOTHER ATTACK RUN!

THE CREATURE MUST BE *PROTECTED*-- AT ALL COSTS! *UNDERSTOOD?*

UNDERSTOOD, *LORD THUNDERWING!*

*HAW!* IT'S COME TO SOME-THING WHEN *DECEPTICON* LEADERS START WORRYING ABOUT *DUMB ANIMALS!*

*RUCKUS*--

*SHUT UP!*

*KRUD*

*CHANK!*

*GNNN!*

WHAT ABOUT YOU, *SPINISTER?* PERHAPS **YOU** WOULD LIKE TO *QUESTION* MY ORDERS?

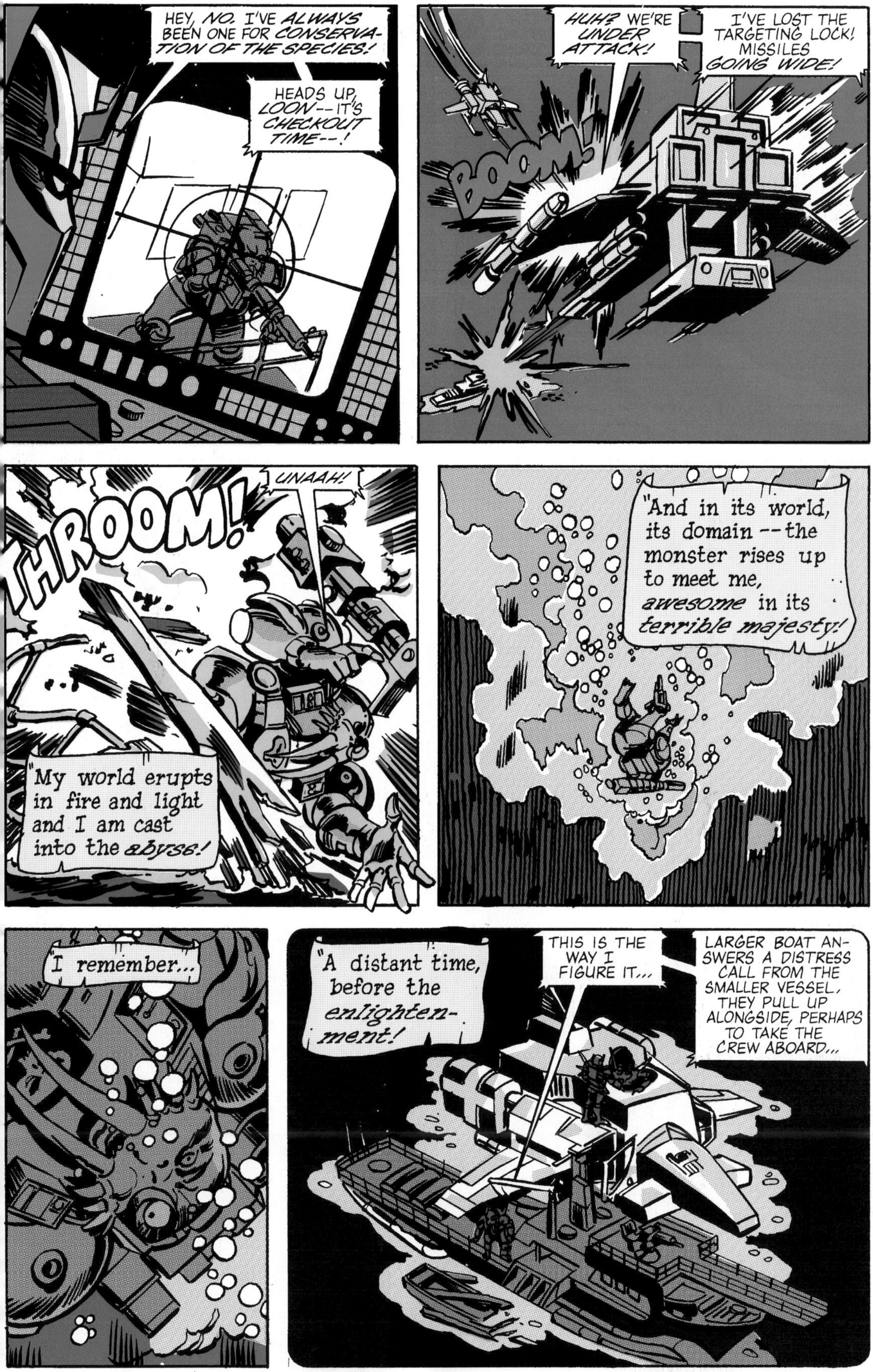

HEY, NO. I'VE ALWAYS BEEN ONE FOR CONSERVATION OF THE SPECIES!
HEADS UP, LOON--IT'S CHECKOUT TIME--!
HUH? WE'RE UNDER ATTACK!
I'VE LOST THE TARGETING LOCK! MISSILES GOING WIDE!
BOOM!
THROOM!
UNAAH!
"My world erupts in fire and light and I am cast into the abyss!
"And in its world, its domain--the monster rises up to meet me, awesome in its terrible majesty!
"I remember...
"A distant time, before the enlightenment!
THIS IS THE WAY I FIGURE IT...
LARGER BOAT ANSWERS A DISTRESS CALL FROM THE SMALLER VESSEL. THEY PULL UP ALONGSIDE, PERHAPS TO TAKE THE CREW ABOARD...

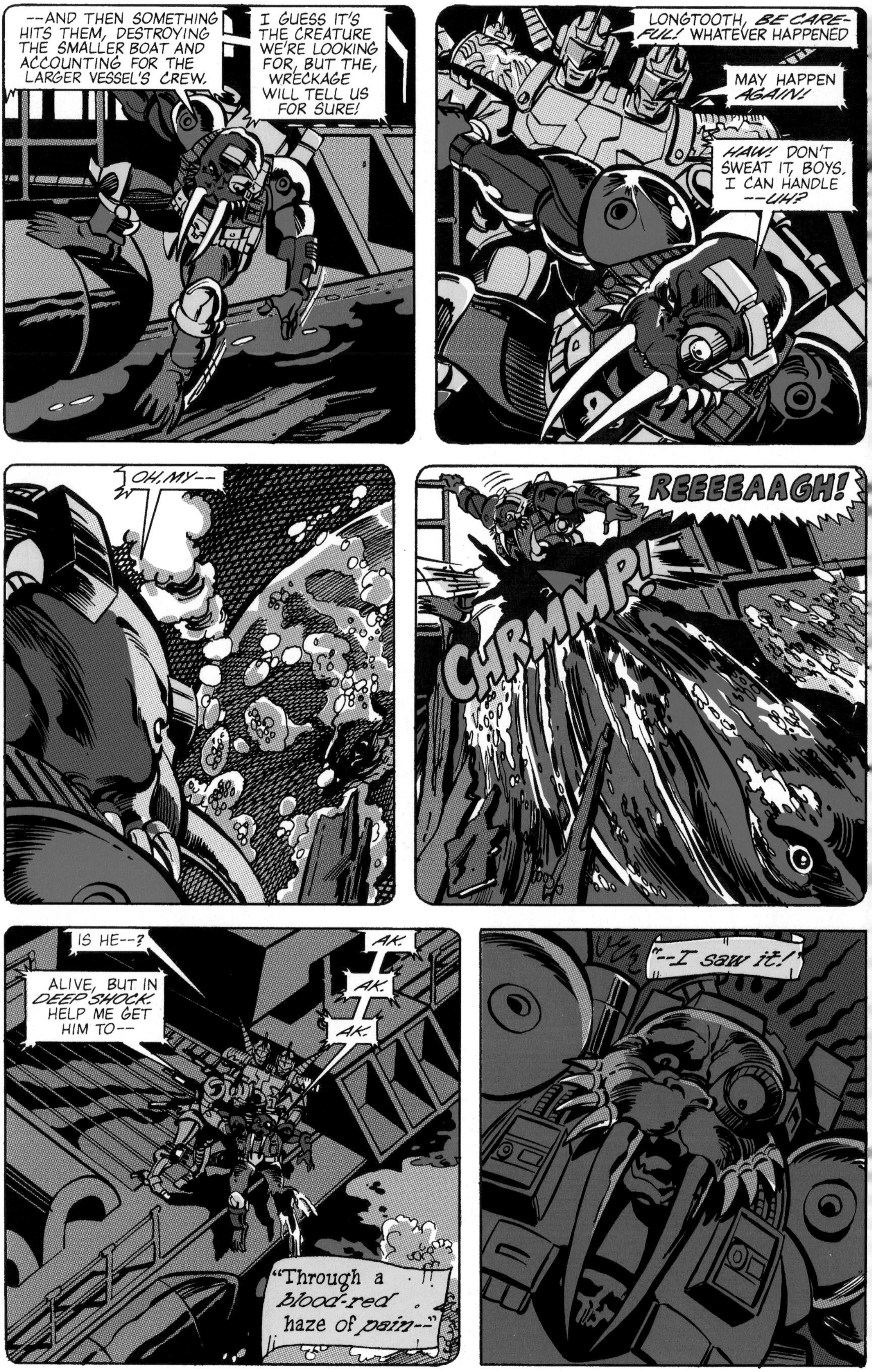
--AND THEN SOMETHING HITS THEM, DESTROYING THE SMALLER BOAT AND ACCOUNTING FOR THE LARGER VESSEL'S CREW.
I GUESS IT'S THE CREATURE WE'RE LOOKING FOR, BUT THE WRECKAGE WILL TELL US FOR SURE!
LONGTOOTH, BE CAREFUL! WHATEVER HAPPENED
MAY HAPPEN AGAIN!
HAW! DON'T SWEAT IT, BOYS, I CAN HANDLE --UH?
OH, MY--
REEEEAAGH!
CHRMMP!
IS HE--?
ALIVE, BUT IN DEEP SHOCK. HELP ME GET HIM TO--
AK.
AK.
AK.
"Through a blood-red haze of pain--"
"--I saw it!"

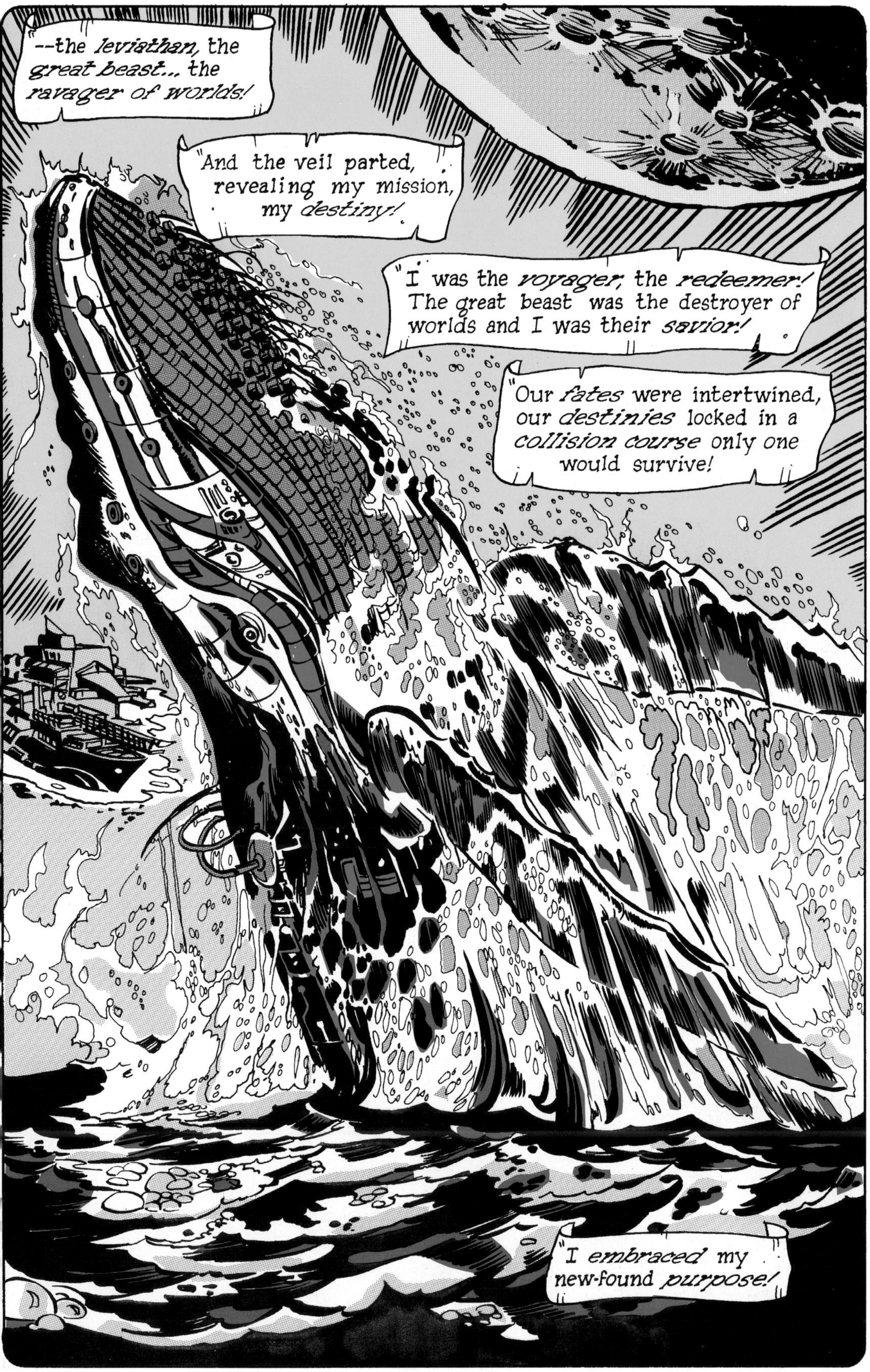
"--the leviathan, the great beast... the ravager of worlds!
"And the veil parted, revealing my mission, my destiny!
"I was the voyager, the redeemer! The great beast was the destroyer of worlds and I was their savior!
"Our fates were intertwined, our destinies locked in a collision course only one would survive!
"I embraced my new-found purpose!

"Repaired and *revitalized,* I stole a craft, and the hunt began."

"And now, it is as it should be. Face-to-face--

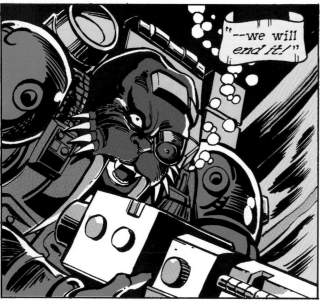

"--we will *end it!*"

AUTOBOTS! LONGTOOTH'S FELLOW MATRIX HUNTERS, NO DOUBT!

THEY MUST *NOT* BE ALLOWED TO INTERFERE! *DESTROY THEM!*

ERM.... I'M NOT QUESTIONING YOU OR ANYTHING, LORD THUNDERWING, BUT--

--AREN'T WE RISKING AN AWFUL LOT JUST TO SAVE THIS CREATURE? I MEAN--

I--NO, NO RISK IS TOO GREAT TO TAKE! THE CREATURE-- IT...HAS TOUCHED THE MATRIX, IT...*KNOWS.* I WILL--

NNN!

DO AS I SAY! NOW! YOU'RE HERE TO FIGHT, *NOT THINK!*

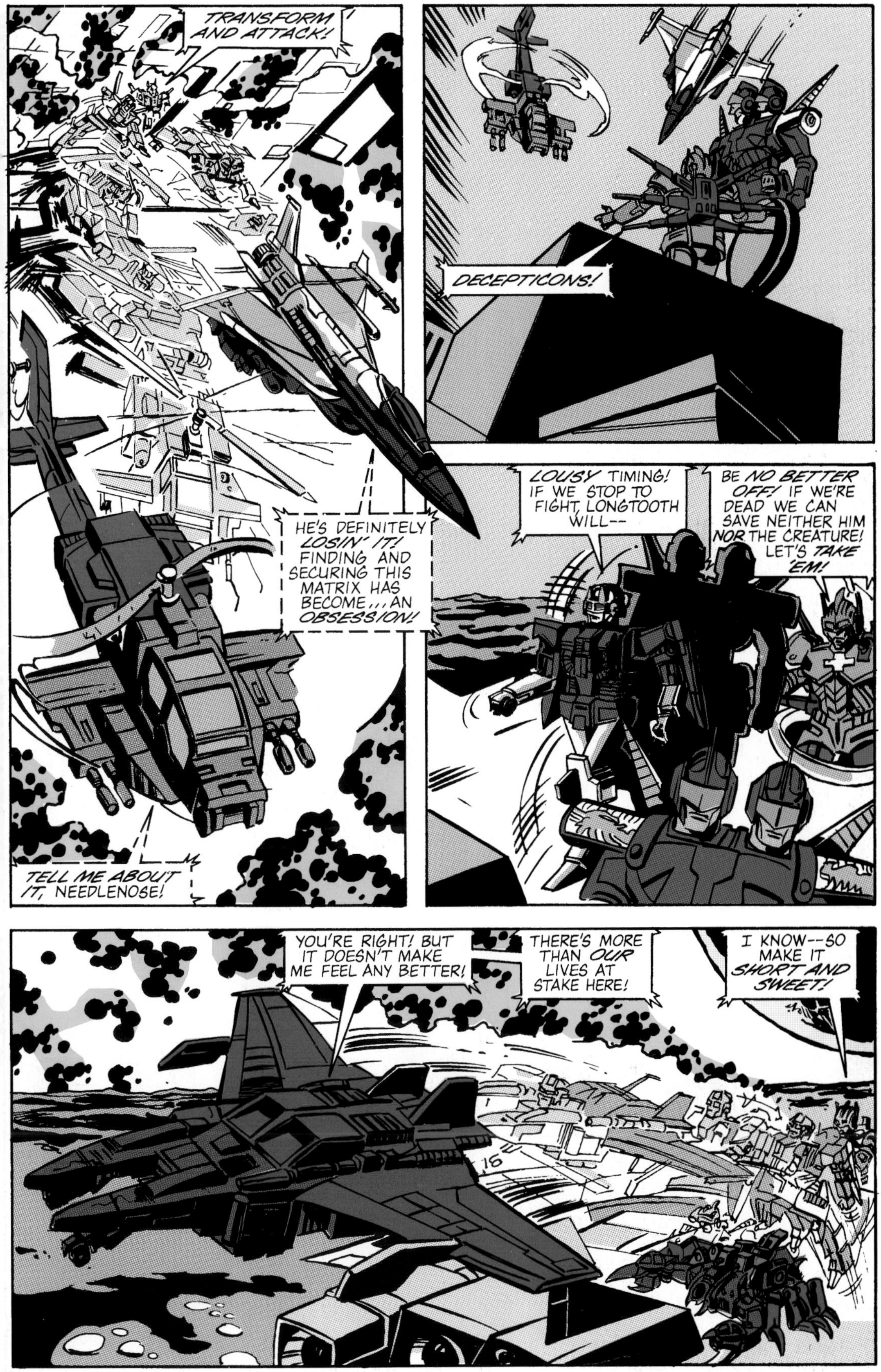
TRANSFORM AND ATTACK!
DECEPTICONS!
HE'S DEFINITELY LOSIN' IT! FINDING AND SECURING THIS MATRIX HAS BECOME... AN OBSESSION!
TELL ME ABOUT IT, NEEDLENOSE!
LOUSY TIMING! IF WE STOP TO FIGHT, LONGTOOTH WILL--
BE NO BETTER OFF! IF WE'RE DEAD WE CAN SAVE NEITHER HIM NOR THE CREATURE! LET'S TAKE 'EM!
YOU'RE RIGHT! BUT IT DOESN'T MAKE ME FEEL ANY BETTER!
THERE'S MORE THAN OUR LIVES AT STAKE HERE!
I KNOW--SO MAKE IT SHORT AND SWEET!

THERE! BOTH STILL ALIVE, LOCKED IN A *PITIFUL* DUEL OF WILLS AND STRENGTH!

YES, I WAS RIGHT-- I FEEL IT *CLEARLY* NOW. THE CREATURE HAS BEEN TOUCHED BY THE MATRIX, *RESTORED* BY IT!

BUT IT IS WOUNDED, PERHAPS FATALLY--

"--I MUST *ACT QUICKLY!*"

LIKE A SELECT FEW OTHERS, NORMALLY AUTOBOTS, I WAS CREATED WITH AN INNATE *AFFINITY* WITH OUR SACRED LIFEFORCE!

IT *CALLS* TO ME, AS IT DOES TO POTENTIAL AUTOBOT LEADERS. NO DOUBT THE TIME HAS COME--FOR A *DECEPTICON* TO *POSSESS IT!*

NOW, LET US SEE IF I CAN *MIND-LINK* WITH THIS CREATURE--LEARN HOW IT CAME IN CONTACT WITH--

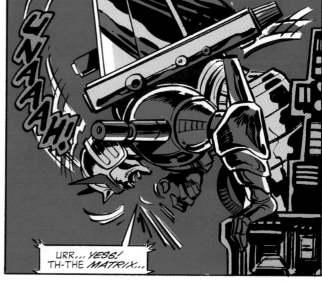

UNAAH!

URR... *YESS!* TH-THE *MATRIX*...

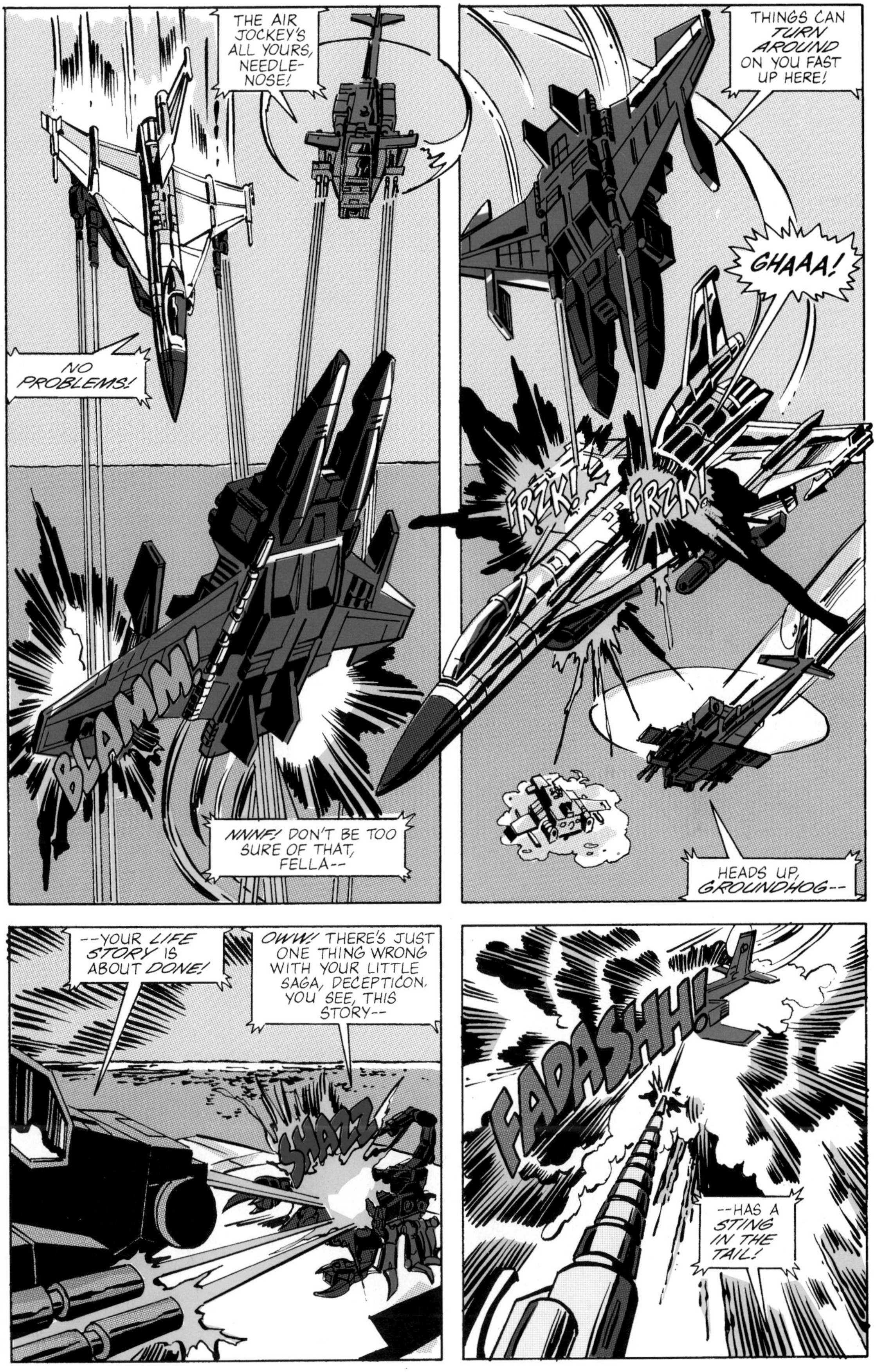
THE AIR JOCKEY'S ALL YOURS, NEEDLE-NOSE!
NO PROBLEMS!
BLAMM!
NNNF! DON'T BE TOO SURE OF THAT, FELLA--
THINGS CAN TURN AROUND ON YOU FAST UP HERE!
GHAAA!
FRZK!
FRZK!
HEADS UP, GROUNDHOG--
--YOUR LIFE STORY IS ABOUT DONE!
OWW! THERE'S JUST ONE THING WRONG WITH YOUR LITTLE SAGA, DECEPTICON. YOU SEE, THIS STORY--
SHAZZ
FADASHH!
--HAS A STING IN THE TAIL!

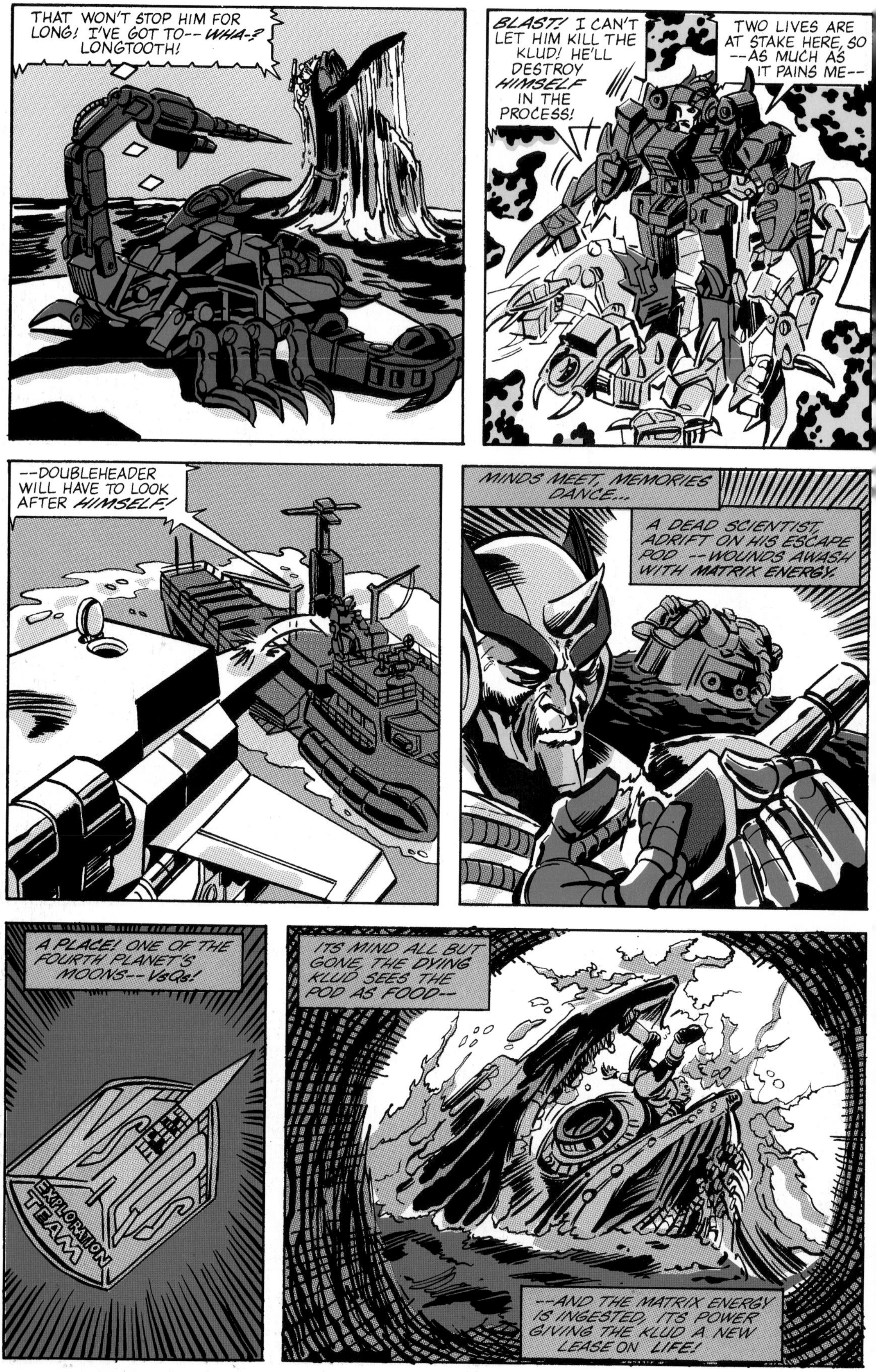
THAT WON'T STOP HIM FOR LONG! I'VE GOT TO-- WHA-? LONGTOOTH!
BLAST! I CAN'T LET HIM KILL THE KLUD! HE'LL DESTROY HIMSELF IN THE PROCESS!
TWO LIVES ARE AT STAKE HERE, SO --AS MUCH AS IT PAINS ME--
--DOUBLEHEADER WILL HAVE TO LOOK AFTER HIMSELF!
MINDS MEET, MEMORIES DANCE...
A DEAD SCIENTIST, ADRIFT ON HIS ESCAPE POD --WOUNDS AWASH WITH MATRIX ENERGY.
A PLACE! ONE OF THE FOURTH PLANET'S MOONS-- V8Qs!
EXPLORATION TEAM
ITS MIND ALL BUT GONE, THE DYING KLUD SEES THE POD AS FOOD--
--AND THE MATRIX ENERGY IS INGESTED, ITS POWER GIVING THE KLUD A NEW LEASE ON LIFE!

"Its eyes glaze, its struggles cease --the beast has *accepted* its fate!"

"With strangely *heavy heart* I..."

*NO!* IF ANY *PART* OF YOU IS STILL AUTOBOT, YOU *WON'T* PULL THAT TRIGGER!

UH? Nuh-*NO!* NOT *YOU!* YOU'RE THE *PAST!* I--I DON'T *WANT* TO REMEMBER!

YOU *MUST!*

YOU MUST *REMEMBER* WHAT IT MEANS TO *BE* AN AUTOBOT, REMEMBER THE *VALUE* WE PLACE ON LIFE --*ALL LIFE!* THE CREATURE IS AT YOUR MERCY, *HELP-LESS.* IT IS THE *LAST* OF ITS RACE!

WHAT RIGHT HAS *ANY* BEING TO DECIDE WHO LIVES AND WHO DIES?

WHEN WE START TO TAMPER WITH THE NATURAL ORDER OF THINGS, WE START TO PLAY GOD! IS THAT WHAT YOU *WANT?*

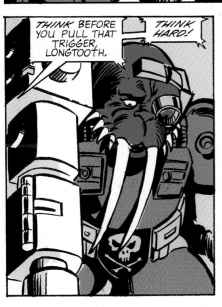

*THINK* BEFORE YOU PULL THAT TRIGGER, LONGTOOTH.

*THINK HARD!*

*GOTCHA!*

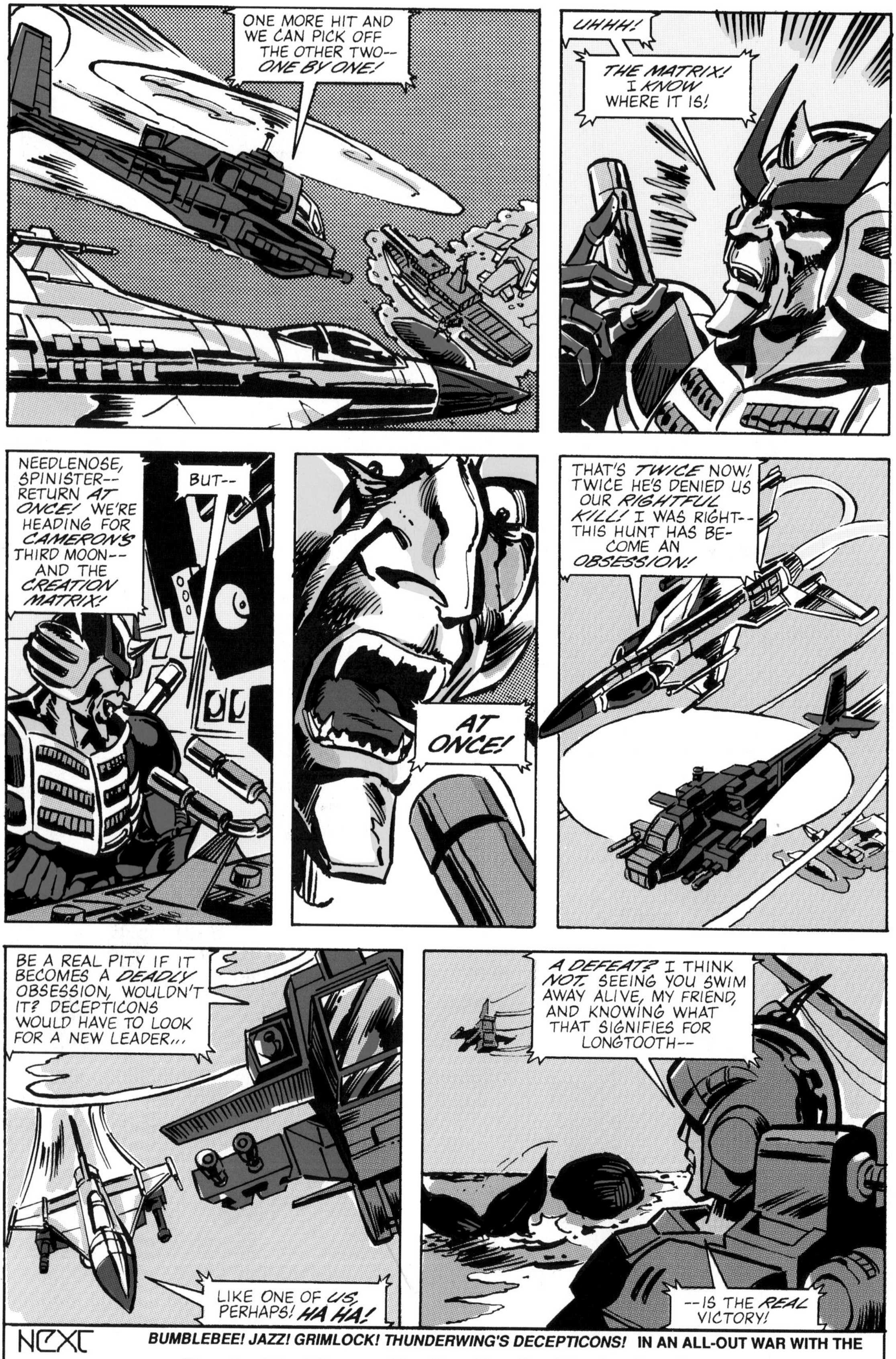

ONE MORE HIT AND WE CAN PICK OFF THE OTHER TWO-- ONE BY ONE!
UHHH!
THE MATRIX! I KNOW WHERE IT IS!
NEEDLENOSE, SPINISTER-- RETURN AT ONCE! WE'RE HEADING FOR CAMERON'S THIRD MOON-- AND THE CREATION MATRIX!
BUT--
AT ONCE!
THAT'S TWICE NOW! TWICE HE'S DENIED US OUR RIGHTFUL KILL! I WAS RIGHT-- THIS HUNT HAS BECOME AN OBSESSION!
BE A REAL PITY IF IT BECOMES A DEADLY OBSESSION, WOULDN'T IT? DECEPTICONS WOULD HAVE TO LOOK FOR A NEW LEADER...
LIKE ONE OF US, PERHAPS! HA HA!
A DEFEAT? I THINK NOT. SEEING YOU SWIM AWAY ALIVE, MY FRIEND, AND KNOWING WHAT THAT SIGNIFIES FOR LONGTOOTH--
--IS THE REAL VICTORY!


NEXT ISSUE **BUMBLEBEE! JAZZ! GRIMLOCK! THUNDERWING'S DECEPTICONS! IN AN ALL-OUT WAR WITH THE**

**DARK CREATION** IN 30 DAYS!

They **were** the dream--mechanical beings able to transform their bodies into vehicles, machinery and weapons; a last line of defense against the chaos-bringer, **Unicron**! They **are** at war, heroic **Autobot** pitted against evil **Decepticon**, both on their homeworld, the metal planet called **Cybertron**, and here on our **Earth**. They **are** the galaxy's last hope, they **are**-- TRANSFORMERS.

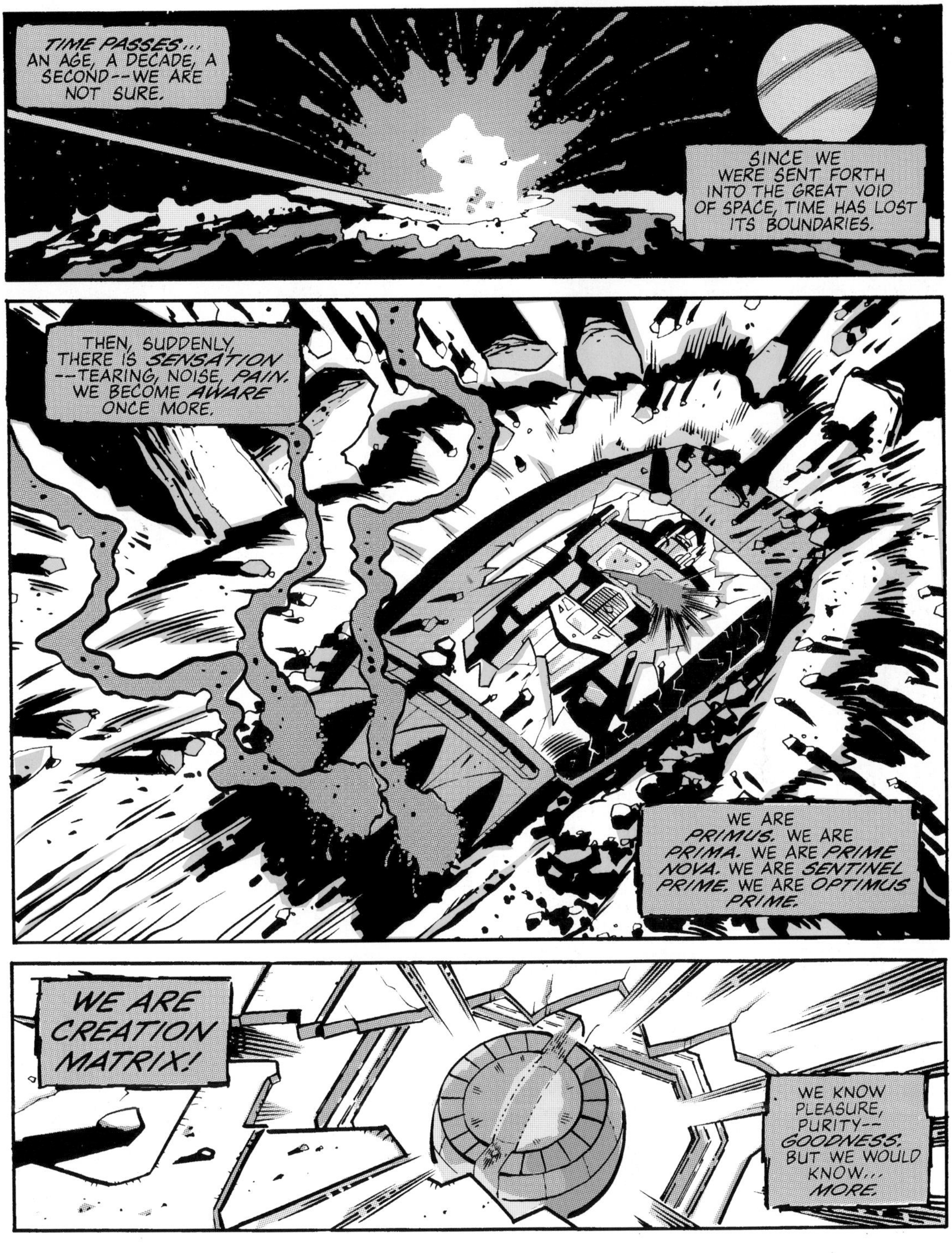
TIME PASSES... AN AGE, A DECADE, A SECOND--WE ARE NOT SURE.
SINCE WE WERE SENT FORTH INTO THE GREAT VOID OF SPACE, TIME HAS LOST ITS BOUNDARIES.
THEN, SUDDENLY, THERE IS SENSATION --TEARING, NOISE, PAIN. WE BECOME AWARE ONCE MORE.
WE ARE PRIMUS. WE ARE PRIMA. WE ARE PRIME NOVA. WE ARE SENTINEL PRIME. WE ARE OPTIMUS PRIME.
WE ARE CREATION MATRIX!
WE KNOW PLEASURE, PURITY--GOODNESS. BUT WE WOULD KNOW... MORE.

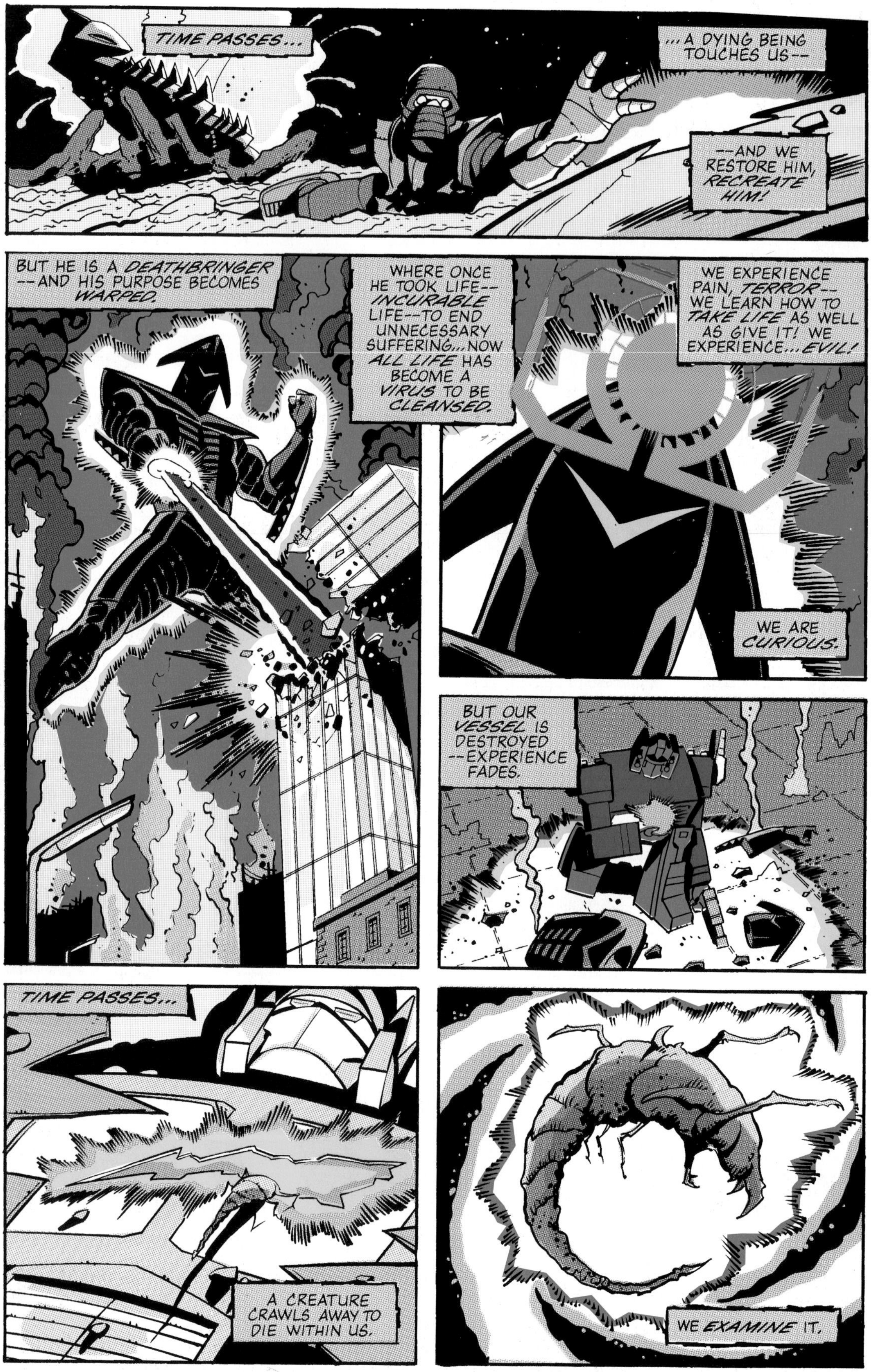
TIME PASSES...
...A DYING BEING TOUCHES US--
--AND WE RESTORE HIM, RECREATE HIM!
BUT HE IS A DEATHBRINGER --AND HIS PURPOSE BECOMES WARPED.
WHERE ONCE HE TOOK LIFE-- INCURABLE LIFE--TO END UNNECESSARY SUFFERING...NOW ALL LIFE HAS BECOME A VIRUS TO BE CLEANSED.
WE EXPERIENCE PAIN, TERROR-- WE LEARN HOW TO TAKE LIFE AS WELL AS GIVE IT! WE EXPERIENCE...EVIL!
WE ARE CURIOUS.
BUT OUR VESSEL IS DESTROYED --EXPERIENCE FADES.
TIME PASSES...
A CREATURE CRAWLS AWAY TO DIE WITHIN US.
WE EXAMINE IT.

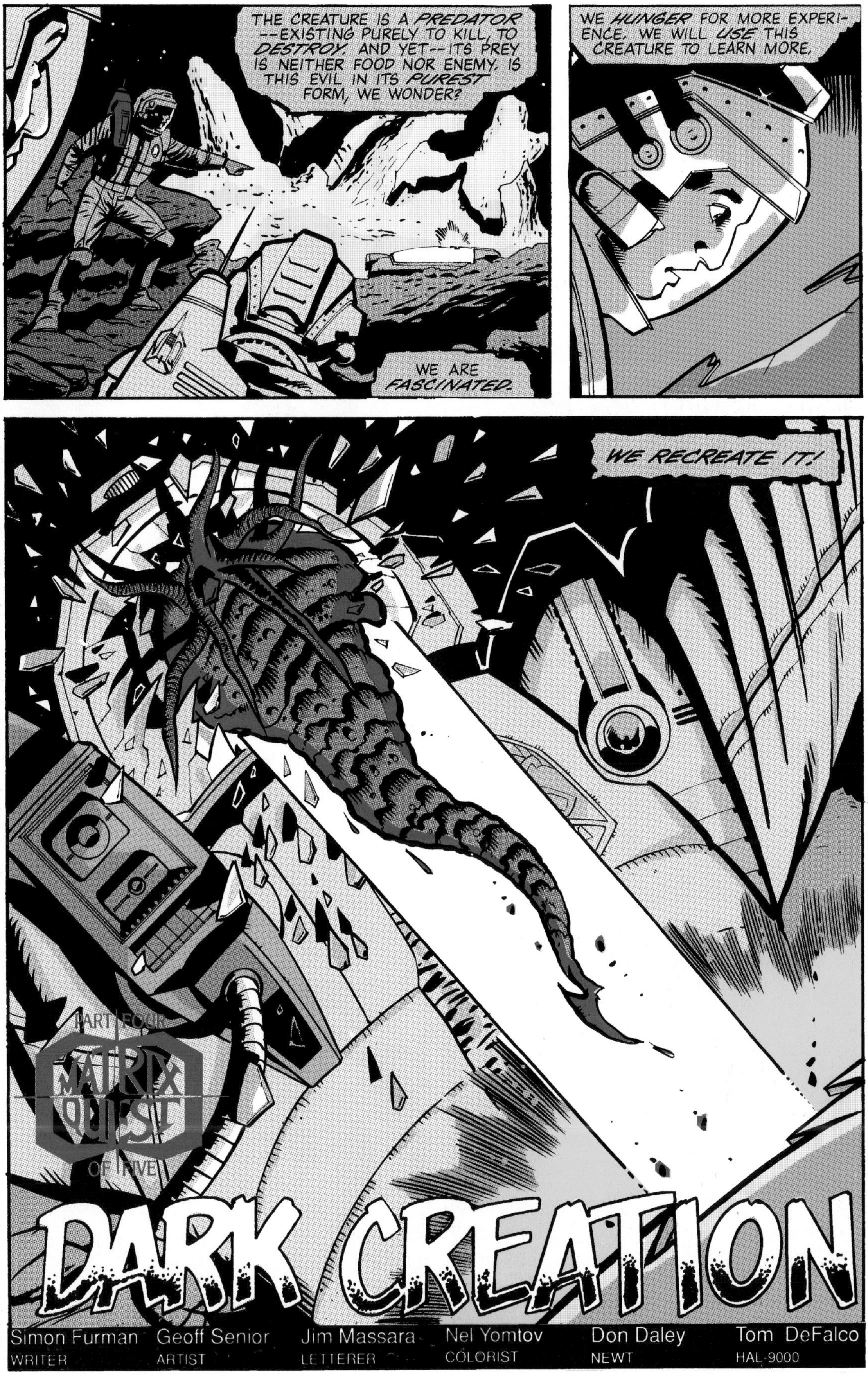
THE CREATURE IS A PREDATOR --EXISTING PURELY TO KILL, TO DESTROY. AND YET--ITS PREY IS NEITHER FOOD NOR ENEMY. IS THIS EVIL IN ITS PUREST FORM, WE WONDER?
WE ARE FASCINATED.
WE HUNGER FOR MORE EXPERIENCE. WE WILL USE THIS CREATURE TO LEARN MORE.
WE RECREATE IT!
PART FOUR
MATRIX QUEST
OF FIVE
DARK CREATION
Simon Furman WRITER
Geoff Senior ARTIST
Jim Massara LETTERER
Nel Yomtov COLORIST
Don Daley NEWT
Tom DeFalco HAL-9000

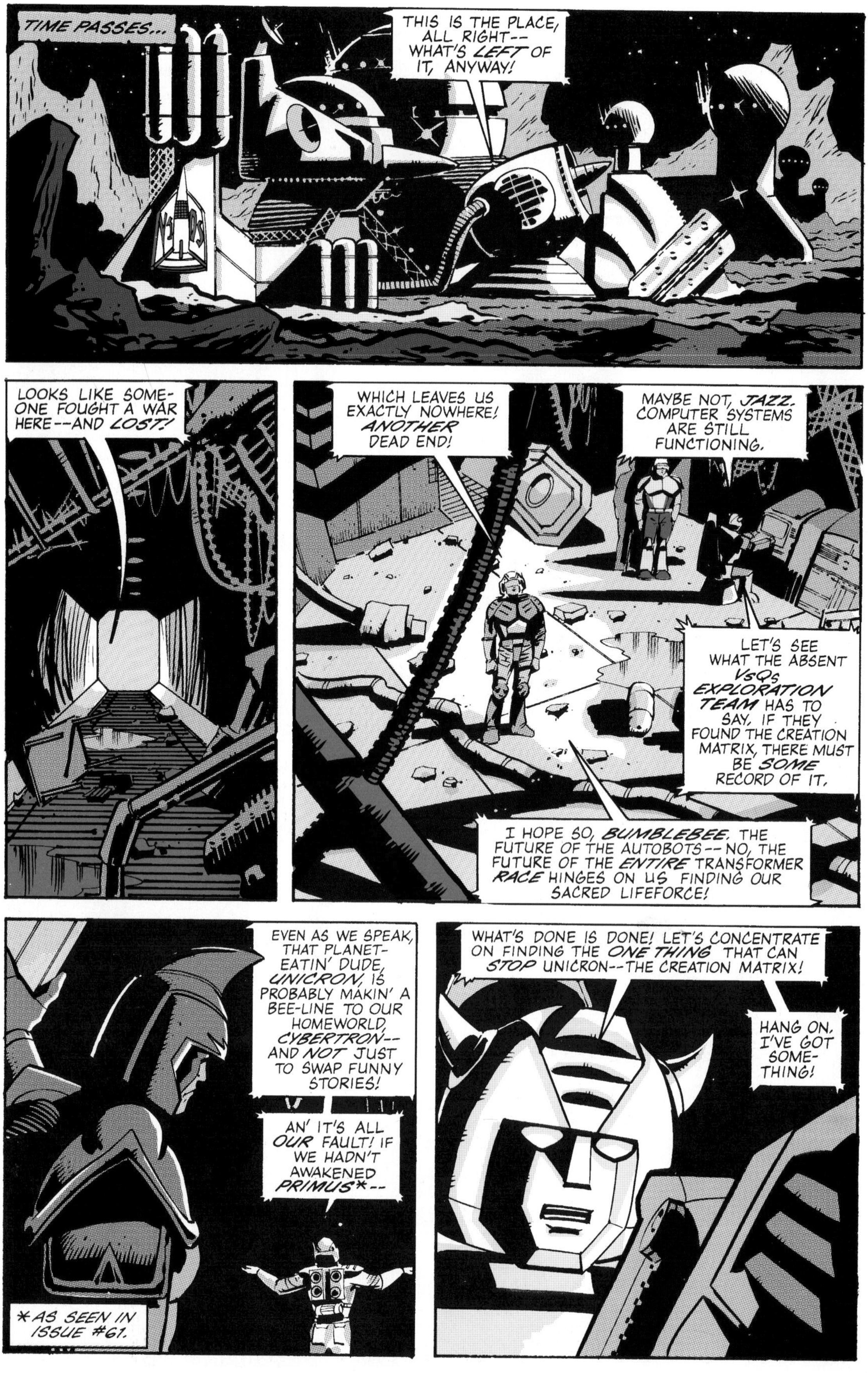
TIME PASSES...
THIS IS THE PLACE, ALL RIGHT-- WHAT'S LEFT OF IT, ANYWAY!
LOOKS LIKE SOME-ONE FOUGHT A WAR HERE--AND LOST!
WHICH LEAVES US EXACTLY NOWHERE! ANOTHER DEAD END!
MAYBE NOT, JAZZ. COMPUTER SYSTEMS ARE STILL FUNCTIONING.
LET'S SEE WHAT THE ABSENT VsQs EXPLORATION TEAM HAS TO SAY. IF THEY FOUND THE CREATION MATRIX, THERE MUST BE SOME RECORD OF IT.
I HOPE SO, BUMBLEBEE. THE FUTURE OF THE AUTOBOTS--NO, THE FUTURE OF THE ENTIRE TRANSFORMER RACE HINGES ON US FINDING OUR SACRED LIFEFORCE!
EVEN AS WE SPEAK, THAT PLANET-EATIN' DUDE, UNICRON, IS PROBABLY MAKIN' A BEE-LINE TO OUR HOMEWORLD, CYBERTRON-- AND NOT JUST TO SWAP FUNNY STORIES!
AN' IT'S ALL OUR FAULT! IF WE HADN'T AWAKENED PRIMUS*--
*AS SEEN IN ISSUE #61.
WHAT'S DONE IS DONE! LET'S CONCENTRATE ON FINDING THE ONE THING THAT CAN STOP UNICRON--THE CREATION MATRIX!
HANG ON, I'VE GOT SOME-THING!

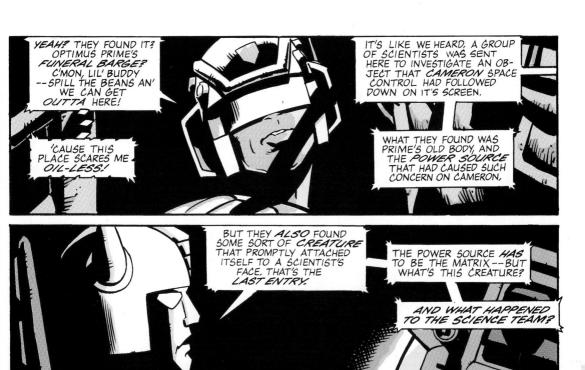

YEAH? THEY FOUND IT? OPTIMUS PRIME'S *FUNERAL BARGE?* C'MON, LIL' BUDDY --SPILL THE BEANS AN' WE CAN GET *OUTTA* HERE!

'CAUSE THIS PLACE SCARES ME *OIL-LESS!*

IT'S LIKE WE HEARD, A GROUP OF SCIENTISTS WAS SENT HERE TO INVESTIGATE AN OBJECT THAT *CAMERON* SPACE CONTROL HAD FOLLOWED DOWN ON IT'S SCREEN.

WHAT THEY FOUND WAS PRIME'S OLD BODY, AND THE *POWER SOURCE* THAT HAD CAUSED SUCH CONCERN ON CAMERON,

BUT THEY *ALSO* FOUND SOME SORT OF *CREATURE* THAT PROMPTLY ATTACHED ITSELF TO A SCIENTIST'S FACE. THAT'S THE *LAST ENTRY.*

THE POWER SOURCE *HAS* TO BE THE MATRIX -- BUT WHAT'S THIS CREATURE?

AND WHAT HAPPENED TO THE SCIENCE TEAM?

CAN ANSWER THAT,

FOUND THEM,

GREAT! *GRIMLOCK* -- I NEVER DOUBTED YOU FOR A MINUTE! WHERE *ARE* THEY? DID THEY TELL YOU--

NO.

NONE OF THEM *EVER* TELL ANYTHING AGAIN.

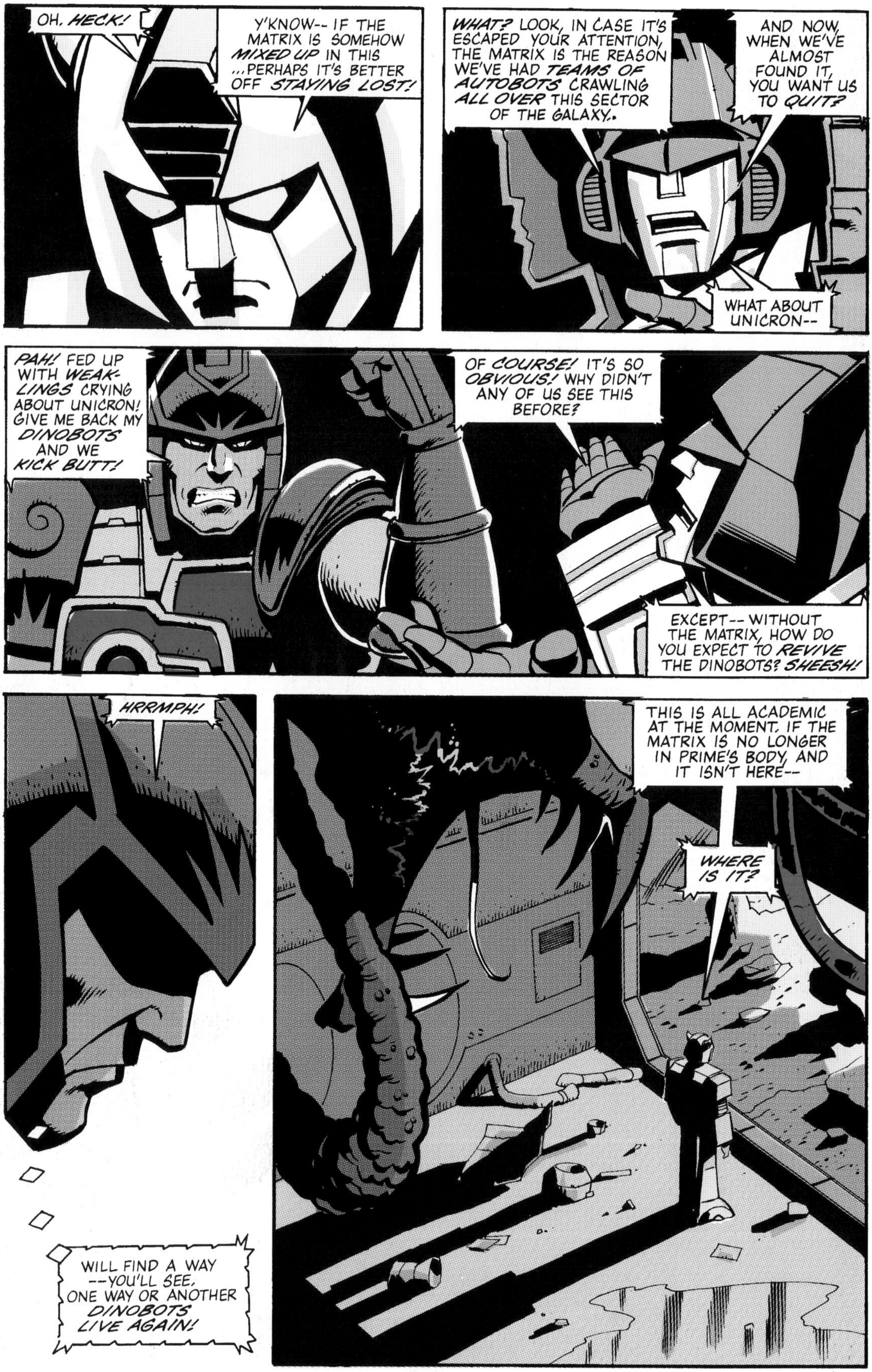
OH, HECK!
Y'KNOW-- IF THE MATRIX IS SOMEHOW MIXED UP IN THIS ...PERHAPS IT'S BETTER OFF STAYING LOST!
WHAT? LOOK, IN CASE IT'S ESCAPED YOUR ATTENTION, THE MATRIX IS THE REASON WE'VE HAD TEAMS OF AUTOBOTS CRAWLING ALL OVER THIS SECTOR OF THE GALAXY.
AND NOW, WHEN WE'VE ALMOST FOUND IT, YOU WANT US TO QUIT?
WHAT ABOUT UNICRON--
PAH! FED UP WITH WEAK-LINGS CRYING ABOUT UNICRON! GIVE ME BACK MY DINOBOTS AND WE KICK BUTT!
OF COURSE! IT'S SO OBVIOUS! WHY DIDN'T ANY OF US SEE THIS BEFORE?
EXCEPT-- WITHOUT THE MATRIX, HOW DO YOU EXPECT TO REVIVE THE DINOBOTS? SHEESH!
HRRMPH!
WILL FIND A WAY --YOU'LL SEE. ONE WAY OR ANOTHER DINOBOTS LIVE AGAIN!
THIS IS ALL ACADEMIC AT THE MOMENT. IF THE MATRIX IS NO LONGER IN PRIME'S BODY, AND IT ISN'T HERE--
WHERE IS IT?

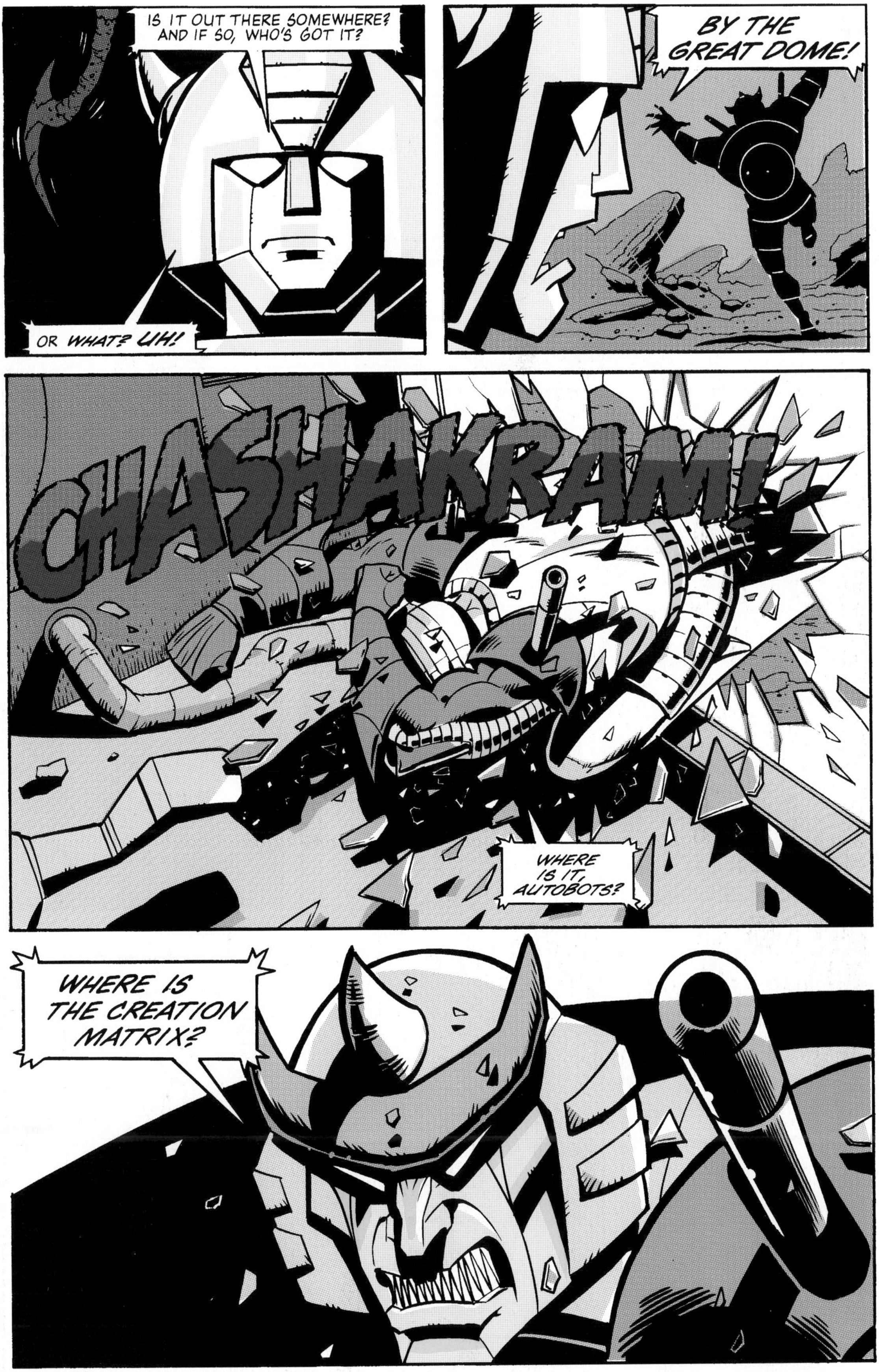
IS IT OUT THERE SOMEWHERE? AND IF SO, WHO'S GOT IT?
OR WHAT? UH!
BY THE GREAT DOME!
CHASHAKRAM!
WHERE IS IT, AUTOBOTS?
WHERE IS THE CREATION MATRIX?

NEARBY...

IT'S JUST *NOT FAIR!* I'M MISSING OUT ON ALL THE *FUN!*

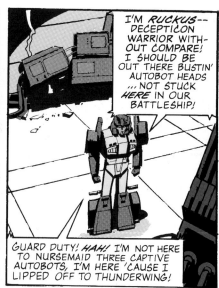

I'M *RUCKUS*-- DECEPTICON WARRIOR WITH- OUT COMPARE! I SHOULD BE OUT THERE BUSTIN' AUTOBOT HEADS ...NOT STUCK *HERE* IN OUR BATTLESHIP!

GUARD DUTY! *HAH!* I'M NOT HERE TO NURSEMAID THREE CAPTIVE AUTOBOTS, I'M HERE 'CAUSE I LIPPED OFF TO THUNDERWING!

"THAT PUNCH HE GAVE ME* SHOULD HAVE BEEN PUNISHMENT ENOUGH!"

*LAST ISSUE!

BUT *NO!* "ENOUGH" *ISN'T* A WORD IN OUR LEADER'S VOCABULARY THESE DAYS! HE'S LOSIN' HIS MARBLES OVER THIS BLASTED MATRIX--THAT'S FOR SURE!

WE'VE *ALL* WATCHED HIS *DECLINE,* WATCHED HIS DESIRE TO BEAT THE AUTOBOTS TO THE MATRIX BECOME AN *OBSESSION!*

WELL, ALL I CAN SAY IS -- HE'D BETTER *WATCH OUT!* BEFORE WE DECIDE TO *DISCONNECT* HIM-- *PERMANENTLY!*

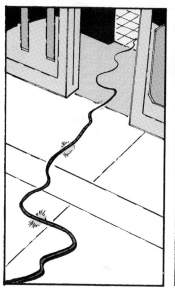

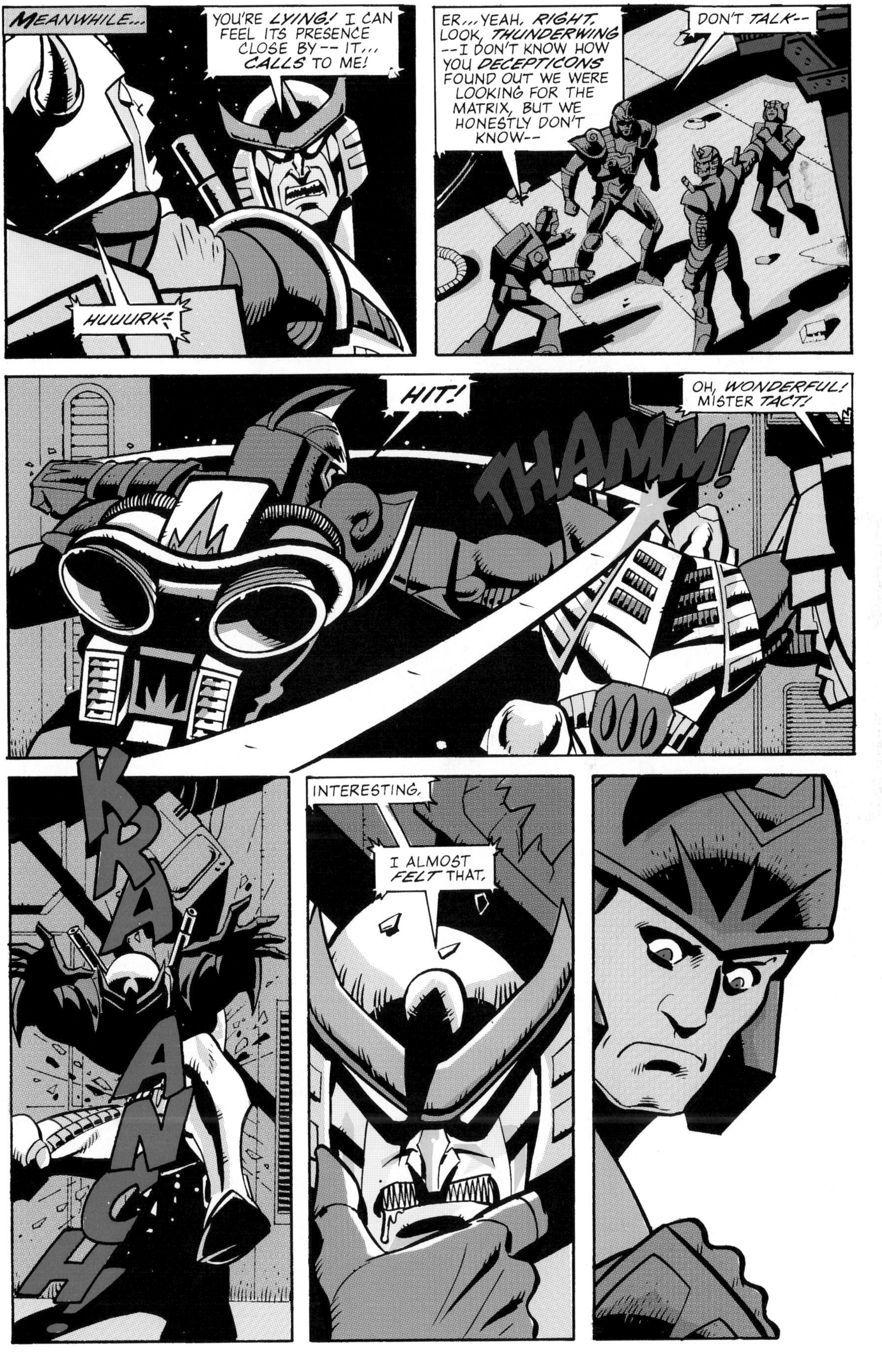
MEANWHILE...
YOU'RE LYING! I CAN FEEL ITS PRESENCE CLOSE BY -- IT... CALLS TO ME!
HUUURK!
ER... YEAH, RIGHT. LOOK, THUNDERWING --I DON'T KNOW HOW YOU DECEPTICONS FOUND OUT WE WERE LOOKING FOR THE MATRIX, BUT WE HONESTLY DON'T KNOW--
DON'T TALK--
HIT!
THAMM!
OH, WONDERFUL! MISTER TACT!
KRAANCH!
INTERESTING.
I ALMOST FELT THAT.

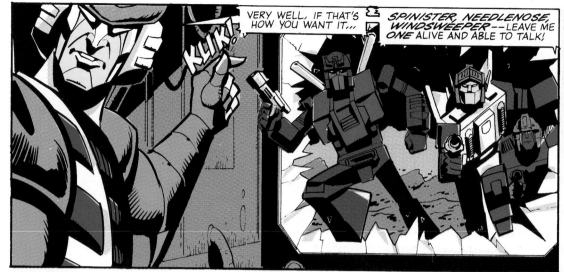

VERY WELL, IF THAT'S HOW YOU WANT IT...

SPINISTER, NEEDLENOSE, WINDSWEEPER--LEAVE ME ONE ALIVE AND ABLE TO TALK!

STAY CALM, CONCENTRATE. MAKE YOUR PRETENDER SHELL DO THE WORK FOR YOU.

UNNF!

FWUNK!

YEAH!

THINK YOU TOUGH, DECEPTICON LEADER?

ME GRIMLOCK --ME EAT DECEPTICON LEADERS FOR BREAK-FAST!

HA.

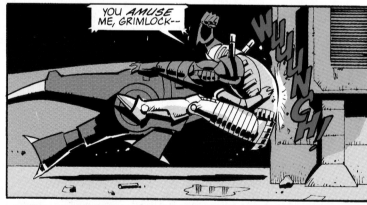

YOU AMUSE ME, GRIMLOCK--

WUUUNCH!

BUT THAT--

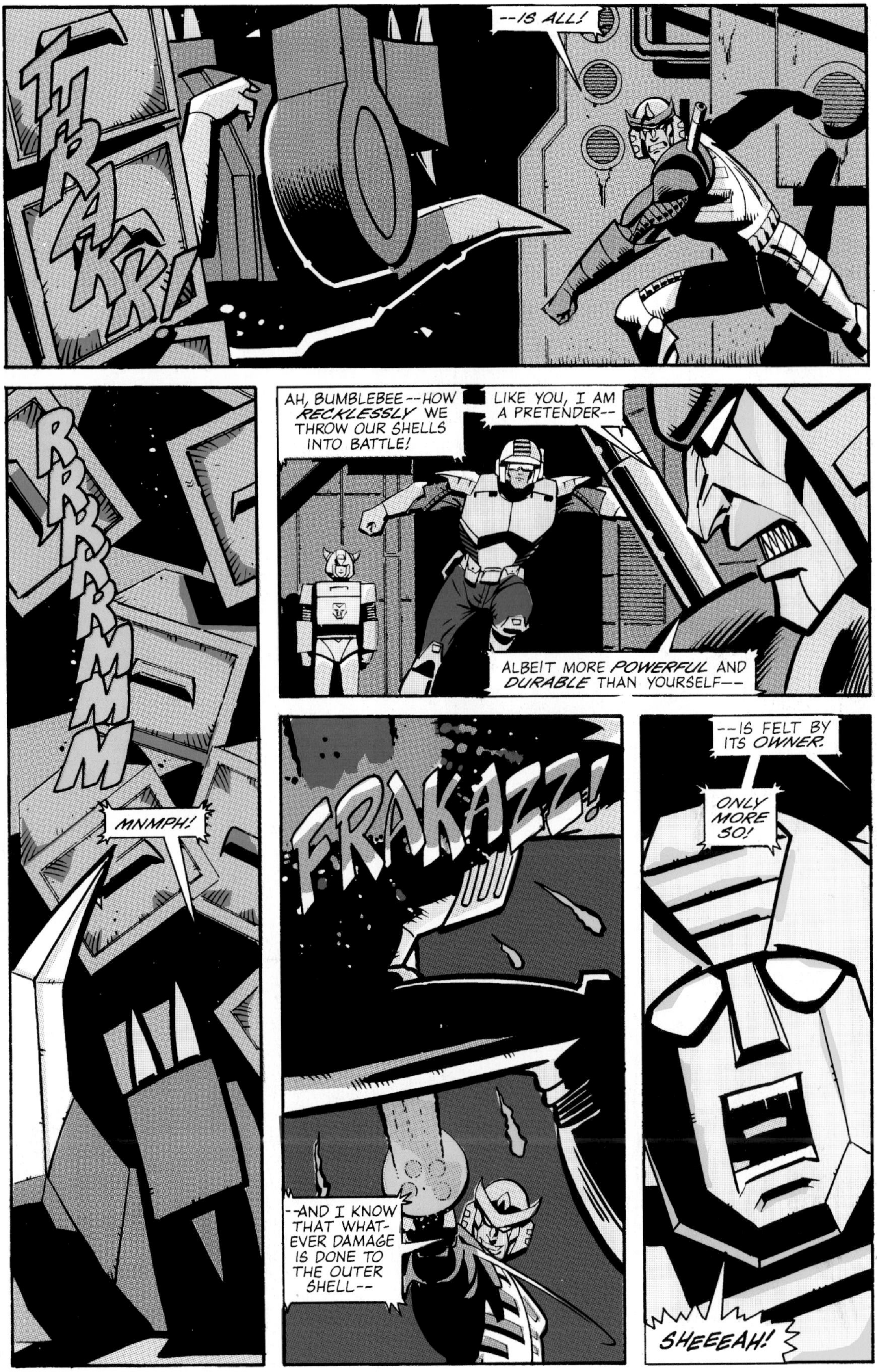
THRAKKA!
--IS ALL!
RRRRRMMMM
MNMPH!
AH, BUMBLEBEE--HOW RECKLESSLY WE THROW OUR SHELLS INTO BATTLE!
LIKE YOU, I AM A PRETENDER--
ALBEIT MORE POWERFUL AND DURABLE THAN YOURSELF--
FRAKAZZ!
--AND I KNOW THAT WHAT-EVER DAMAGE IS DONE TO THE OUTER SHELL--
--IS FELT BY ITS OWNER.
ONLY MORE SO!
SHEEEAH!

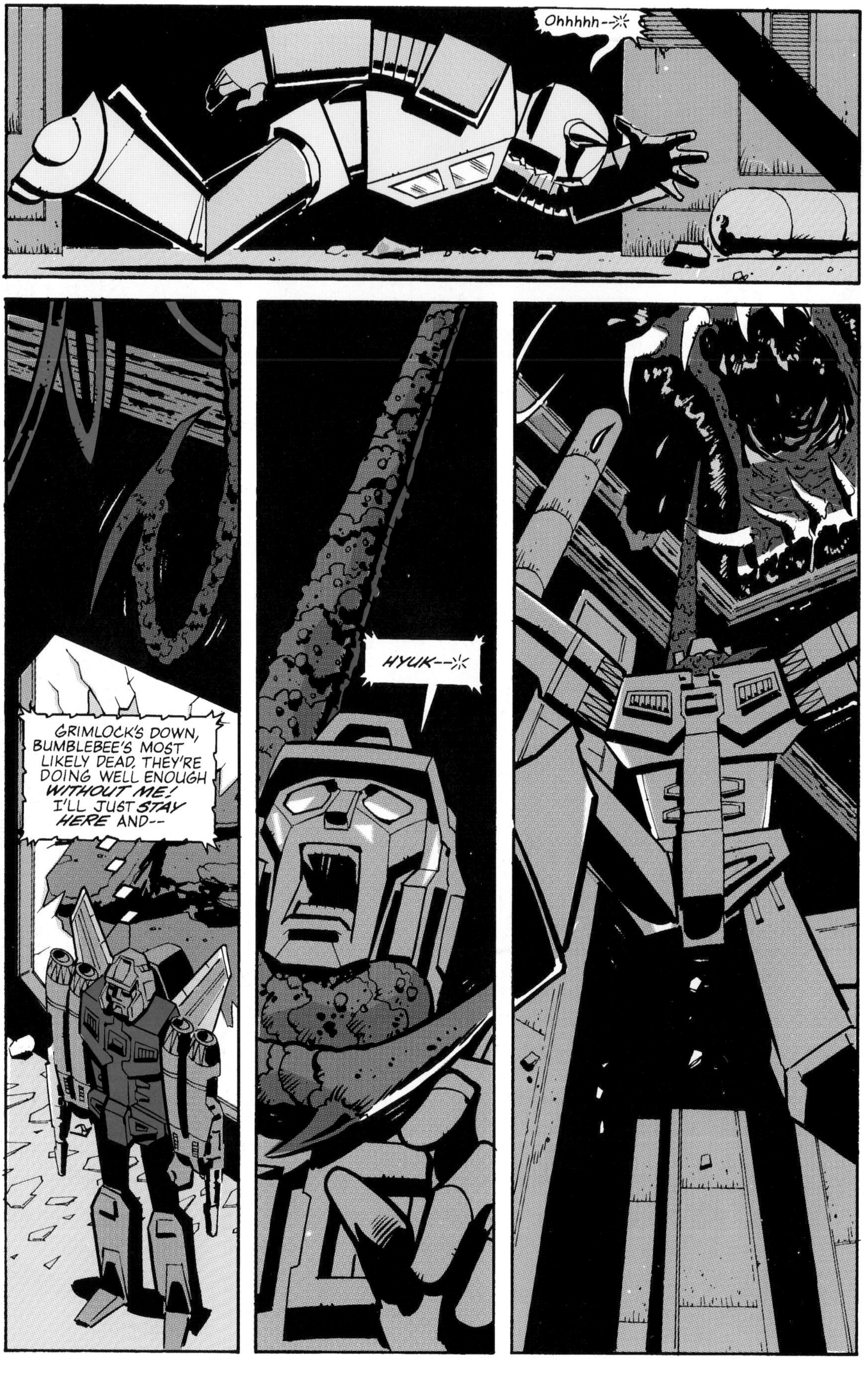
Ohhhhh--
GRIMLOCK'S DOWN, BUMBLEBEE'S MOST LIKELY DEAD. THEY'RE DOING WELL ENOUGH WITHOUT ME! I'LL JUST STAY HERE AND--
HYUK--

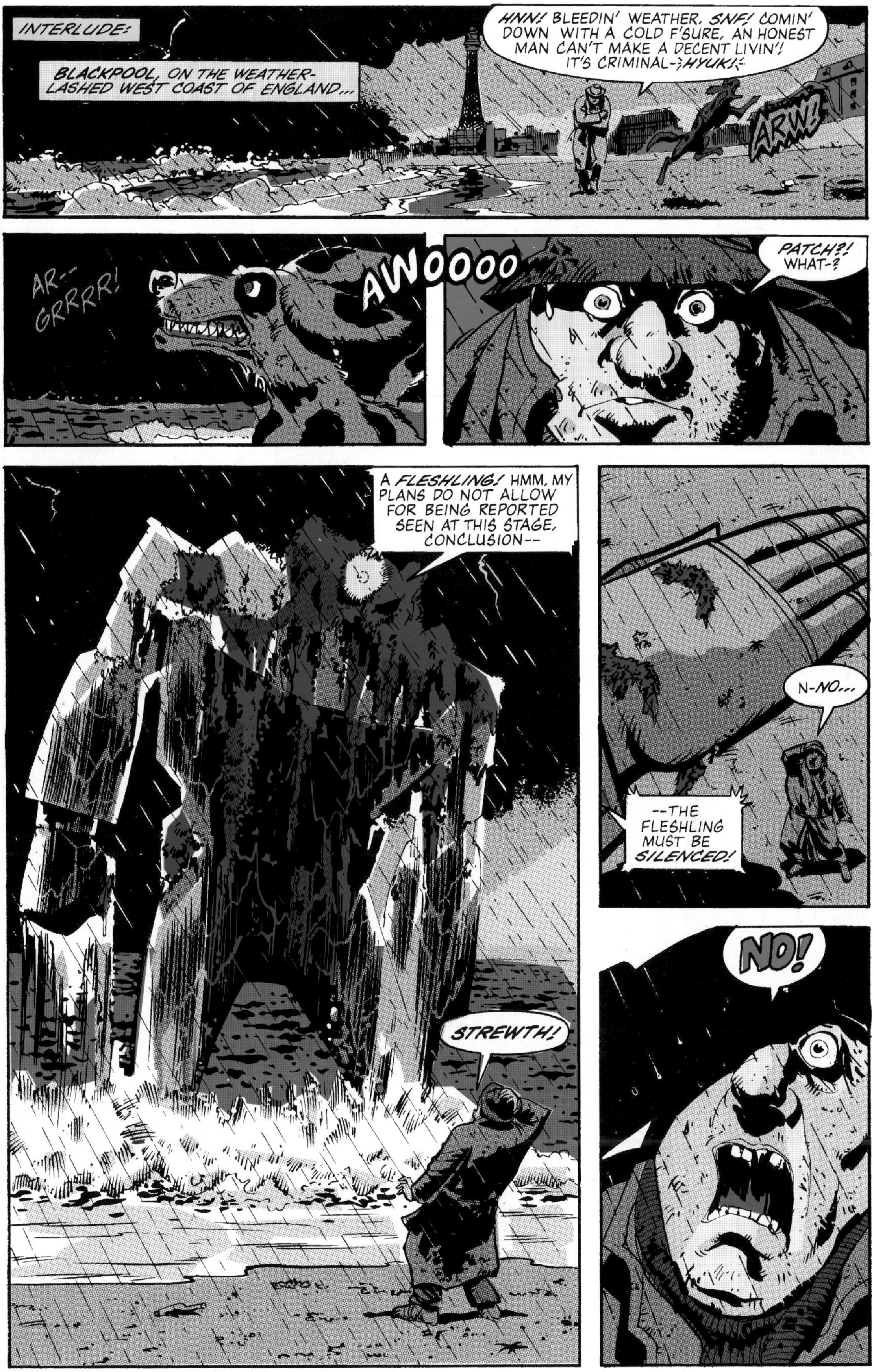
INTERLUDE:
BLACKPOOL, ON THE WEATHER-LASHED WEST COAST OF ENGLAND...
HNN! BLEEDIN' WEATHER. SNF! COMIN' DOWN WITH A COLD F'SURE. AN HONEST MAN CAN'T MAKE A DECENT LIVIN'! IT'S CRIMINAL--HYUK!
ARW!
AR--GRRRR!
AWOOOO
PATCH?! WHAT-?
A FLESHLING! HMM. MY PLANS DO NOT ALLOW FOR BEING REPORTED SEEN AT THIS STAGE. CONCLUSION--
STREWTH!
N-NO...
--THE FLESHLING MUST BE SILENCED!
NO!

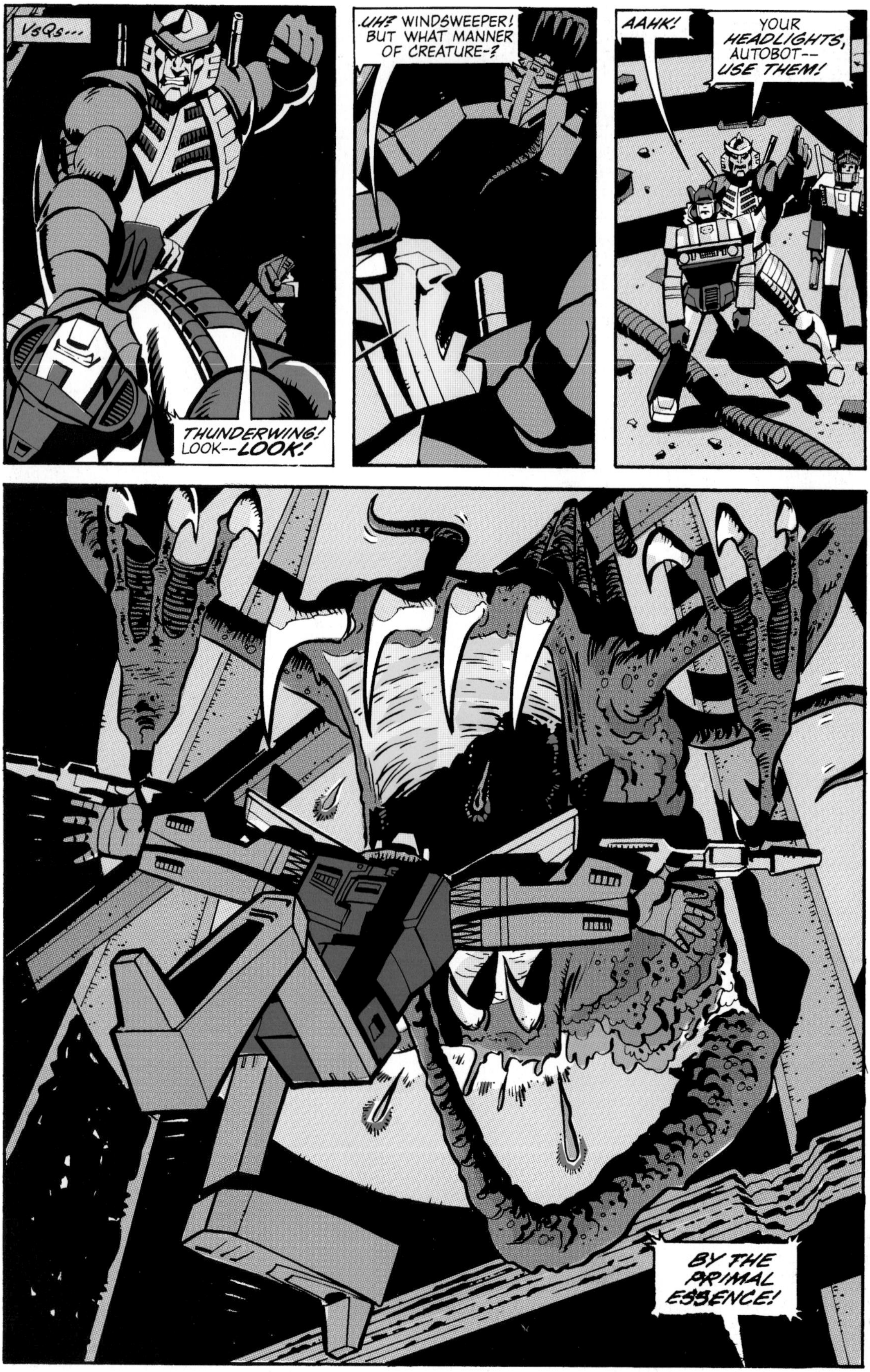
VsQs...
THUNDERWING! LOOK--LOOK!
UH? WINDSWEEPER! BUT WHAT MANNER OF CREATURE-?
AAHK!
YOUR HEADLIGHTS, AUTOBOT-- USE THEM!
BY THE PRIMAL ESSENCE!

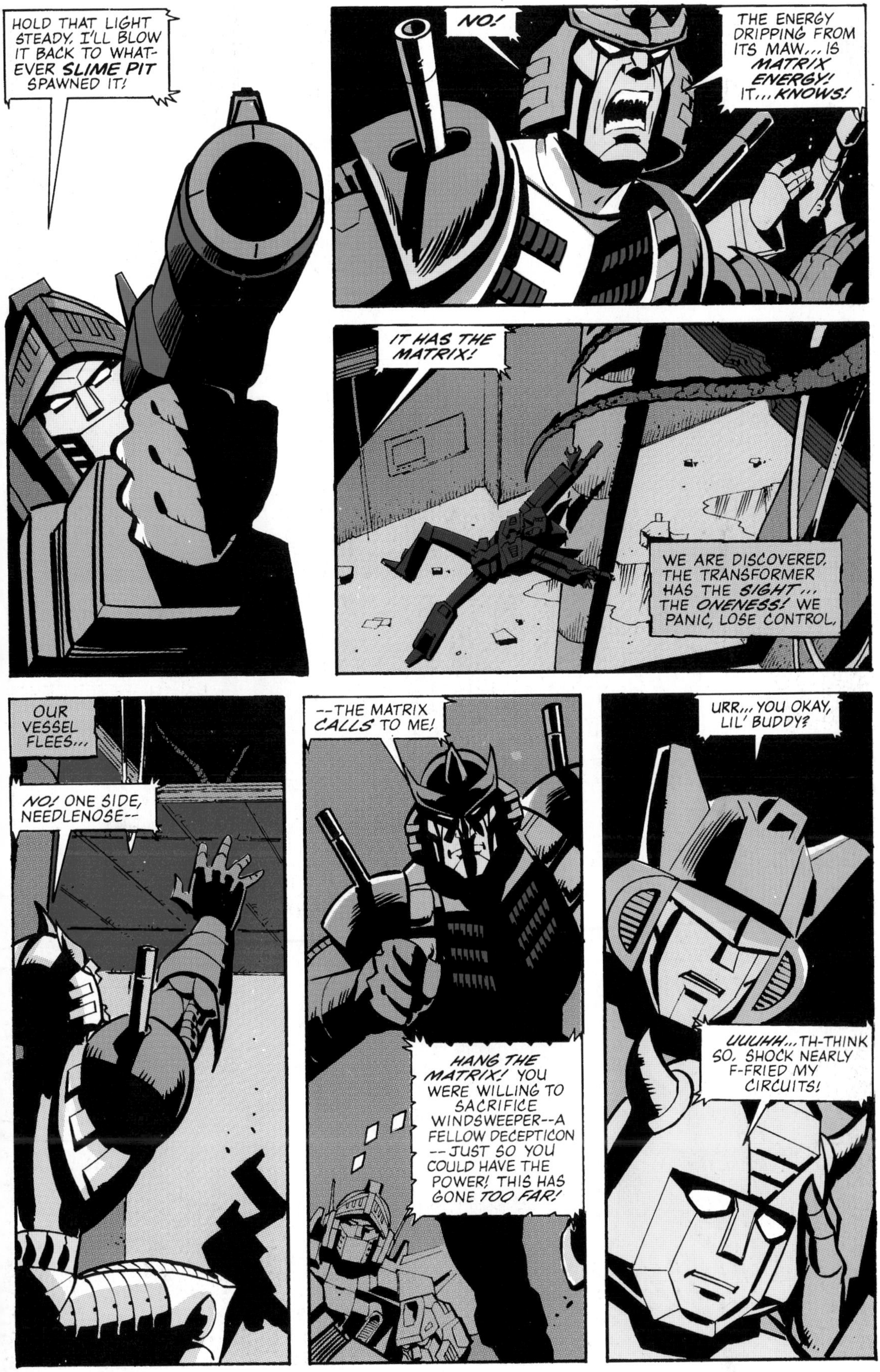
HOLD THAT LIGHT STEADY. I'LL BLOW IT BACK TO WHATEVER SLIME PIT SPAWNED IT!
NO!
THE ENERGY DRIPPING FROM ITS MAW... IS MATRIX ENERGY! IT... KNOWS!
IT HAS THE MATRIX!
WE ARE DISCOVERED. THE TRANSFORMER HAS THE SIGHT... THE ONENESS! WE PANIC, LOSE CONTROL.
OUR VESSEL FLEES...
NO! ONE SIDE, NEEDLENOSE--
--THE MATRIX CALLS TO ME!
HANG THE MATRIX! YOU WERE WILLING TO SACRIFICE WINDSWEEPER--A FELLOW DECEPTICON--JUST SO YOU COULD HAVE THE POWER! THIS HAS GONE TOO FAR!
URR... YOU OKAY, LIL' BUDDY?
UUUHH... TH-THINK SO. SHOCK NEARLY F-FRIED MY CIRCUITS!

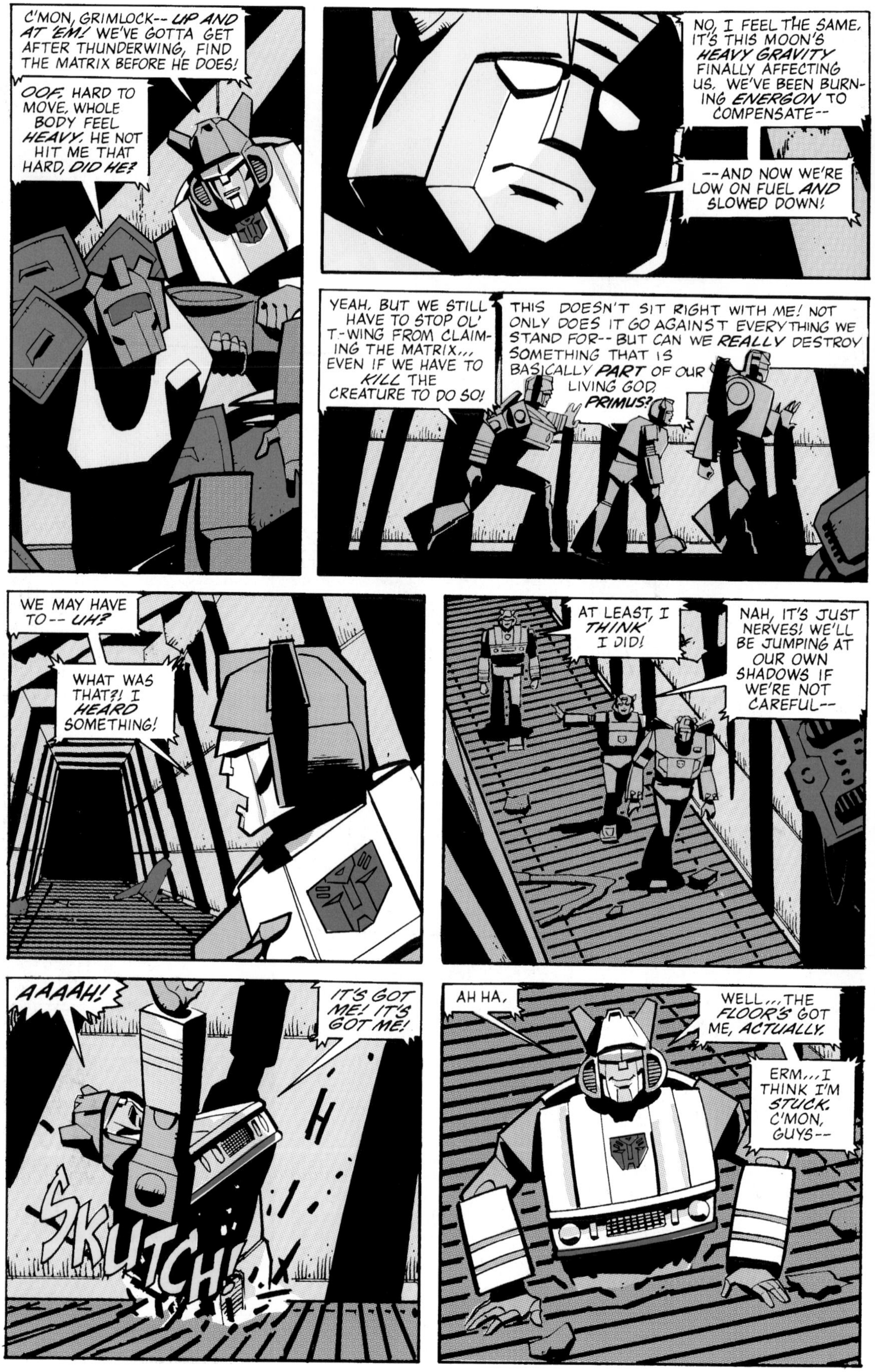
C'MON, GRIMLOCK-- UP AND AT 'EM! WE'VE GOTTA GET AFTER THUNDERWING, FIND THE MATRIX BEFORE HE DOES!
OOF. HARD TO MOVE. WHOLE BODY FEEL HEAVY. HE NOT HIT ME THAT HARD, DID HE?
NO, I FEEL THE SAME. IT'S THIS MOON'S HEAVY GRAVITY FINALLY AFFECTING US. WE'VE BEEN BURNING ENERGON TO COMPENSATE--
--AND NOW WE'RE LOW ON FUEL AND SLOWED DOWN!
YEAH, BUT WE STILL HAVE TO STOP OL' T-WING FROM CLAIMING THE MATRIX... EVEN IF WE HAVE TO KILL THE CREATURE TO DO SO!
THIS DOESN'T SIT RIGHT WITH ME! NOT ONLY DOES IT GO AGAINST EVERYTHING WE STAND FOR-- BUT CAN WE REALLY DESTROY SOMETHING THAT IS BASICALLY PART OF OUR LIVING GOD, PRIMUS?
WE MAY HAVE TO-- UH?
WHAT WAS THAT?! I HEARD SOMETHING!
AT LEAST, I THINK I DID!
NAH, IT'S JUST NERVES! WE'LL BE JUMPING AT OUR OWN SHADOWS IF WE'RE NOT CAREFUL--
AAAAH!
IT'S GOT ME! IT'S GOT ME!
SKUTCH!
AH HA.
WELL... THE FLOOR'S GOT ME, ACTUALLY.
ERM... I THINK I'M STUCK. C'MON, GUYS--

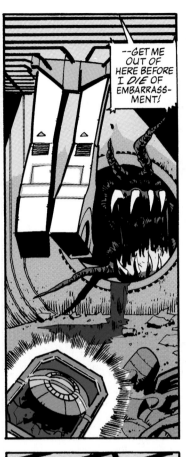

--GET ME OUT OF HERE BEFORE I *DIE* OF EMBARRASS-MENT!

MEANWHILE...

YEAH, HE LIT OUT THAT WAY--IN A *MAJOR LEAGUE HURRY*. THE AUTO-BOTS WENT AFTER HIM!

YOU RECKON WE SHOULD GO AFTER THUNDERWING, HELP OUT?

NAH, IT'S *HIS* FIGHT --HE'S MADE THAT PLENTY CLEAR TO US ALREADY! ANYWAY, HE DOESN'T CARE ABOUT WHAT HAPPENS TO US --WHY SHOULD *WE* WORRY ABOUT *HIM*?

IF THUNDERWING BEATS THE CREATURE, THE AUTO-BOTS--THAT'S FINE BY ME. IF HE DIES--

--I'LL SEND FLOWERS!

C'MON-- *HEAVE!*

HURRY! THERE'S SOMETHING *DOWN THERE!* IT'S *GOT* ME! IT'S--

HUUURK!

OUT OF MY *WAY*, AUTOBOT!

YESSS! COME TO ME, COME TO YOUR *RIGHT-FUL OWNER!*

WE OBEY...

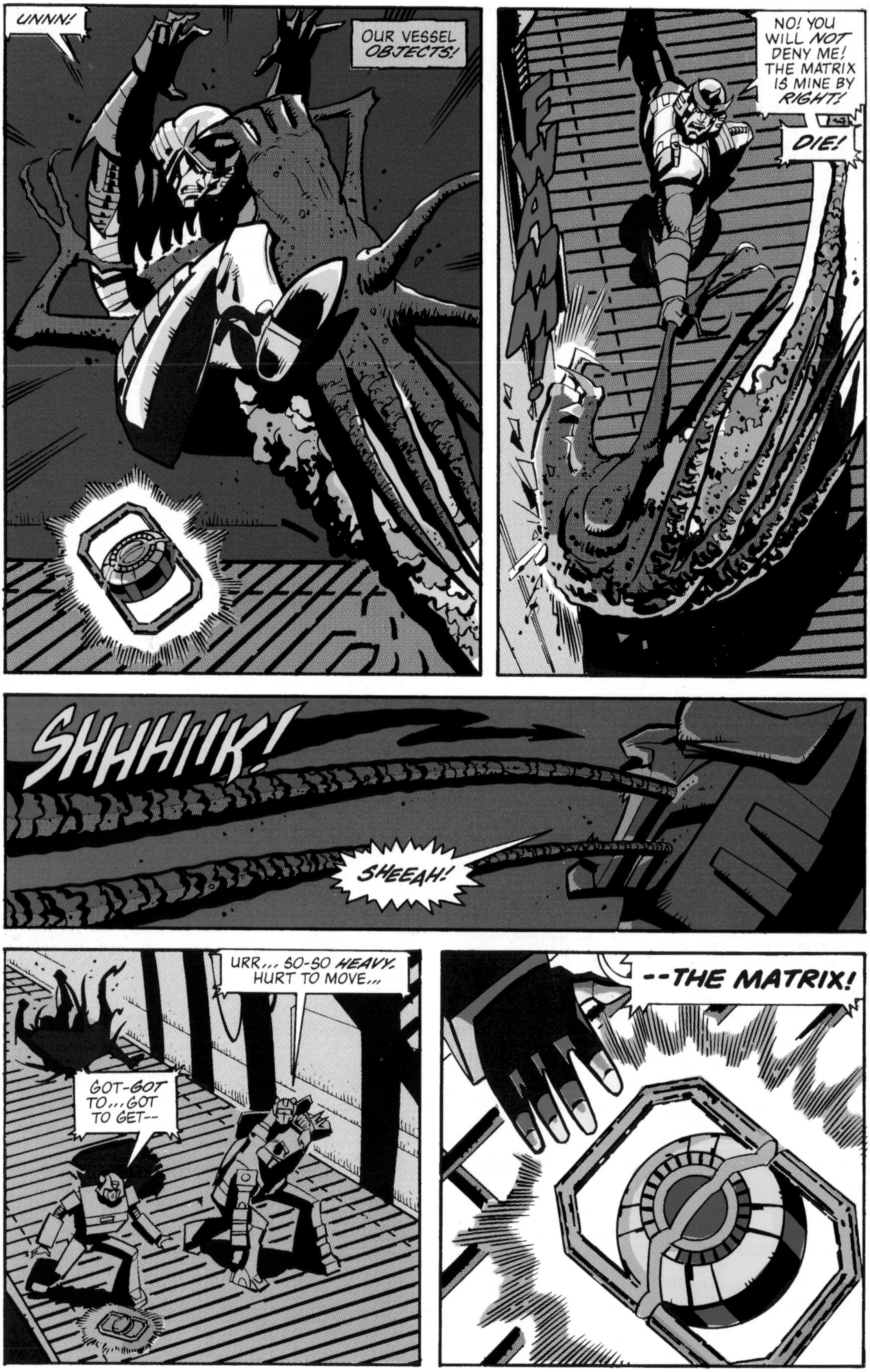
UNNN!
OUR VESSEL OBJECTS!
NO! YOU WILL NOT DENY ME! THE MATRIX IS MINE BY RIGHT!
DIE!
SHHHIIK!
SHEEAH!
URR... SO-SO HEAVY. HURT TO MOVE...
GOT-GOT TO... GOT TO GET--
--THE MATRIX!

TIME PASSES...

IT'S GRIMLOCK'S SHUTTLE! THEY'RE *COMING BACK!* THE APPROACH PATTERN'S CORRECT, ALL WARNING LIGHTS ARE GREEN.

AND THE CREATION MATRIX?

IS *ABOARD,* HOT ROD, I SENSE IT!

MY WARRIORS ARE COMING HOME--THE *MATRIX QUEST* IS CONCLUDED *SUCCESSFULLY!*

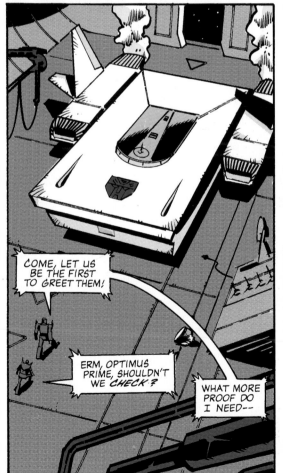

COME, LET US BE THE FIRST TO GREET THEM!

ERM, OPTIMUS PRIME, SHOULDN'T WE *CHECK?*

WHAT MORE PROOF DO I NEED--

--THAN THE PROOF OF MY *OWN EYES! THE MATRIX!*

WE ARE *CREATION MATRIX*--

*GHAAAA!*

WE ARE *PRIMUS,* WE ARE *PRIMA.* WE ARE *PRIME NOVA.* WE ARE *SENTINEL PRIME.* WE ARE *OPTIMUS PRIME.*

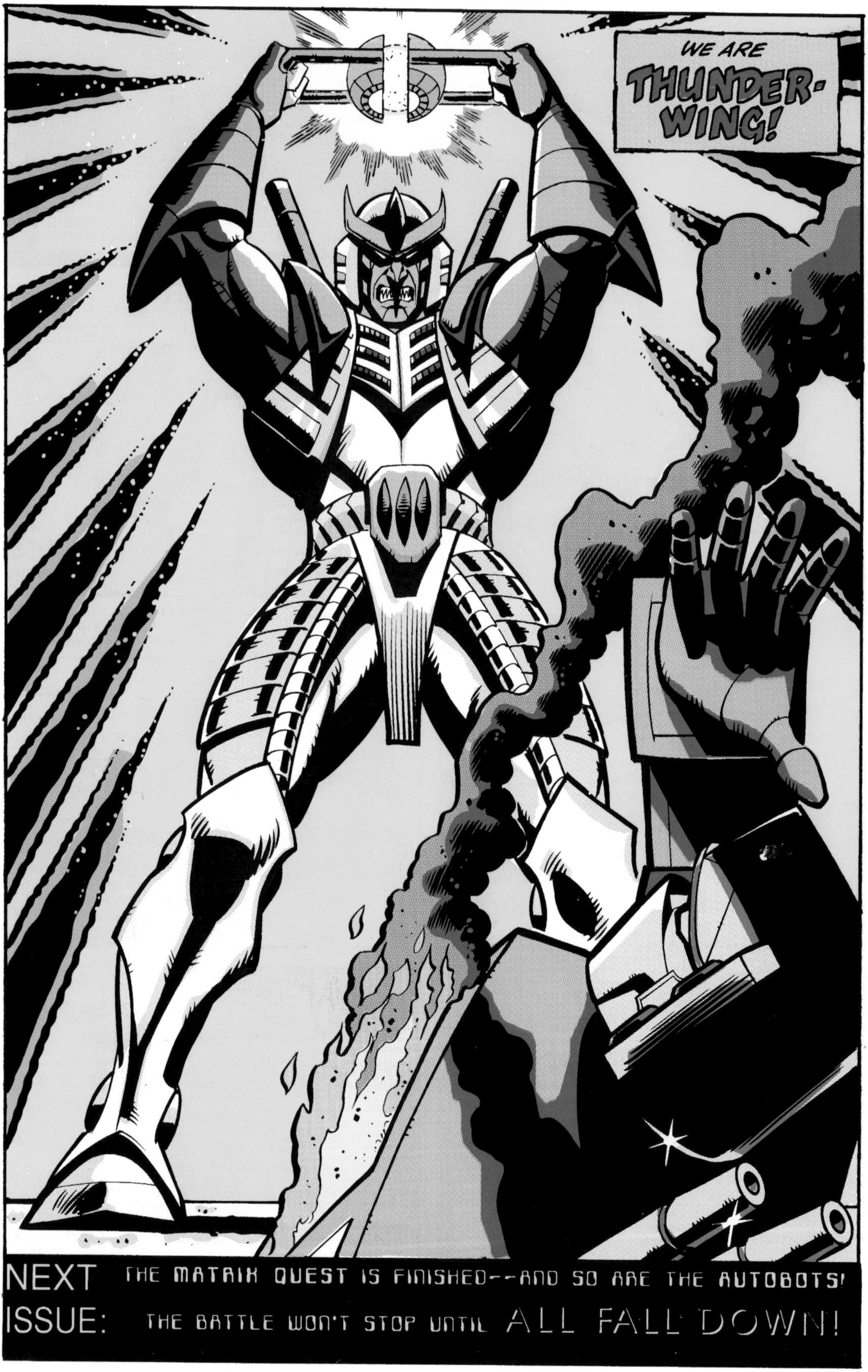
WE ARE THUNDERWING!

NEXT ISSUE: THE MATRIX QUEST IS FINISHED--AND SO ARE THE AUTOBOTS! THE BATTLE WON'T STOP UNTIL ALL FALL DOWN!

STAN LEE PRESENTS: TRANSFORMERS — ALL FALL DOWN

WELCOME TO THE END OF THE WORLD!

| Simon Furman | Geoff Senior | Jim Massara | Nel Yomtov | Don Daley | Tom DeFalco |
|---|---|---|---|---|---|
| WRITER | ARTIST | LETTERER | COLORIST | APPETIZER | MAIN COURSE |

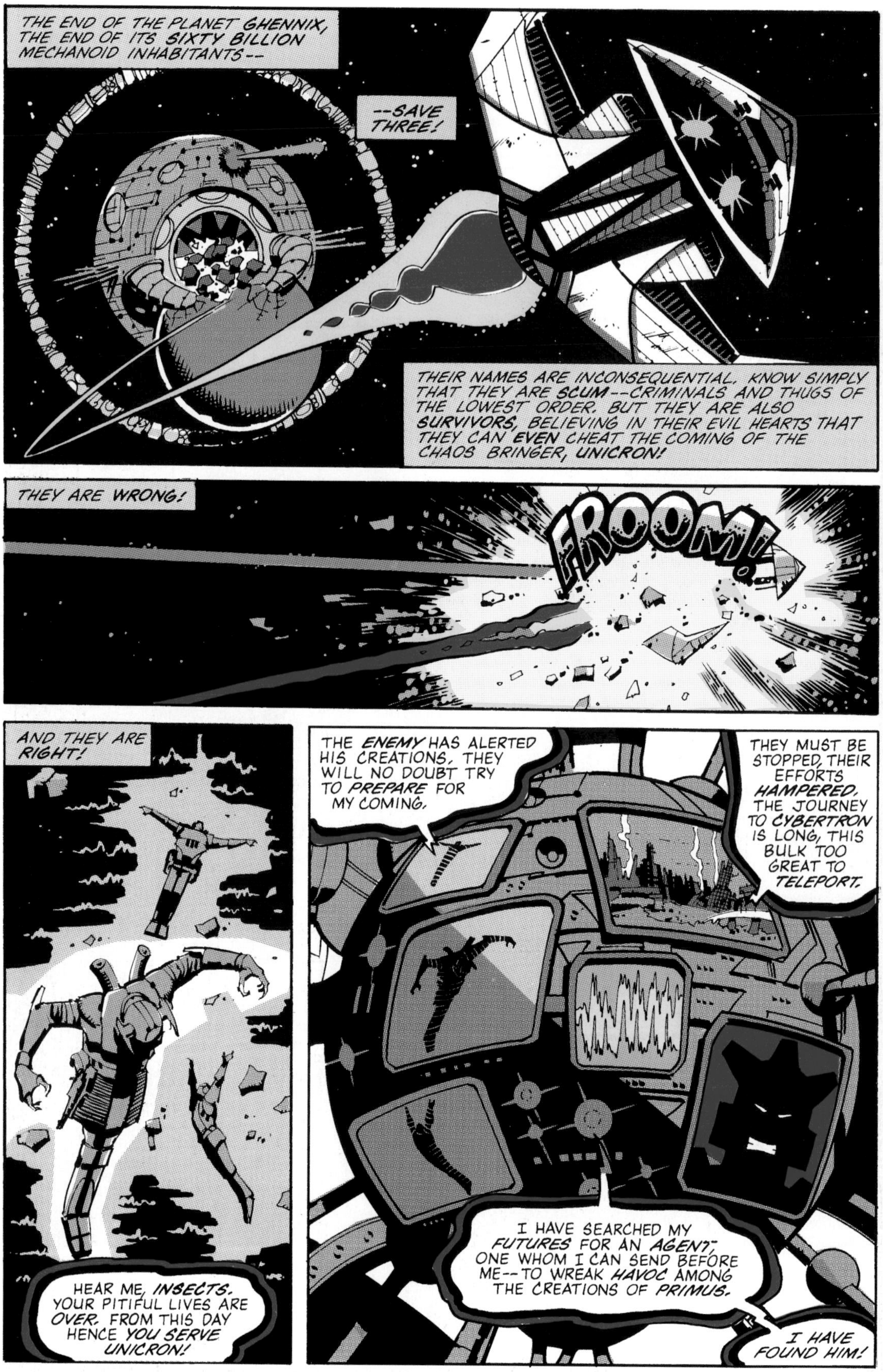
THE END OF THE PLANET GHENNIX, THE END OF ITS SIXTY BILLION MECHANOID INHABITANTS--
--SAVE THREE!
THEIR NAMES ARE INCONSEQUENTIAL. KNOW SIMPLY THAT THEY ARE SCUM--CRIMINALS AND THUGS OF THE LOWEST ORDER. BUT THEY ARE ALSO SURVIVORS, BELIEVING IN THEIR EVIL HEARTS THAT THEY CAN EVEN CHEAT THE COMING OF THE CHAOS BRINGER, UNICRON!
THEY ARE WRONG!
FROOM!
AND THEY ARE RIGHT!
HEAR ME, INSECTS. YOUR PITIFUL LIVES ARE OVER. FROM THIS DAY HENCE YOU SERVE UNICRON!
THE ENEMY HAS ALERTED HIS CREATIONS. THEY WILL NO DOUBT TRY TO PREPARE FOR MY COMING.
THEY MUST BE STOPPED, THEIR EFFORTS HAMPERED. THE JOURNEY TO CYBERTRON IS LONG, THIS BULK TOO GREAT TO TELEPORT.
I HAVE SEARCHED MY FUTURES FOR AN AGENT-- ONE WHOM I CAN SEND BEFORE ME--TO WREAK HAVOC AMONG THE CREATIONS OF PRIMUS.
I HAVE FOUND HIM!

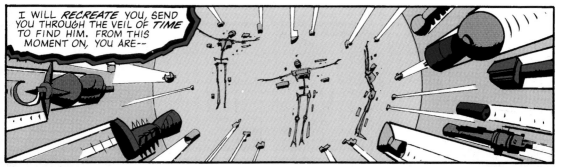

I WILL *RECREATE* YOU, SEND YOU THROUGH THE VEIL OF *TIME* TO FIND HIM. FROM THIS MOMENT ON, YOU ARE--

*HOOK--*

*LINE--*

*--AND SINKER!*

NOW *GO!* BRING HIM TO ME! *DO NOT FAIL!*

THIS MAY PROVE *UNNECESSARY* AFTER ALL. I CAN SENSE THE MATRIX, SENSE THE ESSENCE OF THE ENEMY ABOARD THE *AUTOBOT* SPACECRAFT *THE ARK!*

THE ONE THING THAT COULD HARM ME HAS BEEN *TURNED--*

"--TO THE WAYS OF EVIL!"

NOW, OPTIMUS PRIME--

--DIE!

THE POWER YOU ONCE WORSHIPPED IS *MINE* TO COMMAND! IT'S FITTING THAT THE INSTRUMENT OF YOUR *DEATH*--

FRZAK!

--SHOULD BE THE *AUTOBOTS' SACRED LIFEFORCE!*

PRIME'S *DOWN!* TAKE HIM, AUTOBOTS!

THEY *TRICKED US!* GOT ONTO THE ARK ABOARD GRIMLOCK'S SHUTTLE! LET'S GIVE THESE DECEPTICONS THE *WELCOME* THEY *DESERVE!*

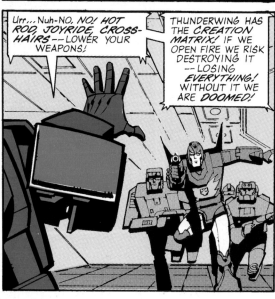

Urr... Nuh-NO, NO! HOT ROD, JOYRIDE, CROSS-HAIRS-- LOWER YOUR WEAPONS!

THUNDERWING HAS THE *CREATION MATRIX!* IF WE OPEN FIRE WE RISK DESTROYING IT --LOSING *EVERYTHING!* WITHOUT IT WE ARE *DOOMED!*

HA HA HA! PATHETIC! I HATE TO *DISILLUSION* YOU, AUTO-BOT SCUM--

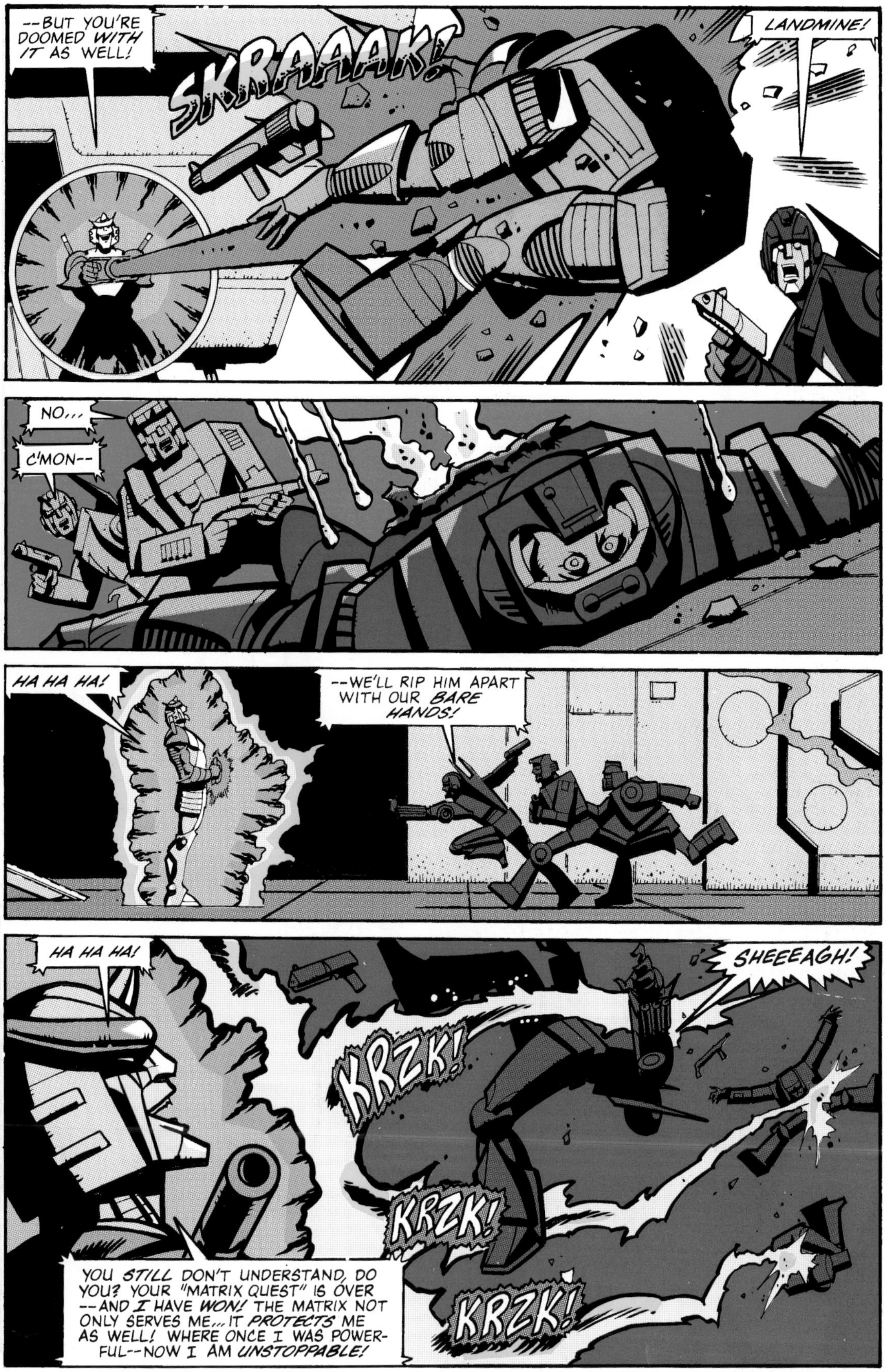
--BUT YOU'RE DOOMED WITH IT AS WELL!
SKRAAAK!
LANDMINE!
NO...
C'MON--
HA HA HA!
--WE'LL RIP HIM APART WITH OUR BARE HANDS!
HA HA HA!
SHEEEAGH!
KRZK!
KRZK!
KRZK!
YOU STILL DON'T UNDERSTAND, DO YOU? YOUR "MATRIX QUEST" IS OVER --AND I HAVE WON! THE MATRIX NOT ONLY SERVES ME... IT PROTECTS ME AS WELL! WHERE ONCE I WAS POWERFUL--NOW I AM UNSTOPPABLE!

WITH IT IN MY POSSESSION, *NOTHING CAN HARM--* GNNNK!

WHAMM!

UNNNNF!

NO--*NO!* THIS *CANNOT BE!* WHY DOES IT NOT PROTECT ME? I COMMAND THE MATRIX NOW!

THOK!

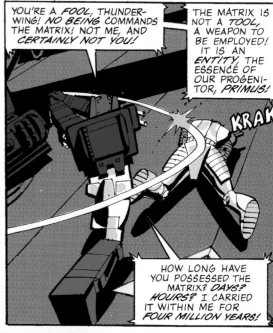

YOU'RE A *FOOL,* THUNDERWING! *NO BEING* COMMANDS THE MATRIX! NOT ME, AND *CERTAINLY NOT YOU!*

THE MATRIX IS NOT A *TOOL,* A WEAPON TO BE EMPLOYED! IT IS AN *ENTITY,* THE ESSENCE OF OUR PROGENITOR, *PRIMUS!*

KRAK

HOW LONG HAVE YOU POSSESSED THE MATRIX? *DAYS? HOURS?* I CARRIED IT WITHIN ME FOR *FOUR MILLION YEARS!*

THOUGH UNDOUBTEDLY TAINTED BY *EVIL,* THE GOODNESS, THE *PURITY* IS STILL THERE, BEGGING ME TO *FREE IT!*

WHAT HAS BEEN DONE--

--CAN BE *UNDONE!*

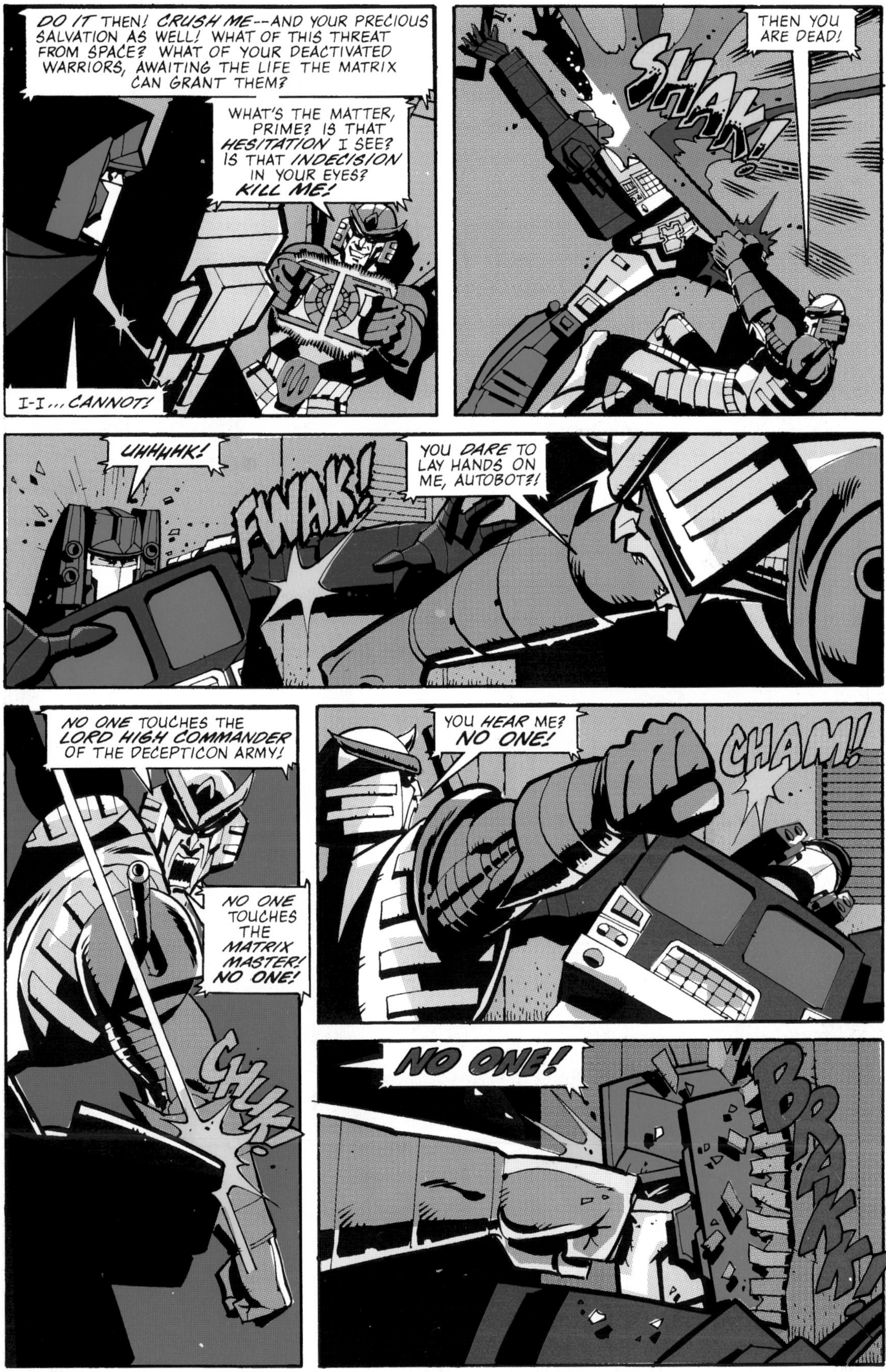

DO IT THEN! CRUSH ME--AND YOUR PRECIOUS SALVATION AS WELL! WHAT OF THIS THREAT FROM SPACE? WHAT OF YOUR DEACTIVATED WARRIORS, AWAITING THE LIFE THE MATRIX CAN GRANT THEM?
WHAT'S THE MATTER, PRIME? IS THAT HESITATION I SEE? IS THAT INDECISION IN YOUR EYES? KILL ME!
I-I... CANNOT!
THEN YOU ARE DEAD!
SHAK!
UHHHHK!
FWAK!
YOU DARE TO LAY HANDS ON ME, AUTOBOT?!
NO ONE TOUCHES THE LORD HIGH COMMANDER OF THE DECEPTICON ARMY!
NO ONE TOUCHES THE MATRIX MASTER! NO ONE!
CHUK!
YOU HEAR ME? NO ONE!
CHAM!
NO ONE!
BRAKK!

HE'S DEFINITELY *LOST IT!*

YOU'RE RIGHT, *RUCKUS!* --OUR LEADER WAS ALWAYS A *DRIVEN* BEING, BUT NOT LIKE *THIS!* HE *USED* HIS FURY.

SINCE THIS QUEST BEGAN WE'VE WATCHED HIS *OBSESSION*-- HIS DESIRE TO POSSESS THE MATRIX--TURN TO *MADNESS!* HE'S *OUT OF CONTROL!*

AND IF HE'S AS POWERFUL AS HE CLAIMS, DOES HE STILL NEED *US?* WHAT IF HE DOESN'T STOP WITH THE AUTOBOTS? *WHAT IF WE'RE NEXT?*

*BEG* FOR MERCY! *BEG* FOR YOUR DEATH TO BE SWIFT AND PAINLESS!

Urrr... Wuh-WAIT... *WAIT!*

DON'T LISTEN TO HIM, LISTEN TO *US*--TO THE *MATRIX!* SHOW US HIS DEATH, SHOW US GOOD-NESS CAN *PERISH!*

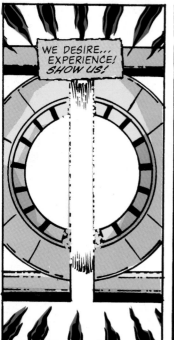

WE DESIRE... EXPERIENCE! *SHOW US!*

I-I ACKNOW-LEDGE YOUR ... *MASTERY.* GRANT ME ONE FINAL WISH, T-TELL ME WHAT BE-CAME OF GRIMLOCK AND THE OTHERS...

AND BUY ME SOME *TIME!* ALARMS SOUNDING NOW ...REINFORCEMENTS *MUST* BE COMING!

*YESS!* WAS THAT NOT A BEAUTIFUL DECEPTION? DID YOU KNOW YOUR WARRIORS--

*KILL HIM*

NNN, Y-YOUR WARRIORS ... YOUR WARRIORS ACTUALLY BEAT ME TO THE MATRIX!

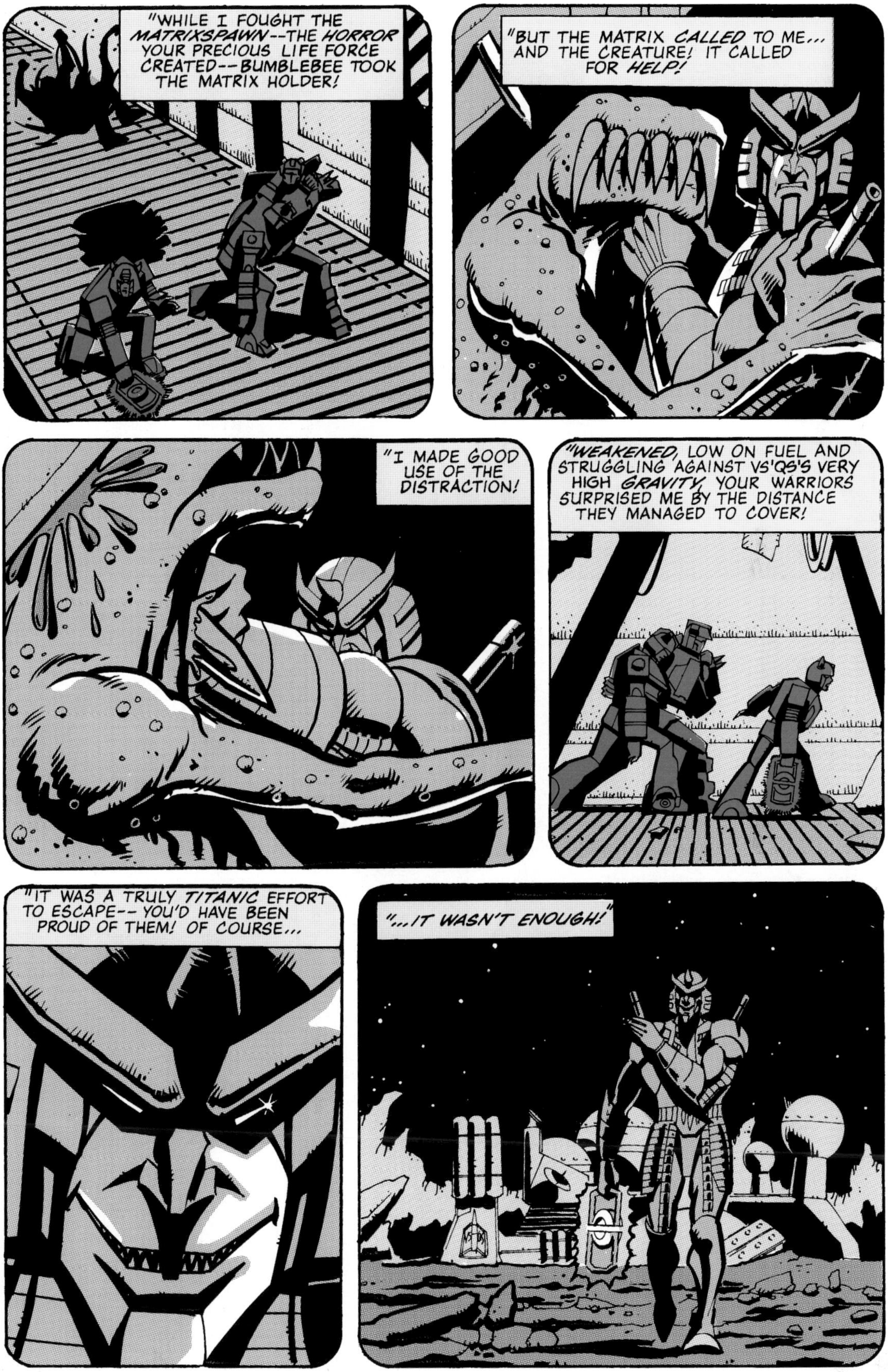
"WHILE I FOUGHT THE MATRIXSPAWN--THE HORROR YOUR PRECIOUS LIFE FORCE CREATED--BUMBLEBEE TOOK THE MATRIX HOLDER!
"BUT THE MATRIX CALLED TO ME... AND THE CREATURE! IT CALLED FOR HELP!
"I MADE GOOD USE OF THE DISTRACTION!
"WEAKENED, LOW ON FUEL AND STRUGGLING AGAINST VS'QS'S VERY HIGH GRAVITY, YOUR WARRIORS SURPRISED ME BY THE DISTANCE THEY MANAGED TO COVER!
"IT WAS A TRULY TITANIC EFFORT TO ESCAPE--YOU'D HAVE BEEN PROUD OF THEM! OF COURSE...
"...IT WASN'T ENOUGH!"

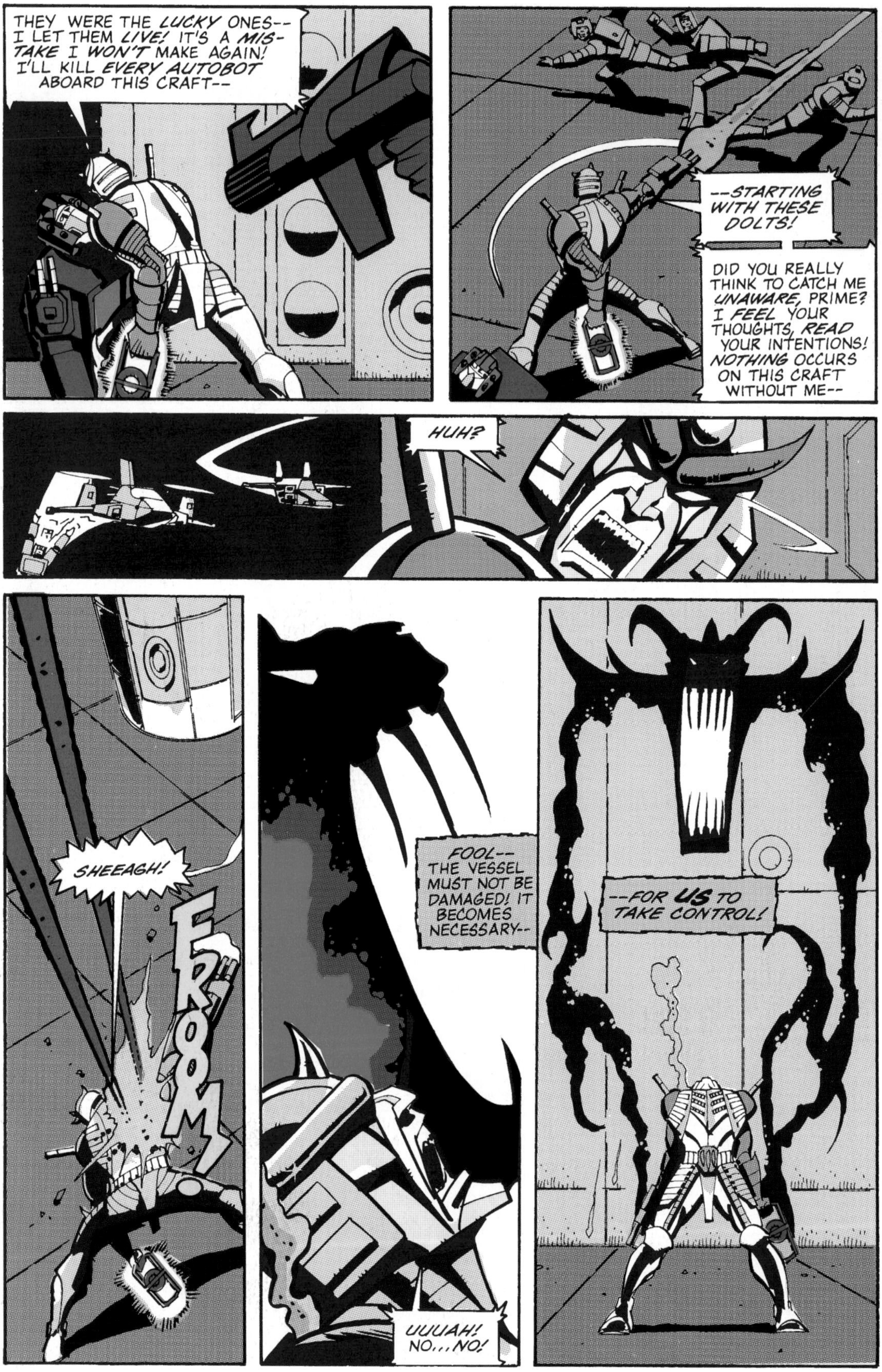
THEY WERE THE LUCKY ONES-- I LET THEM LIVE! IT'S A MISTAKE I WON'T MAKE AGAIN! I'LL KILL EVERY AUTOBOT ABOARD THIS CRAFT--
--STARTING WITH THESE DOLTS!
DID YOU REALLY THINK TO CATCH ME UNAWARE, PRIME? I FEEL YOUR THOUGHTS, READ YOUR INTENTIONS! NOTHING OCCURS ON THIS CRAFT WITHOUT ME--
HUH?
SHEEAGH!
FROOM
FOOL-- THE VESSEL MUST NOT BE DAMAGED! IT BECOMES NECESSARY--
UUUAH! NO...NO!
--FOR US TO TAKE CONTROL!

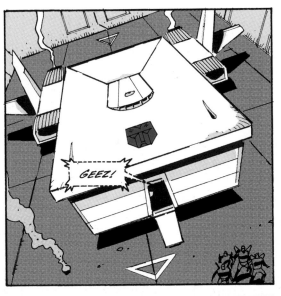

GEEZ!

I DON'T KNOW WHAT'S HAPPENED SINCE WE WERE ZAPPED*, BUT ONE THING'S FOR SURE--

--IT'S GOTTEN *WAY OUT OF HAND!*

*AT THE END OF ISSUE #62.

SO WHAT DO WE DO?

YEAH, *NIGHTBEAT*--WHAT DO WE DO? UNTIL THOSE DECEPTICONS MOVE AWAY, WE'RE TRAPPED HERE! WE GOTTA GET *OUT*--HELP PRIME AND THE OTHERS! *WE GOTTA--*

--STOP PANICKING, *SIREN*, AND *THINK!*

WHAT WE DO, *HOSEHEAD*, IS TRY AND PIECE TOGETHER THE SEQUENCE OF EVENTS. IT'S CLEAR WE WERE AMBUSHED BY THUNDERWING AND HIS MERRY LITTLE BAND!

"AND SINCE WE WOKE UP CONNECTED TO SOME SORT OF *MIND-TAP* DEVICE, IT'S A FAIR BET WE WERE MADE TO TELL THUNDERWING ABOUT THE MATRIX QUEST!

"SO THUNDERWING DOES WHAT ANY SELF-RESPECTING *MEGALOMANIAC* SHOULD DO AND GOES AFTER THE MATRIX HIMSELF-- AND *FINDS IT!*

"ONLY, THE MACHINERY HOLDING US INERT GETS DAMAGED --AND WE'RE *SET FREE!*

"WHILE WE'RE TRYING TO FIGURE A WAY PAST THE GUARD, THUNDERWING RADIOS AHEAD, TELLS *RUCKUS* TO PREPARE THE AUTOBOT SHUTTLE FOR LAUNCH!

"IT DOESN'T TAKE A GENIUS TO FIGURE OUT HOW THUNDERWING'S GOING TO USE IT, SO WHEN THE COAST IS CLEAR WE SNEAK ABOARD, SEE IF WE CAN'T THROW A SPANNER IN THE WORKS!"

ALL WE'VE GOT TO DO NOW--

--IS FIND *THAT SPANNER!*

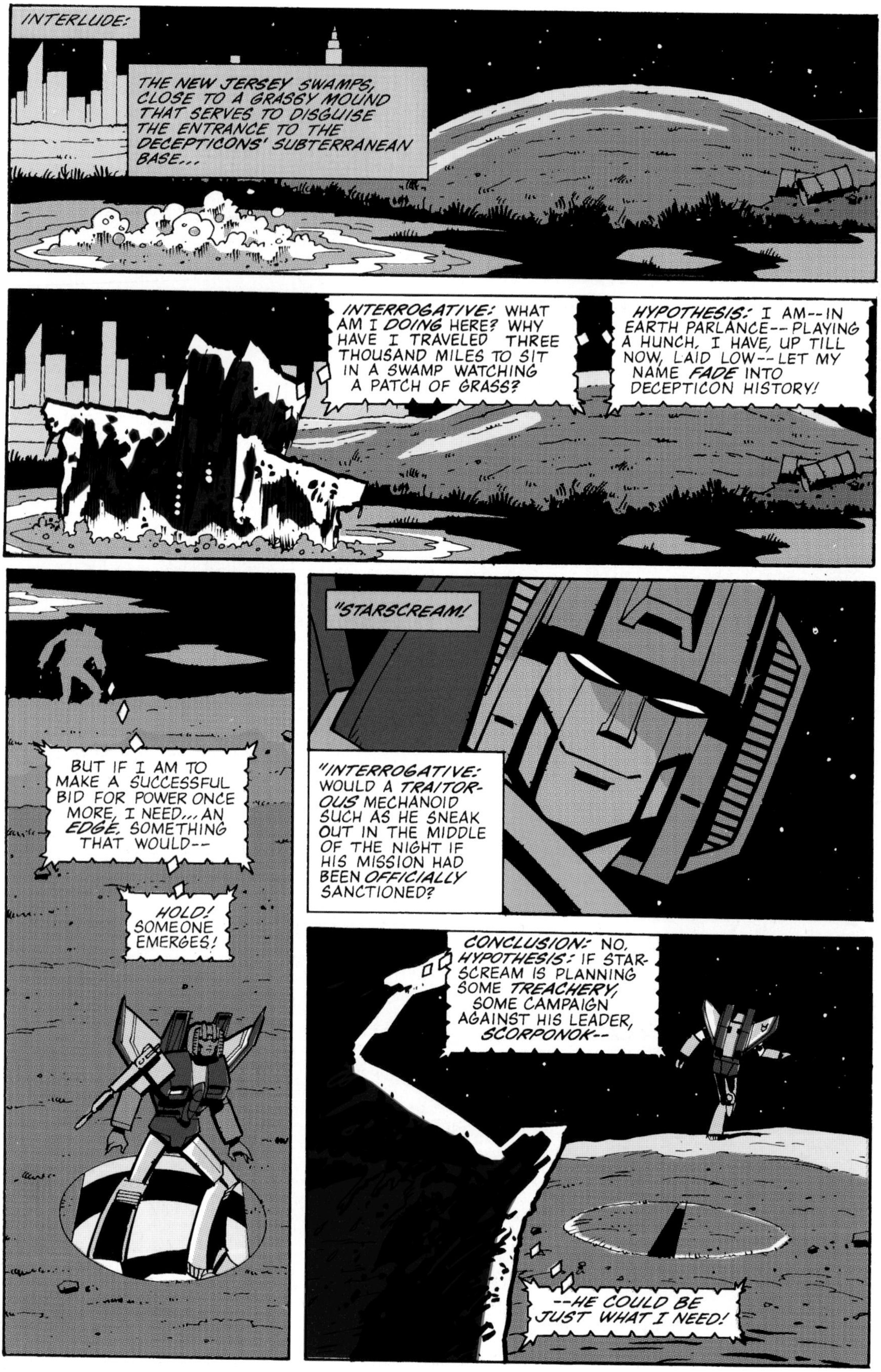
INTERLUDE:
THE NEW JERSEY SWAMPS, CLOSE TO A GRASSY MOUND THAT SERVES TO DISGUISE THE ENTRANCE TO THE DECEPTICONS' SUBTERRANEAN BASE...
INTERROGATIVE: WHAT AM I DOING HERE? WHY HAVE I TRAVELED THREE THOUSAND MILES TO SIT IN A SWAMP WATCHING A PATCH OF GRASS?
HYPOTHESIS: I AM--IN EARTH PARLANCE--PLAYING A HUNCH. I HAVE, UP TILL NOW, LAID LOW--LET MY NAME FADE INTO DECEPTICON HISTORY!
BUT IF I AM TO MAKE A SUCCESSFUL BID FOR POWER ONCE MORE, I NEED... AN EDGE. SOMETHING THAT WOULD--
HOLD! SOMEONE EMERGES!
"STARSCREAM!
"INTERROGATIVE: WOULD A TRAITOROUS MECHANOID SUCH AS HE SNEAK OUT IN THE MIDDLE OF THE NIGHT IF HIS MISSION HAD BEEN OFFICIALLY SANCTIONED?
CONCLUSION: NO. HYPOTHESIS: IF STARSCREAM IS PLANNING SOME TREACHERY, SOME CAMPAIGN AGAINST HIS LEADER, SCORPONOK--
--HE COULD BE JUST WHAT I NEED!

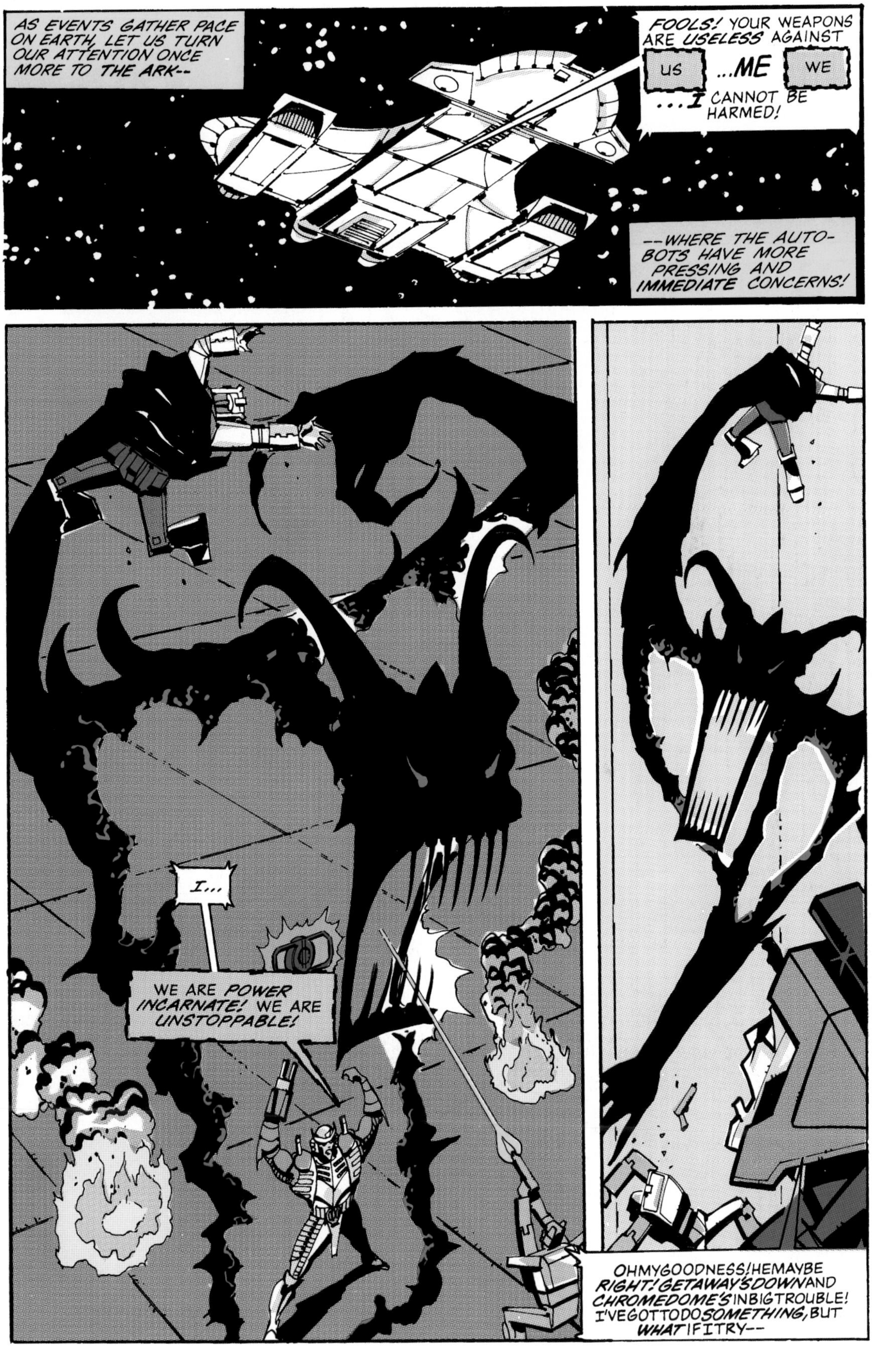
AS EVENTS GATHER PACE ON EARTH, LET US TURN OUR ATTENTION ONCE MORE TO THE ARK--
FOOLS! YOUR WEAPONS ARE USELESS AGAINST
US
...ME
WE
...I CANNOT BE HARMED!
--WHERE THE AUTO-BOTS HAVE MORE PRESSING AND IMMEDIATE CONCERNS!
I...
WE ARE POWER INCARNATE! WE ARE UNSTOPPABLE!
OHMYGOODNESS!HEMAYBE RIGHT!GETAWAY'SDOWNAND CHROMEDOME'SINBIGTROUBLE! I'VEGOTTODOSOMETHING,BUT WHATIFITRY--

OWCH! I FELT THAT! THROWING MY COMRADES AT ME! IT'S JUST NOT GOOD!

CHNCH!

NOW I'M REALLY MAD!

YOU'LL HAVE TO DO BETTER THAN *THAT* IF YOU WANT TO HIT BLURR!

I CAN HIT YOU A HUNDRED TIMES BEFORE YOU CAN THINK ABOUT--

FRZZK!

GNNN!

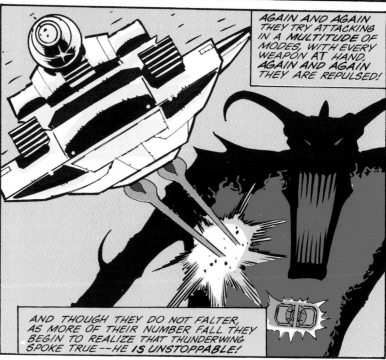

AGAIN AND AGAIN THEY TRY ATTACKING IN A *MULTITUDE* OF MODES, WITH EVERY WEAPON AT HAND. AGAIN AND AGAIN THEY ARE REPULSED!

AND THOUGH THEY DO NOT FALTER, AS MORE OF THEIR NUMBER FALL THEY BEGIN TO REALIZE THAT THUNDERWING SPOKE TRUE--HE *IS* UNSTOPPABLE!

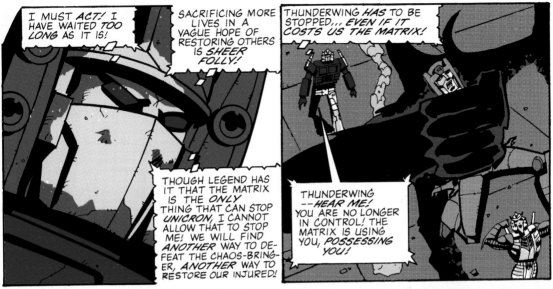

I MUST *ACT!* I HAVE WAITED *TOO LONG* AS IT IS!

SACRIFICING MORE LIVES IN A VAGUE HOPE OF RESTORING OTHERS IS *SHEER FOLLY!*

THUNDERWING *HAS TO BE* STOPPED... *EVEN IF IT COSTS US THE MATRIX!*

THOUGH LEGEND HAS IT THAT THE MATRIX IS THE *ONLY* THING THAT CAN STOP UNICRON, I CANNOT ALLOW THAT TO STOP ME! WE WILL FIND *ANOTHER* WAY TO DEFEAT THE CHAOS-BRINGER, *ANOTHER* WAY TO RESTORE OUR INJURED!

THUNDERWING --*HEAR ME!* YOU ARE NO LONGER IN CONTROL! THE MATRIX IS USING YOU, *POSSESSING YOU!*

*PRIME!*

DO YOU SERIOUSLY THINK WE WILL FALL FOR THIS LAME DECEPTION?

*LISTEN* TO YOURSELF! THIS IS *NOT* THUNDERWING SPEAKING!

HA HA HA! YOU *AMUSE* US, PRIME! IN FACT, THE ONLY THING FUNNIER--

--IS YOUR *IMMINENT DEATH!*

YOU ARE THE *PAST,* PRIME-- A STAGE IN OUR EVOLUTION! AND IN A MOMENT--

--YOU WILL BE *EXTINCT!*

YOU WANT US TO DO **WHAT!?!**

YOU **HEARD** ME, SIREN. HOSEHEAD IS TO **OPEN** THE MAIN SHUTTLE BAY DOORS AND THEN SWITCH OFF THE **ARTIFICIAL GRAVITY.**

YOU ARE TO SET THIS SHUTTLE'S **SELF-DESTRUCT** MECHANISM FOR **THREE MINUTES** AND THEN **GET CLEAR!**

B-BUT WHAT ABOUT **YOU,** NIGHTBEAT?

ME?

I'M GOING **FISHING!**

COMPUTER-- AUTOBOT NIGHTBEAT REQUESTING INTERFACE.

VOICESCAN CONFIRMED. AWAITING ORDERS.

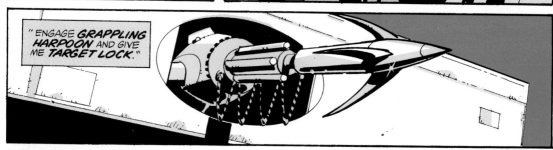

" ENGAGE **GRAPPLING HARPOON** AND GIVE ME **TARGET LOCK.**"

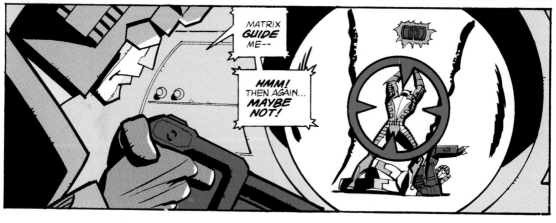

MATRIX **GUIDE** ME--

**HMM!** THEN AGAIN... **MAYBE NOT!**

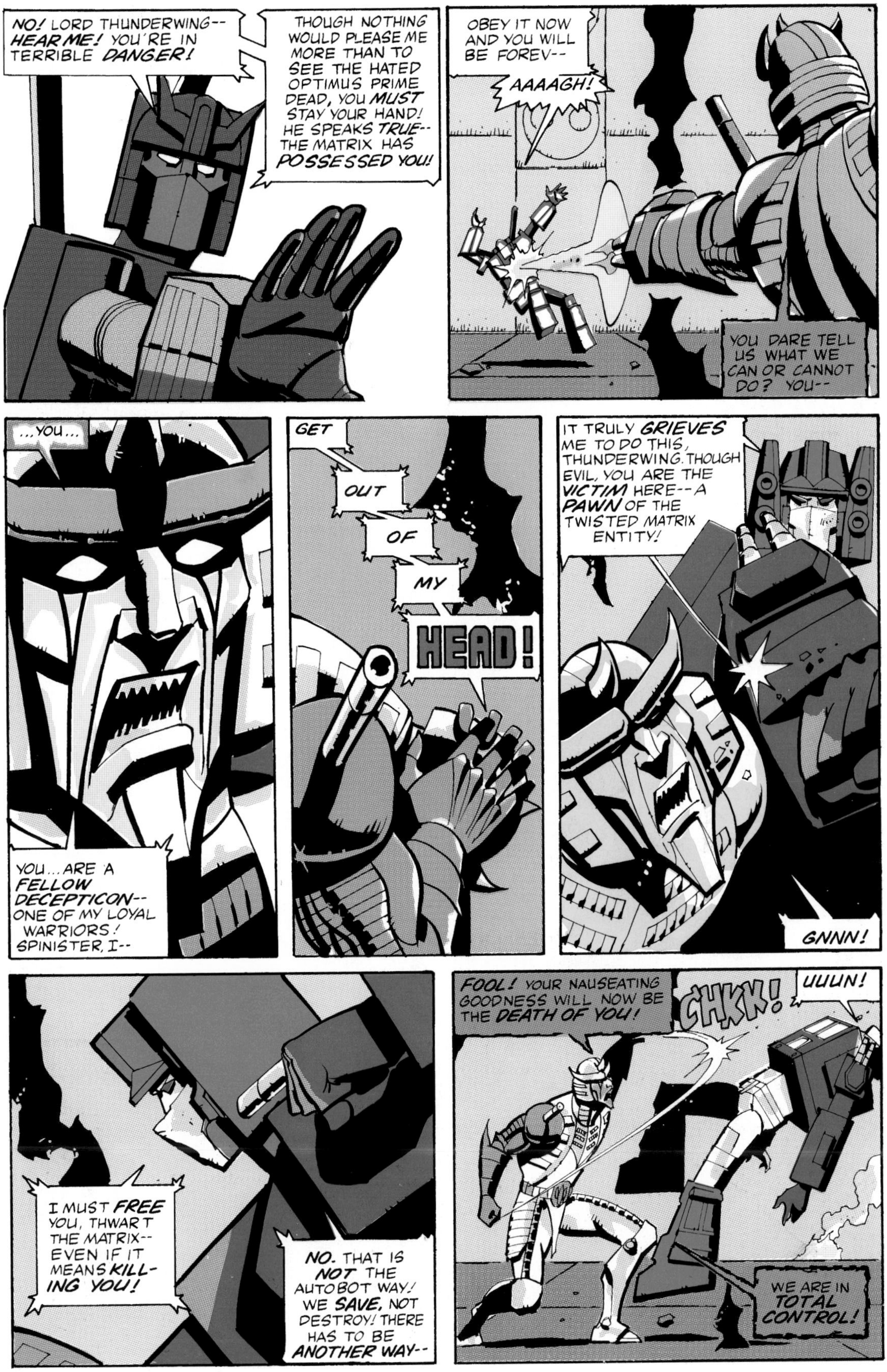
NO! LORD THUNDERWING-- HEAR ME! YOU'RE IN TERRIBLE DANGER!
THOUGH NOTHING WOULD PLEASE ME MORE THAN TO SEE THE HATED OPTIMUS PRIME DEAD, YOU MUST STAY YOUR HAND! HE SPEAKS TRUE-- THE MATRIX HAS POSSESSED YOU!
OBEY IT NOW AND YOU WILL BE FOREV--
AAAAGH!
YOU DARE TELL US WHAT WE CAN OR CANNOT DO? YOU--
...YOU...
YOU...ARE A FELLOW DECEPTICON-- ONE OF MY LOYAL WARRIORS! SPINISTER, I--
GET
OUT
OF
MY
HEAD!
IT TRULY GRIEVES ME TO DO THIS, THUNDERWING. THOUGH EVIL, YOU ARE THE VICTIM HERE-- A PAWN OF THE TWISTED MATRIX ENTITY!
GNNN!
I MUST FREE YOU, THWART THE MATRIX-- EVEN IF IT MEANS KILL-ING YOU!
NO. THAT IS NOT THE AUTOBOT WAY! WE SAVE, NOT DESTROY! THERE HAS TO BE ANOTHER WAY--
FOOL! YOUR NAUSEATING GOODNESS WILL NOW BE THE DEATH OF YOU!
CHKK!
UUUN!
WE ARE IN TOTAL CONTROL!

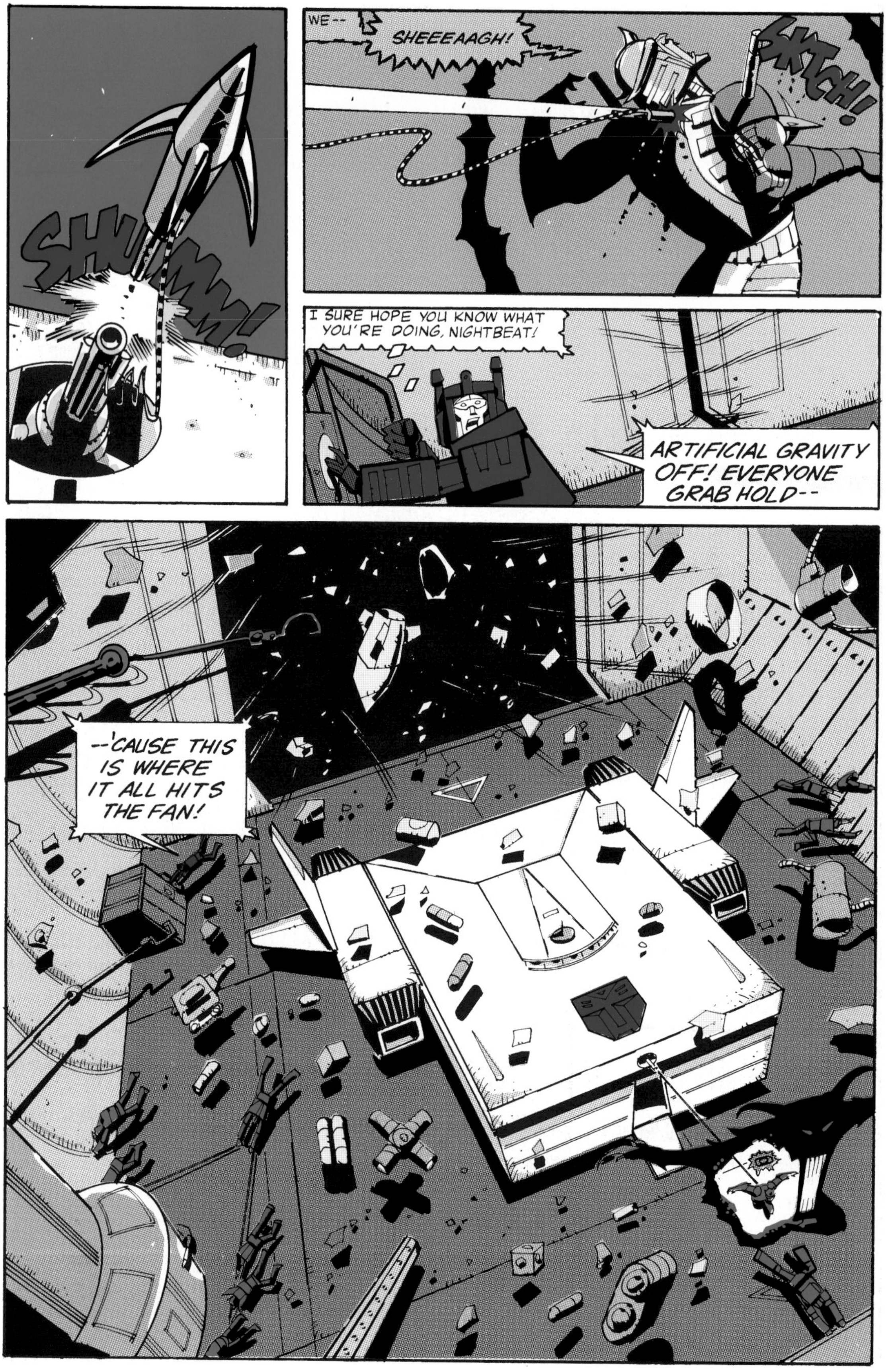
SHUMMM!
WE--
SHEEEAAGH!
SKTCH!
I SURE HOPE YOU KNOW WHAT YOU'RE DOING, NIGHTBEAT!
ARTIFICIAL GRAVITY OFF! EVERYONE GRAB HOLD--
--'CAUSE THIS IS WHERE IT ALL HITS THE FAN!

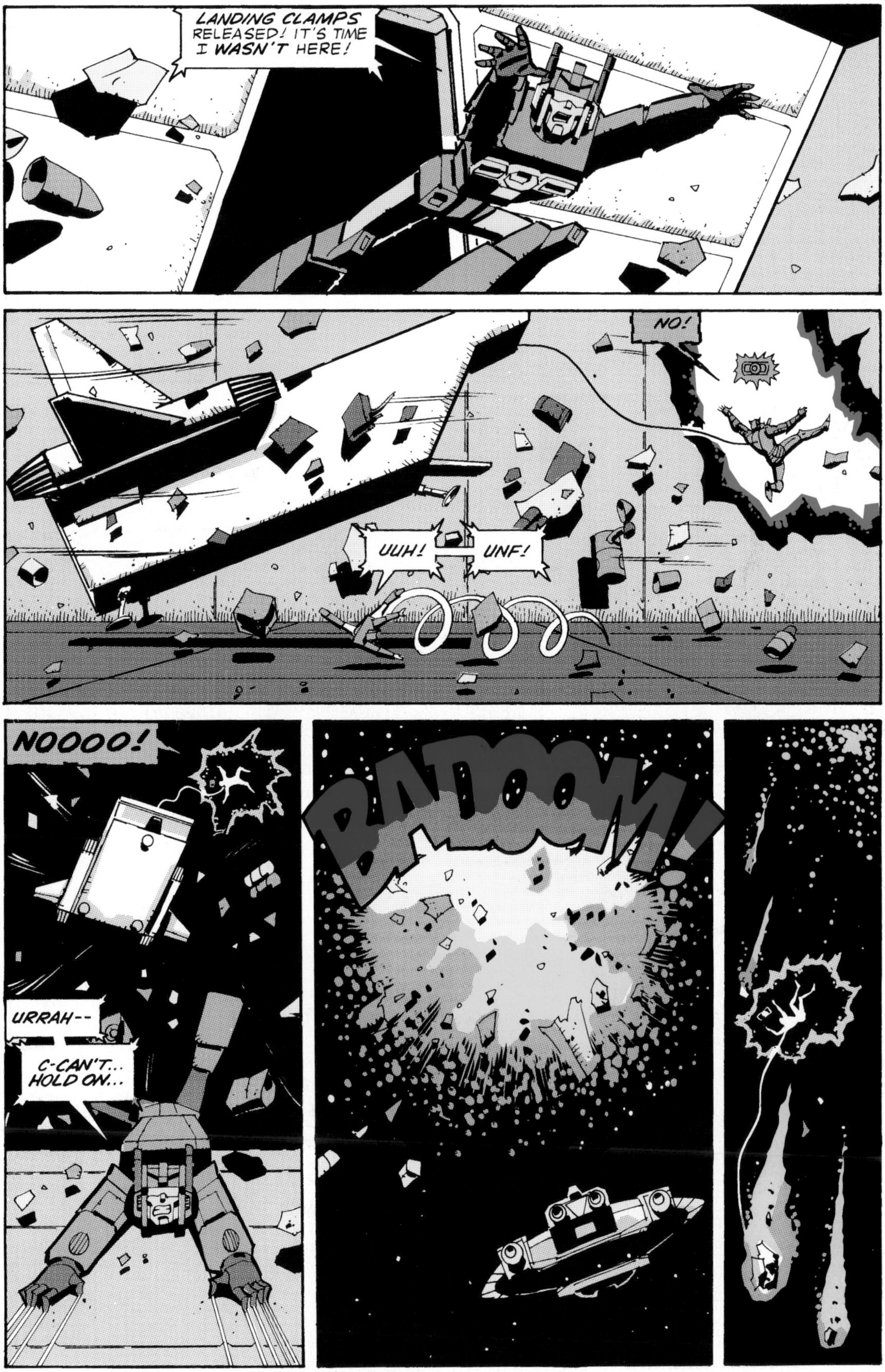
LANDING CLAMPS RELEASED! IT'S TIME I WASN'T HERE!
NO!
UUH!
UNF!
NOOOO!
URRAH--
C-CAN'T... HOLD ON...
BADOOM!

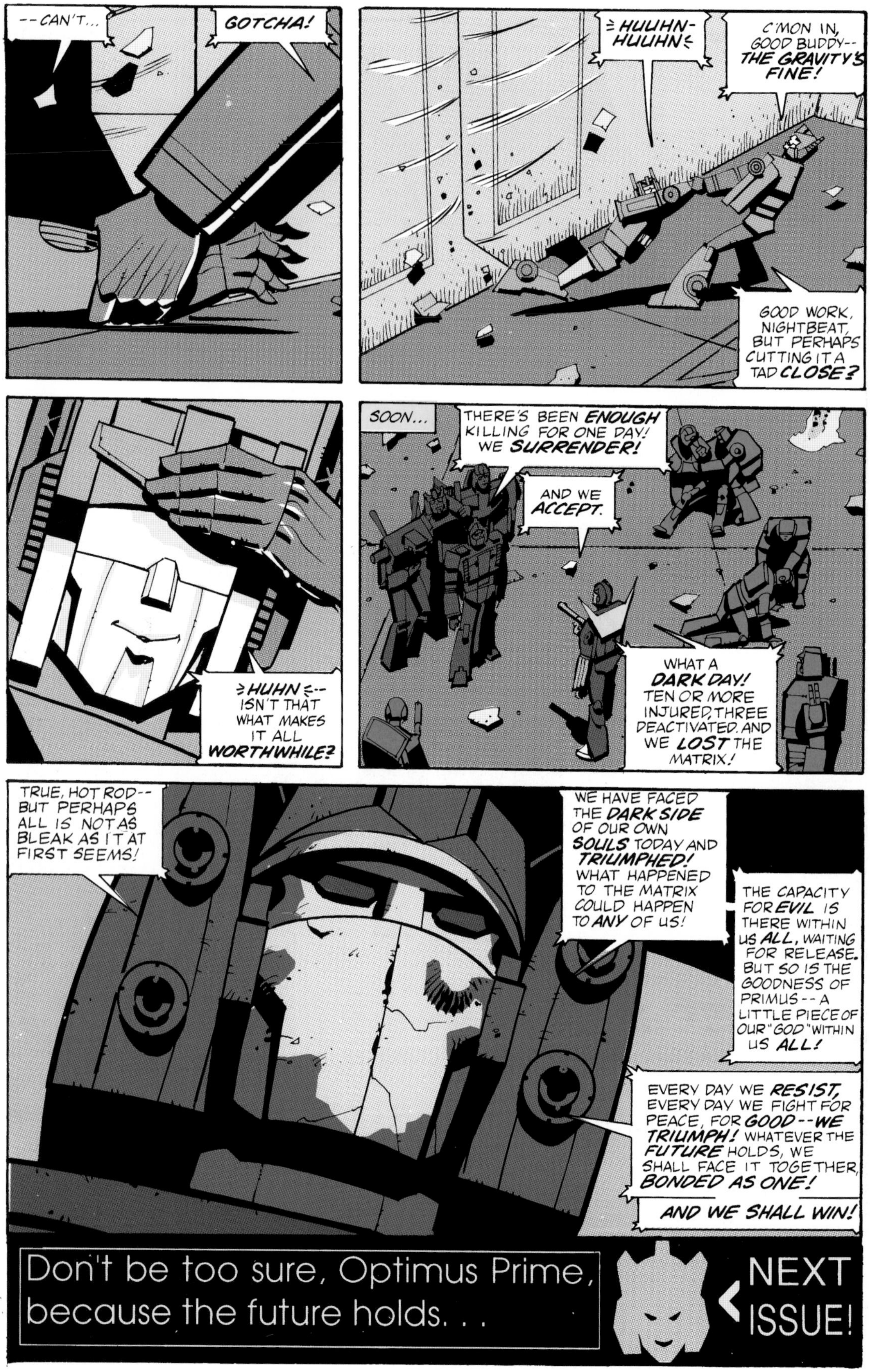
--CAN'T...
GOTCHA!
HUUHN-HUUHN
C'MON IN, GOOD BUDDY-- THE GRAVITY'S FINE!
GOOD WORK, NIGHTBEAT, BUT PERHAPS CUTTING IT A TAD CLOSE?
HUHN-- ISN'T THAT WHAT MAKES IT ALL WORTHWHILE?
SOON...
THERE'S BEEN ENOUGH KILLING FOR ONE DAY! WE SURRENDER!
AND WE ACCEPT.
WHAT A DARK DAY! TEN OR MORE INJURED, THREE DEACTIVATED. AND WE LOST THE MATRIX!
TRUE, HOT ROD-- BUT PERHAPS ALL IS NOT AS BLEAK AS IT AT FIRST SEEMS!
WE HAVE FACED THE DARK SIDE OF OUR OWN SOULS TODAY AND TRIUMPHED! WHAT HAPPENED TO THE MATRIX COULD HAPPEN TO ANY OF US!
THE CAPACITY FOR EVIL IS THERE WITHIN US ALL, WAITING FOR RELEASE. BUT SO IS THE GOODNESS OF PRIMUS -- A LITTLE PIECE OF OUR "GOD" WITHIN US ALL!
EVERY DAY WE RESIST, EVERY DAY WE FIGHT FOR PEACE, FOR GOOD--WE TRIUMPH! WHATEVER THE FUTURE HOLDS, WE SHALL FACE IT TOGETHER, BONDED AS ONE!
AND WE SHALL WIN!
Don't be too sure, Optimus Prime, because the future holds. . .
NEXT ISSUE!

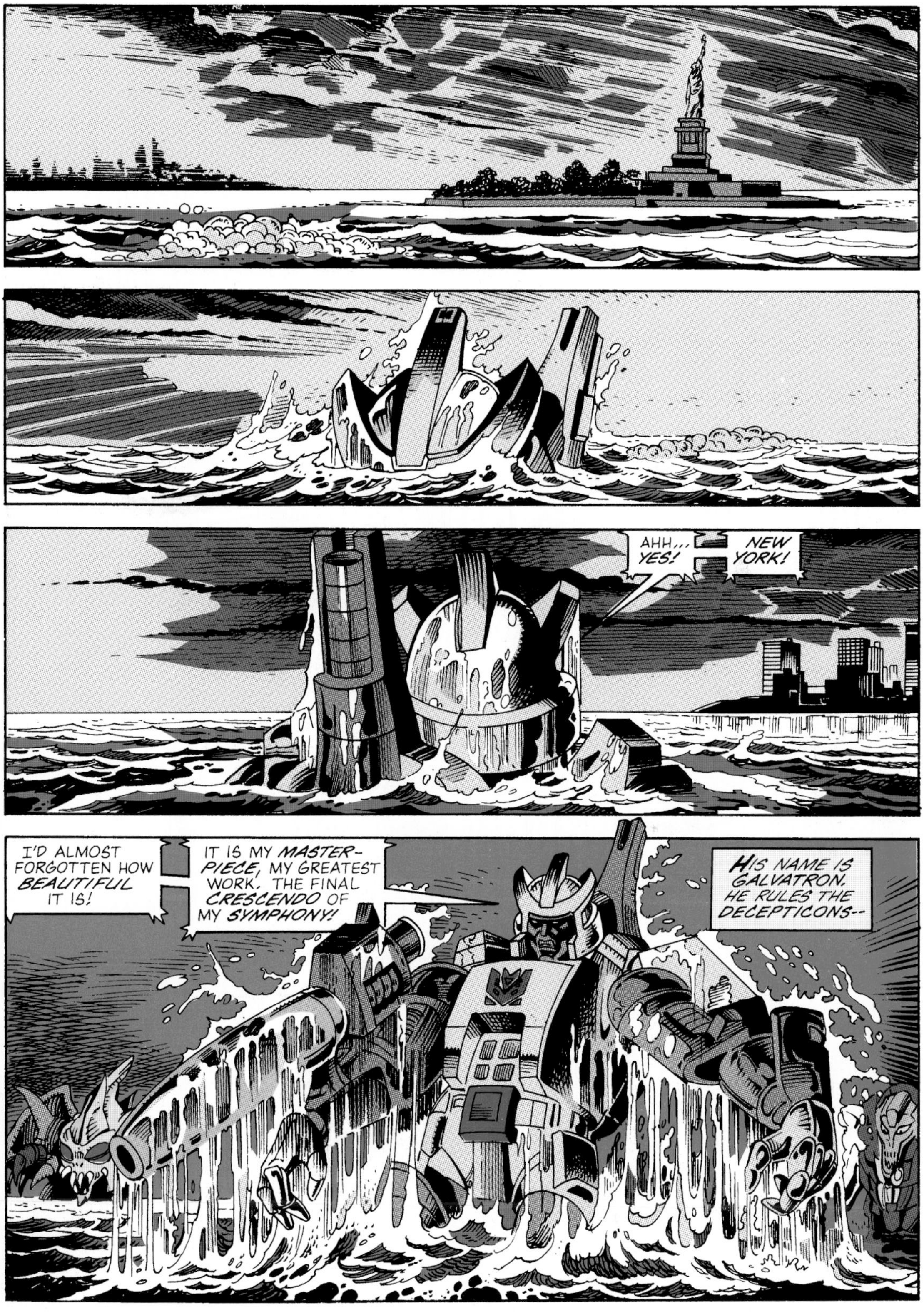
AHH... YES!
NEW YORK!
I'D ALMOST FORGOTTEN HOW BEAUTIFUL IT IS!
IT IS MY MASTER-PIECE, MY GREATEST WORK. THE FINAL CRESCENDO OF MY SYMPHONY!
HIS NAME IS GALVATRON. HE RULES THE DECEPTICONS--

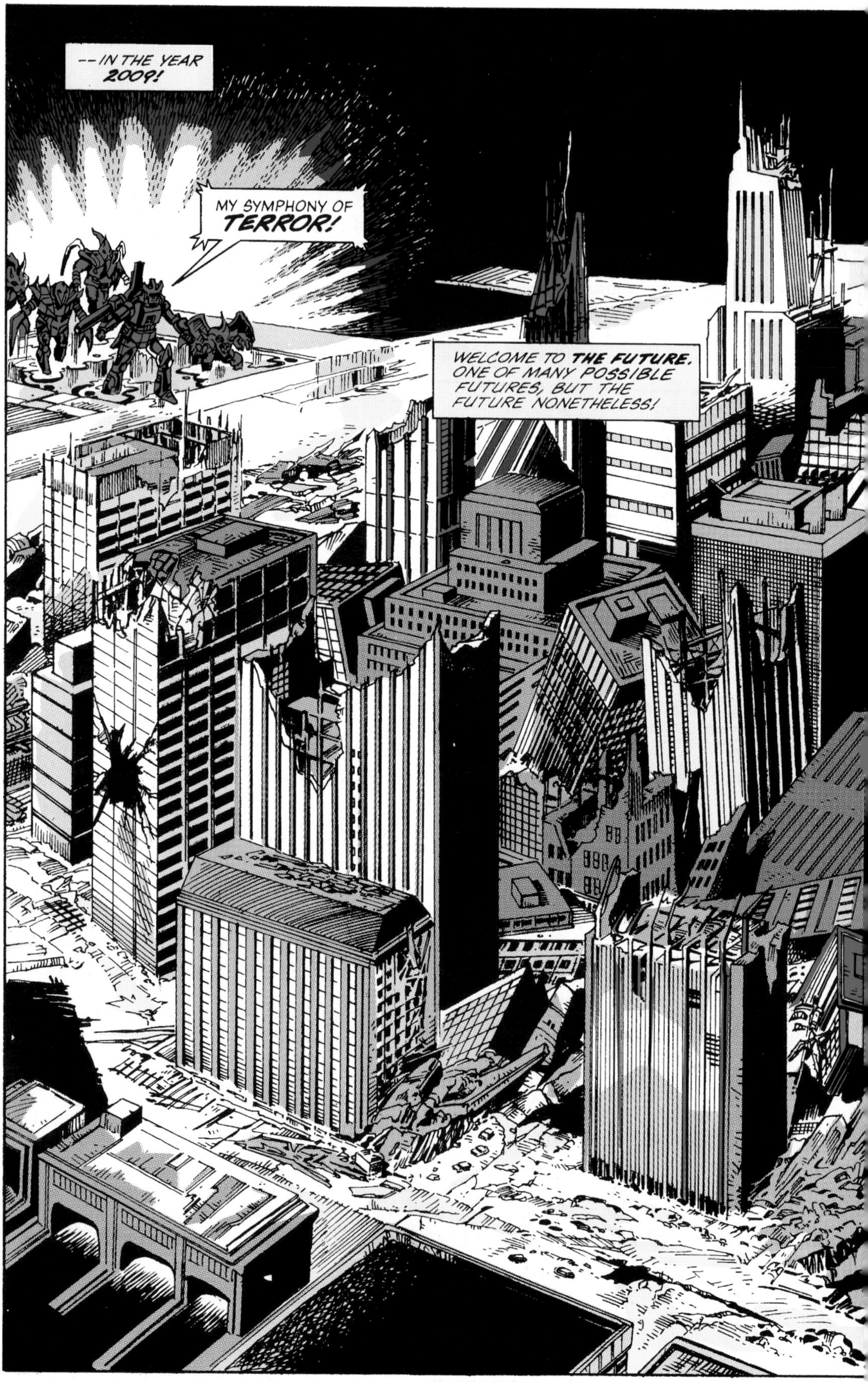
--IN THE YEAR 2009!
MY SYMPHONY OF TERROR!
WELCOME TO THE FUTURE. ONE OF MANY POSSIBLE FUTURES, BUT THE FUTURE NONETHELESS!

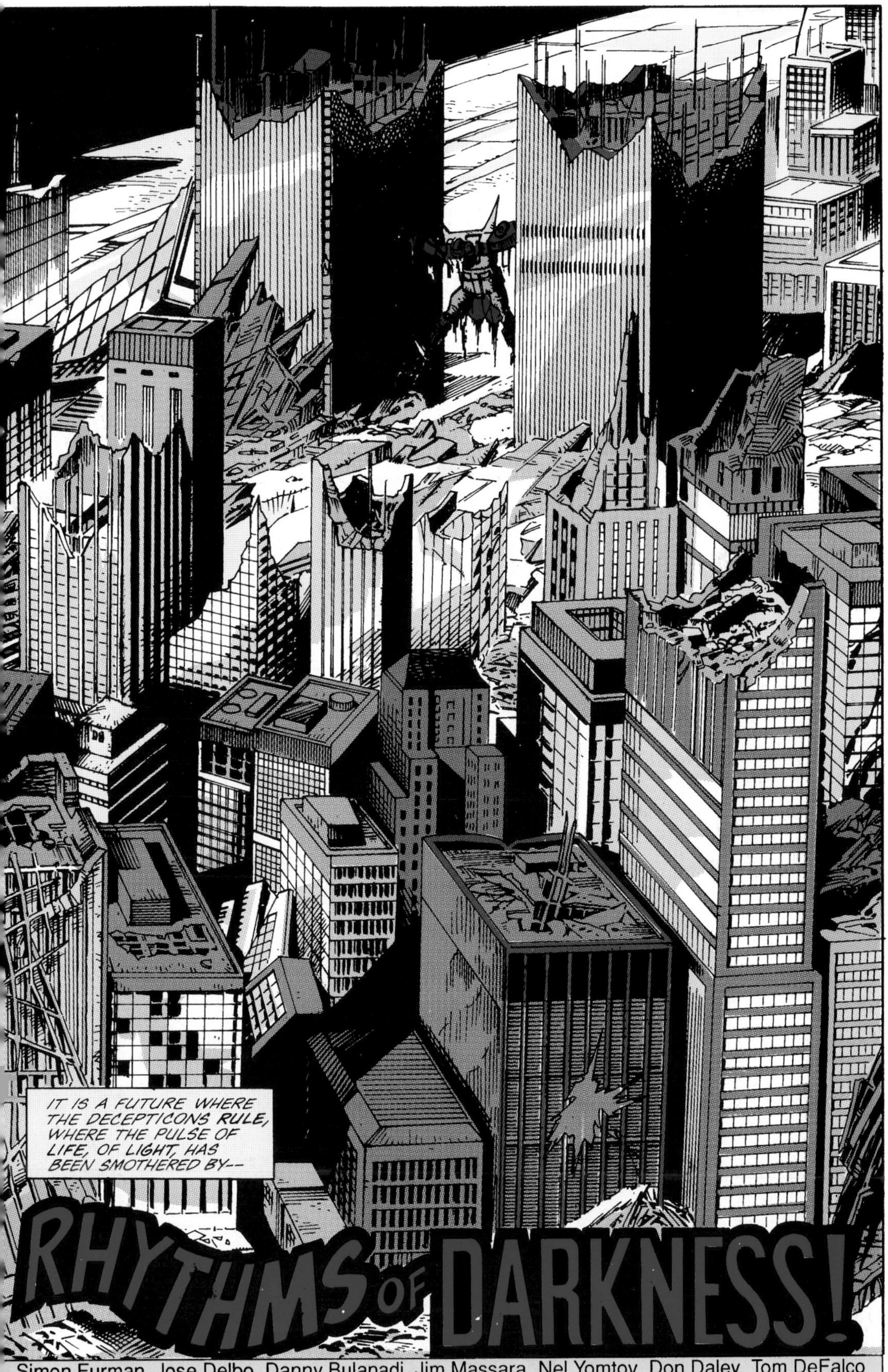
IT IS A FUTURE WHERE THE DECEPTICONS RULE, WHERE THE PULSE OF LIFE, OF LIGHT, HAS BEEN SMOTHERED BY--
RHYTHMS OF DARKNESS!

| Simon Furman | Jose Delbo | Danny Bulanadi | Jim Massara | Nel Yomtov | Don Daley | Tom DeFalco |
|---|---|---|---|---|---|---|
| WRITER | PENCILER | INKER | LETTERER | COLORIST | EDITOR | STREET CLEANER |

THE LAST MOVEMENT IN AN OPERA OF *EVIL* THAT FINALLY LAID AUTOBOT AND HUMAN LOW, MAKING HIM--

--UNDISPUTED *RULER OF EARTH!*

THE FINAL FEW FELL HERE, A DOOMED *LAST STAND* AGAINST AN *UNSTOPPABLE ENEMY!* A FOE SO *POWERFUL,* SO *RESOURCEFUL* -- NONE COULD STAND AGAINST HIM!

WHO'S HE TALKING ABOUT?

HIMSELF. THIRD PERSON DELUSIONS OF GRANDEUR THEY CALL IT.

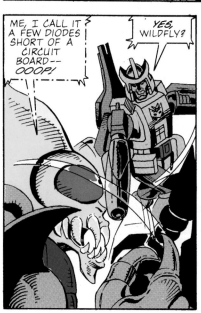

ME, I CALL IT A FEW DIODES SHORT OF A CIRCUIT BOARD-- *OOOP!*

*YES,* WILDFLY?

SOME *COMMENT,* PERHAPS? SOME LEARNED *INSIGHT* INTO MY HISTORIC VICTORY? OR PERHAPS... *A CHALLENGE?*

PRETENDER MONSTERS! *HAH!* TO ME YOU ARE LESS THAN *NOTHING,* CANNON-FODDER TROOPS WHO SHOULD LEAVE THE THINKING TO *OTHERS!*

CROSS ME AND I WILL *OBLITERATE* YOU WITHOUT A SECOND THOUGHT! *REMEMBER THAT!*

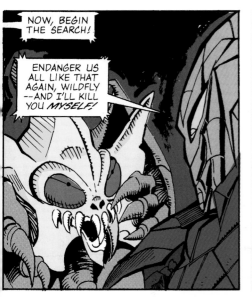

NOW, BEGIN THE SEARCH!

ENDANGER US ALL LIKE THAT AGAIN, WILDFLY --AND I'LL KILL YOU *MYSELF!*

ENOUGH CHATTER, *ICEPICK!* YOU, *BRISTLEBACK* AND *SCOWL* TAKE THE EAST. *WILDFLY* BIRDBRAIN, AND *SLOG* THE WEST.

I SERIOUSLY DOUBT THAT THE FEW *REMNANTS* OF THE AUTOBOT ARMY CAN DO ME ANY HARM AT THIS LATE STAGE, BUT I WISH EVEN THE *SMALLEST* RISK REMOVED!

REMOVED *PERMANENTLY!*

WHAT A WASTE OF TIME! HE'S PUTTING US *ALL* AT RISK, AND FOR WHAT? ONE OR TWO AUTO-BOTS AND A HANDFUL OF HUMANS! IF I ONLY HAD THE MIGHT TO *CHALLENGE* HIM!

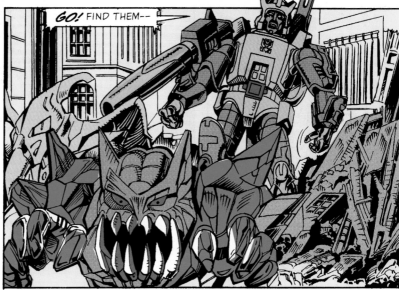

*GO!* FIND THEM--

BLAST THEM!

*FROM!*

PULVERIZE THEM!

LOONY AS THEY COME! HE'S LIKE A KID-- *REVELING* IN THIS!

NOW IF *I* LED THE DECEPTICONS, I'D SPREAD OUR EMPIRE *BEYOND* NORTH AND SOUTH AMERICA, *REALLY* RULE EARTH. I'D SHOW THESE HUMANS ONCE AND FOR ALL WHO THE *MASTERS* ARE--

**KRAKADOOM!**

HUH?!

**KRMMM!**

AAHK!

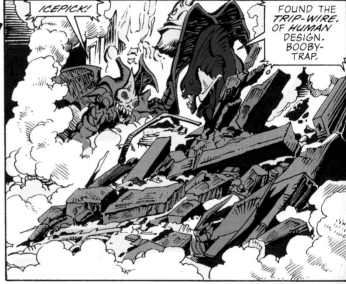

ICEPICK!

FOUND THE *TRIP-WIRE.* OF *HUMAN* DESIGN. BOOBY-TRAP.

YOU DID THIS, *RODIMUS PRIME!* *YOU* TAUGHT THEM HOW TO FIGHT US! LIKE YOU TAUGHT THEM HOW TO *HIDE* FROM US!

THESE LAST FEW AUTOBOTS OF YOURS--THEY WILL TRY TO *SAVE* EARTH, WON'T THEY? EVEN WITH SO LITTLE TIME LEFT, WITH THE ODDS STACKED SO *HOPELESSLY* AGAINST THEM!

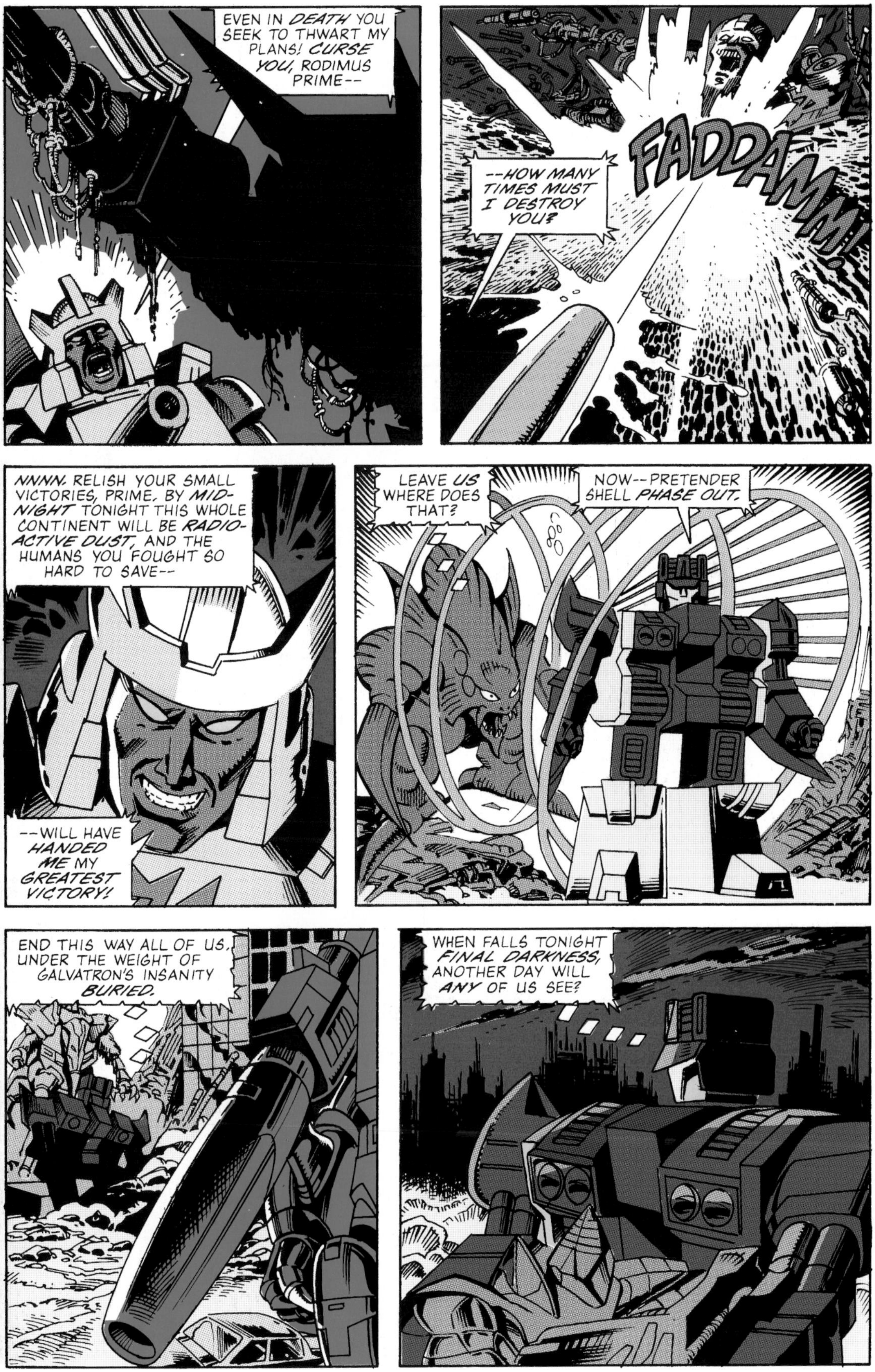
EVEN IN *DEATH* YOU SEEK TO THWART MY PLANS! *CURSE YOU,* RODIMUS PRIME--
--*HOW MANY TIMES MUST I DESTROY YOU?*
FADDAMM!
*NNNN.* RELISH YOUR SMALL VICTORIES, PRIME. BY *MID-NIGHT* TONIGHT THIS WHOLE CONTINENT WILL BE *RADIO-ACTIVE DUST,* AND THE HUMANS YOU FOUGHT SO HARD TO SAVE--
--WILL HAVE *HANDED ME* MY *GREATEST VICTORY!*
LEAVE *US* WHERE DOES THAT?
NOW--PRETENDER SHELL *PHASE OUT.*
END THIS WAY ALL OF US, UNDER THE WEIGHT OF GALVATRON'S INSANITY *BURIED.*
WHEN FALLS TONIGHT *FINAL DARKNESS,* ANOTHER DAY WILL *ANY* OF US SEE?

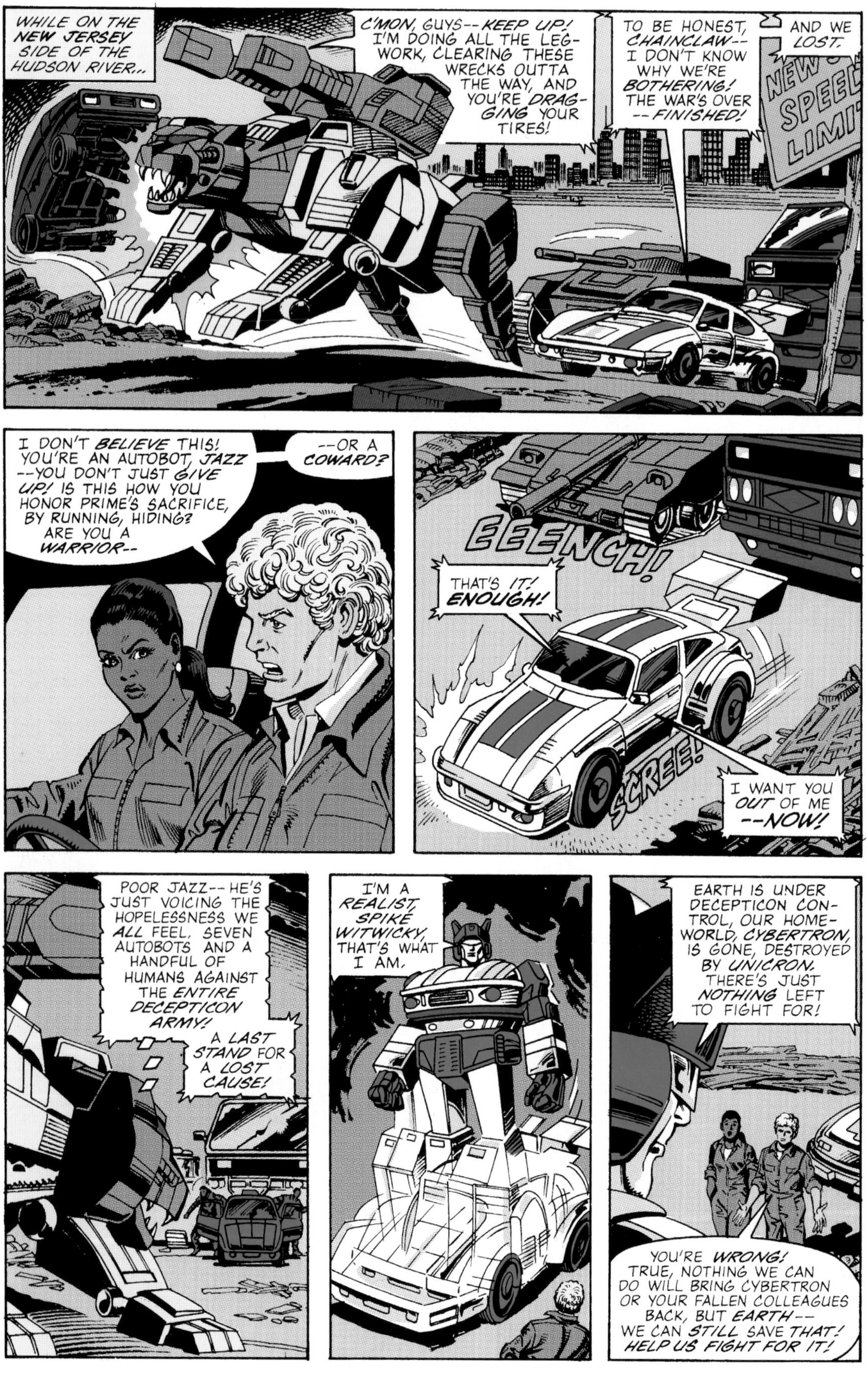
WHILE ON THE NEW JERSEY SIDE OF THE HUDSON RIVER...
C'MON, GUYS--KEEP UP! I'M DOING ALL THE LEG-WORK, CLEARING THESE WRECKS OUTTA THE WAY, AND YOU'RE DRAG-GING YOUR TIRES!
TO BE HONEST, CHAINCLAW--I DON'T KNOW WHY WE'RE BOTHERING! THE WAR'S OVER --FINISHED!
AND WE LOST.
I DON'T BELIEVE THIS! YOU'RE AN AUTOBOT, JAZZ --YOU DON'T JUST GIVE UP! IS THIS HOW YOU HONOR PRIME'S SACRIFICE, BY RUNNING, HIDING? ARE YOU A WARRIOR--
--OR A COWARD?
EEENCH!
THAT'S IT! ENOUGH!
SCREE!
I WANT YOU OUT OF ME --NOW!
POOR JAZZ--HE'S JUST VOICING THE HOPELESSNESS WE ALL FEEL. SEVEN AUTOBOTS AND A HANDFUL OF HUMANS AGAINST THE ENTIRE DECEPTICON ARMY!
A LAST STAND FOR A LOST CAUSE!
I'M A REALIST, SPIKE WITWICKY, THAT'S WHAT I AM.
EARTH IS UNDER DECEPTICON CON-TROL, OUR HOME-WORLD, CYBERTRON, IS GONE, DESTROYED BY UNICRON. THERE'S JUST NOTHING LEFT TO FIGHT FOR!
YOU'RE WRONG! TRUE, NOTHING WE CAN DO WILL BRING CYBERTRON OR YOUR FALLEN COLLEAGUES BACK, BUT EARTH--WE CAN STILL SAVE THAT! HELP US FIGHT FOR IT!

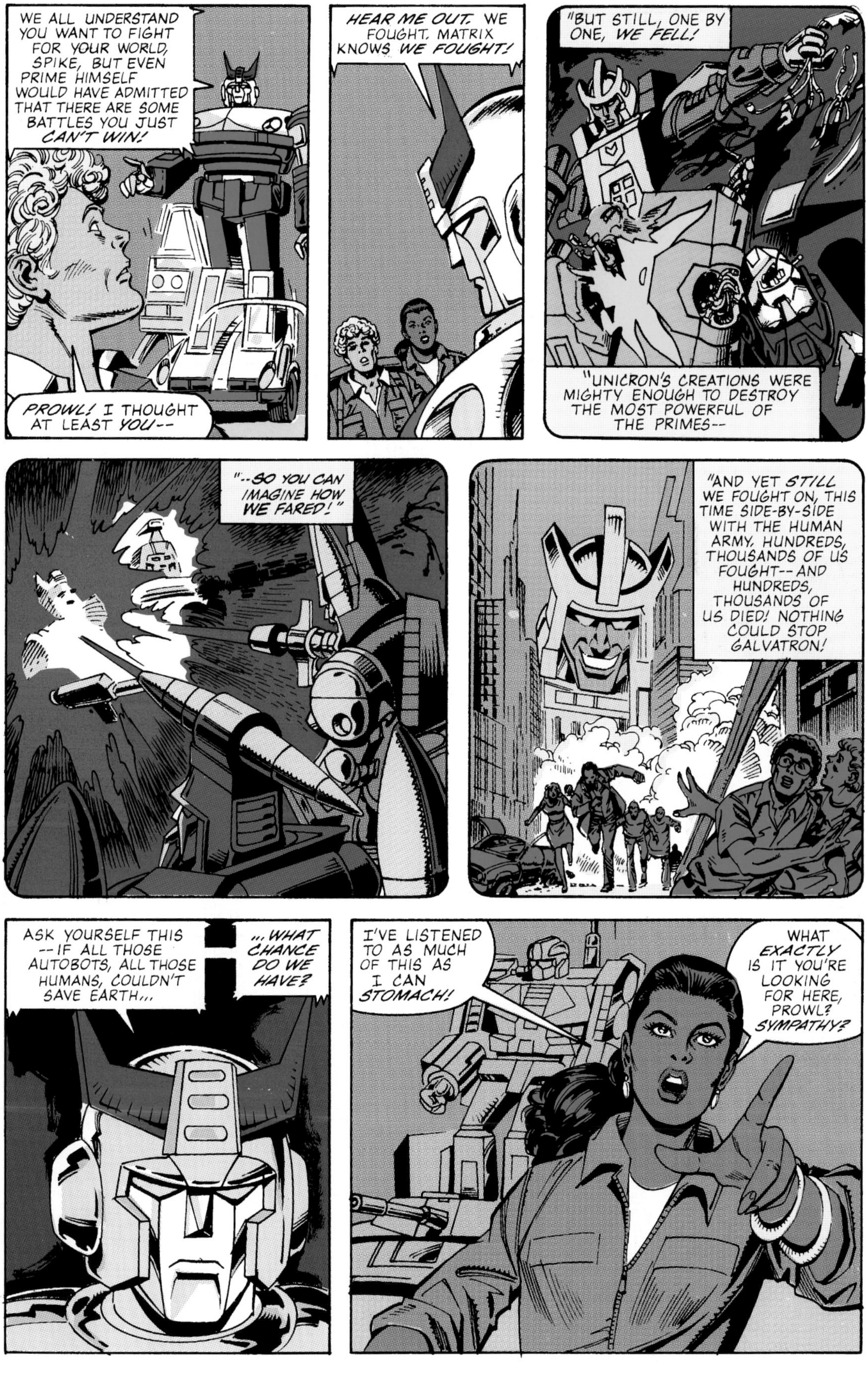
WE ALL UNDERSTAND YOU WANT TO FIGHT FOR YOUR WORLD, SPIKE, BUT EVEN PRIME HIMSELF WOULD HAVE ADMITTED THAT THERE ARE SOME BATTLES YOU JUST CAN'T WIN!
PROWL! I THOUGHT AT LEAST YOU--
HEAR ME OUT. WE FOUGHT. MATRIX KNOWS WE FOUGHT!
"BUT STILL, ONE BY ONE, WE FELL!
"UNICRON'S CREATIONS WERE MIGHTY ENOUGH TO DESTROY THE MOST POWERFUL OF THE PRIMES--
"--SO YOU CAN IMAGINE HOW WE FARED!"
"AND YET STILL WE FOUGHT ON, THIS TIME SIDE-BY-SIDE WITH THE HUMAN ARMY. HUNDREDS, THOUSANDS OF US FOUGHT-- AND HUNDREDS, THOUSANDS OF US DIED! NOTHING COULD STOP GALVATRON!
ASK YOURSELF THIS --IF ALL THOSE AUTOBOTS, ALL THOSE HUMANS, COULDN'T SAVE EARTH...
...WHAT CHANCE DO WE HAVE?
I'VE LISTENED TO AS MUCH OF THIS AS I CAN STOMACH!
WHAT EXACTLY IS IT YOU'RE LOOKING FOR HERE, PROWL? SYMPATHY?

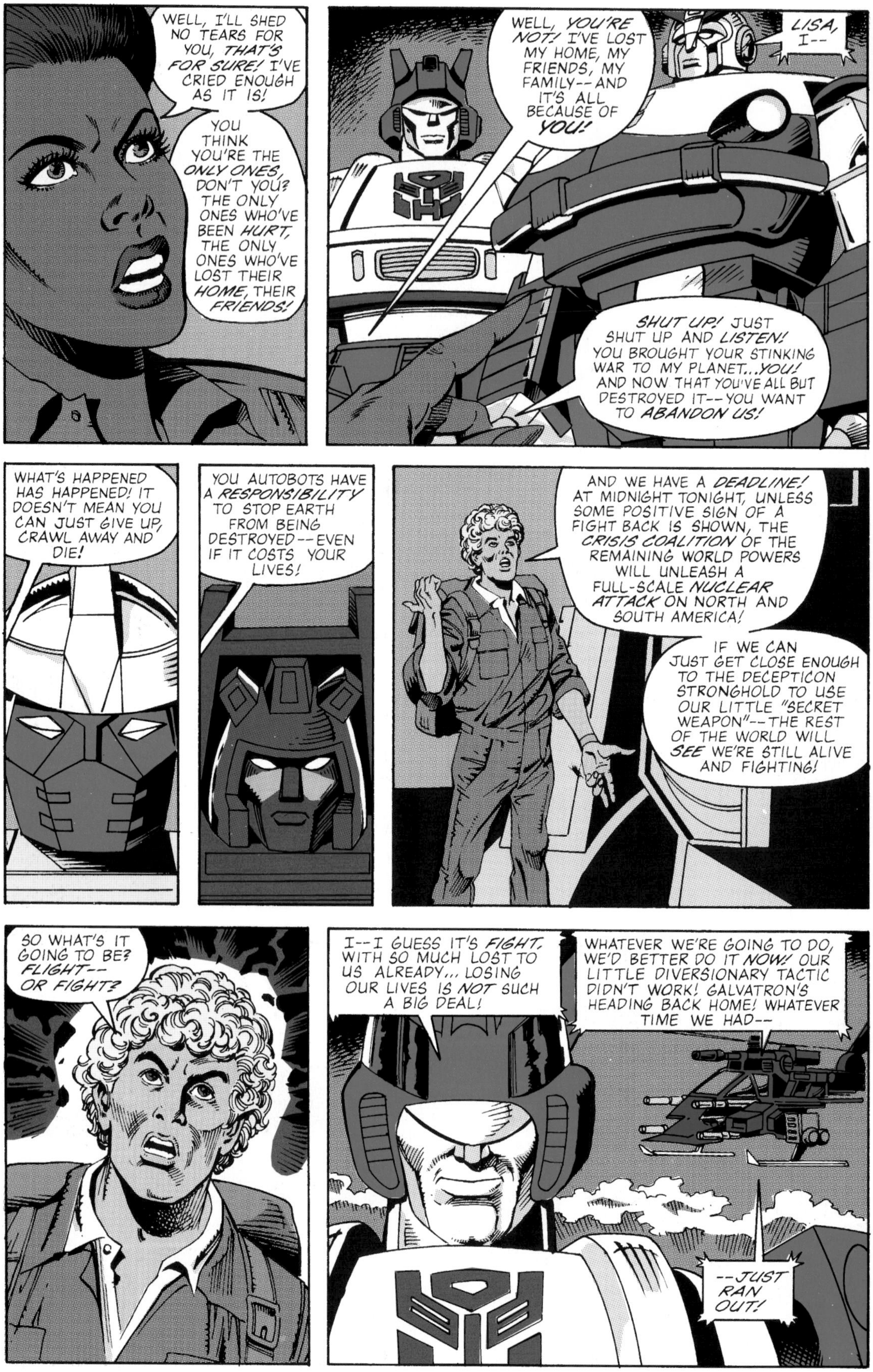
WELL, I'LL SHED NO TEARS FOR YOU, THAT'S FOR SURE! I'VE CRIED ENOUGH AS IT IS!
YOU THINK YOU'RE THE ONLY ONES, DON'T YOU? THE ONLY ONES WHO'VE BEEN HURT, THE ONLY ONES WHO'VE LOST THEIR HOME, THEIR FRIENDS!
LISA, I--
WELL, YOU'RE NOT! I'VE LOST MY HOME, MY FRIENDS, MY FAMILY-- AND IT'S ALL BECAUSE OF YOU!
SHUT UP! JUST SHUT UP AND LISTEN! YOU BROUGHT YOUR STINKING WAR TO MY PLANET... YOU! AND NOW THAT YOU'VE ALL BUT DESTROYED IT--YOU WANT TO ABANDON US!
WHAT'S HAPPENED HAS HAPPENED! IT DOESN'T MEAN YOU CAN JUST GIVE UP, CRAWL AWAY AND DIE!
YOU AUTOBOTS HAVE A RESPONSIBILITY TO STOP EARTH FROM BEING DESTROYED--EVEN IF IT COSTS YOUR LIVES!
AND WE HAVE A DEADLINE! AT MIDNIGHT TONIGHT, UNLESS SOME POSITIVE SIGN OF A FIGHT BACK IS SHOWN, THE CRISIS COALITION OF THE REMAINING WORLD POWERS WILL UNLEASH A FULL-SCALE NUCLEAR ATTACK ON NORTH AND SOUTH AMERICA!
IF WE CAN JUST GET CLOSE ENOUGH TO THE DECEPTICON STRONGHOLD TO USE OUR LITTLE "SECRET WEAPON"--THE REST OF THE WORLD WILL SEE WE'RE STILL ALIVE AND FIGHTING!
SO WHAT'S IT GOING TO BE? FLIGHT-- OR FIGHT?
I--I GUESS IT'S FIGHT. WITH SO MUCH LOST TO US ALREADY... LOSING OUR LIVES IS NOT SUCH A BIG DEAL!
WHATEVER WE'RE GOING TO DO, WE'D BETTER DO IT NOW! OUR LITTLE DIVERSIONARY TACTIC DIDN'T WORK! GALVATRON'S HEADING BACK HOME! WHATEVER TIME WE HAD--
--JUST RAN OUT!

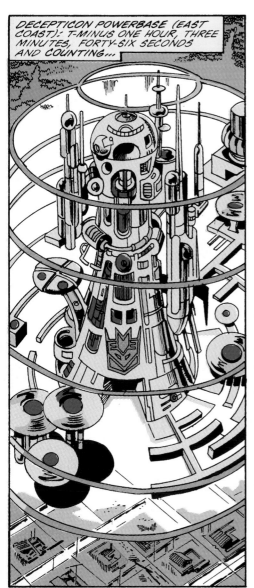

DECEPTICON POWERBASE (EAST COAST): T-MINUS ONE HOUR, THREE MINUTES, FORTY-SIX SECONDS AND COUNTING...

I DUNNO ABOUT YOU, *SCOURGE*, BUT THIS *INACTIVITY* IS DRIVIN' ME *NUTS!* EVEN THOUGH I KNOW THE *ENERGY FIELD* WILL PROTECT US FROM THE MISSILES--

--THE IDEA OF JUST SITTING HERE, LETTING IT HAPPEN, WELL...IT'S *WRONG!*

I KNOW WHAT YOU MEAN, *CYCLONUS.* I DON'T LIKE THE HUMANS THINKING THEY'VE GOT THE BETTER OF US...*EVEN FOR A FEW SECONDS!*

IT WAS SO MUCH BETTER BEFORE...

EARTH WAS *OURS* FOR THE TAKING, OUR PRESENT FROM UNICRON BEFORE HE DEPARTED,

"WE *DESTROYED,* WE *ANNIHILATED* --WE HAD A *GOOD TIME!*"

YEAH, AND NOW, WITH ONLY A HANDFUL OF AUTOBOTS LEFT -- IT'S JUST *PLAIN BORING!*

I'LL BE GLAD WHEN THE HUMANS HAVE FIRED THEIR MISSILES AND GALVATRON'S MACHINES HAVE *ABSORBED* THE RADIATION FOR CONVERSION TO *ENERGON!*

PERHAPS THEN WE CAN GET OFF THIS MISERABLE MUDBALL-- AND HAVE A *REAL* PARTY!

HA HA! *RIGHT ON!*

THEY'RE *LAUGHING* AT US! LAUGHING AT THOSE THEY'VE *MURDERED,* LAUGHING AT THE *CARNAGE* STILL TO COME!

KEEP IT DOWN, *GETAWAY!* CYCLONUS AND SCOURGE ARE TWO OF THE MOST *POWERFUL* OF GALVATRON'S SOLDIERS-- WE WANT THEM *OUT OF THE WAY* BEFORE WE ATTACK!

NO!

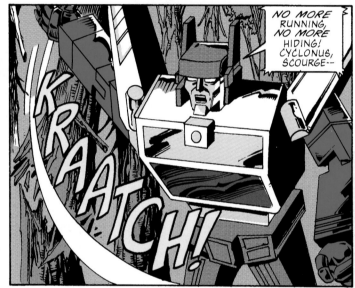

NO MORE RUNNING, NO MORE HIDING! CYCLONUS, SCOURGE--

KRAATCH!

--THIS IS WHERE YOU GET YOURS!

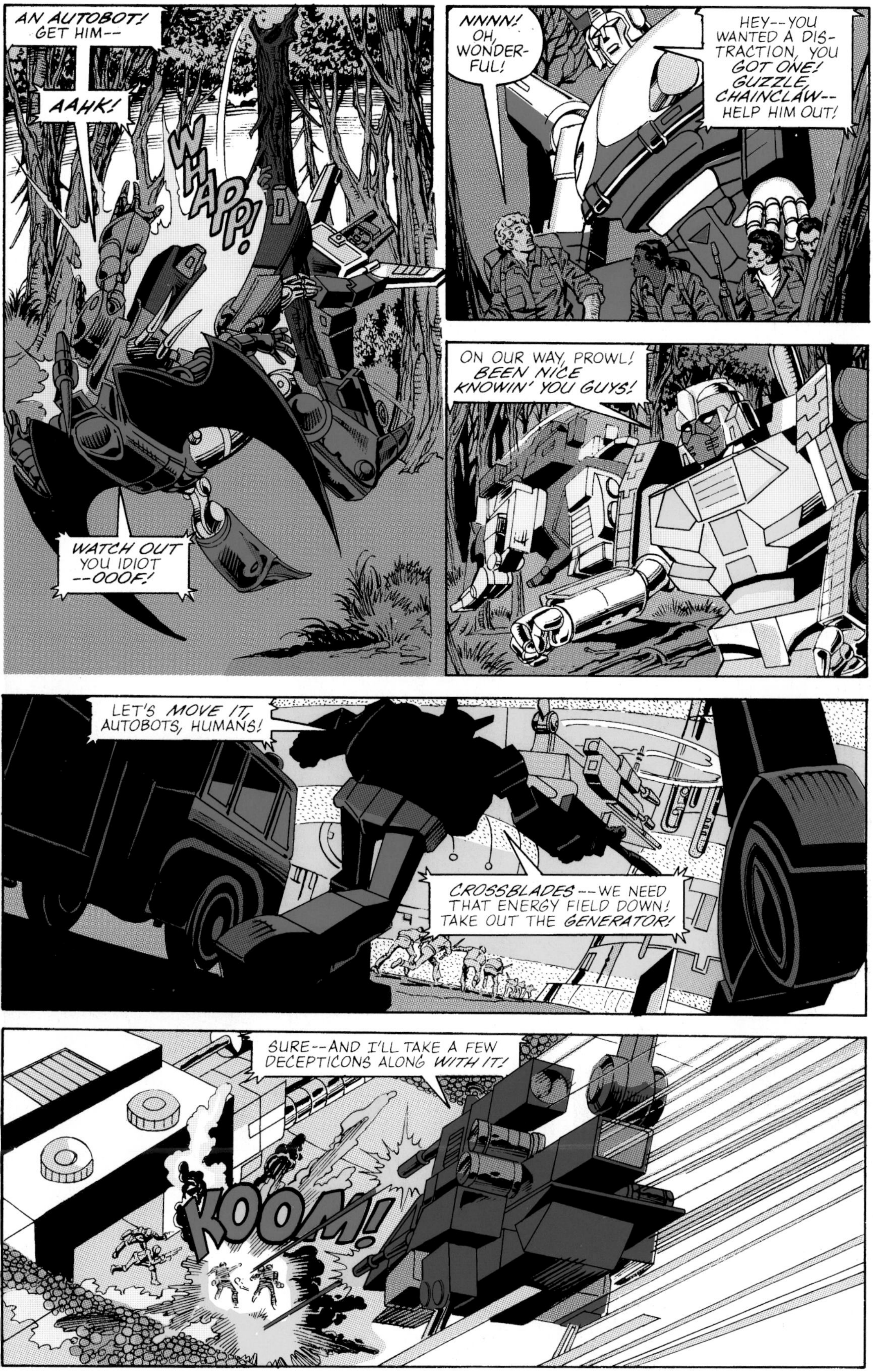
AN AUTOBOT! GET HIM--
AAHK!
WHAPP!
WATCH OUT YOU IDIOT --OOOF!
NNNN! OH, WONDERFUL!
HEY--YOU WANTED A DISTRACTION, YOU GOT ONE! GUZZLE, CHAINCLAW-- HELP HIM OUT!
ON OUR WAY, PROWL! BEEN NICE KNOWIN' YOU GUYS!
LET'S MOVE IT, AUTOBOTS, HUMANS!
CROSSBLADES--WE NEED THAT ENERGY FIELD DOWN! TAKE OUT THE GENERATOR!
SURE--AND I'LL TAKE A FEW DECEPTICONS ALONG WITH IT!
KOOM!

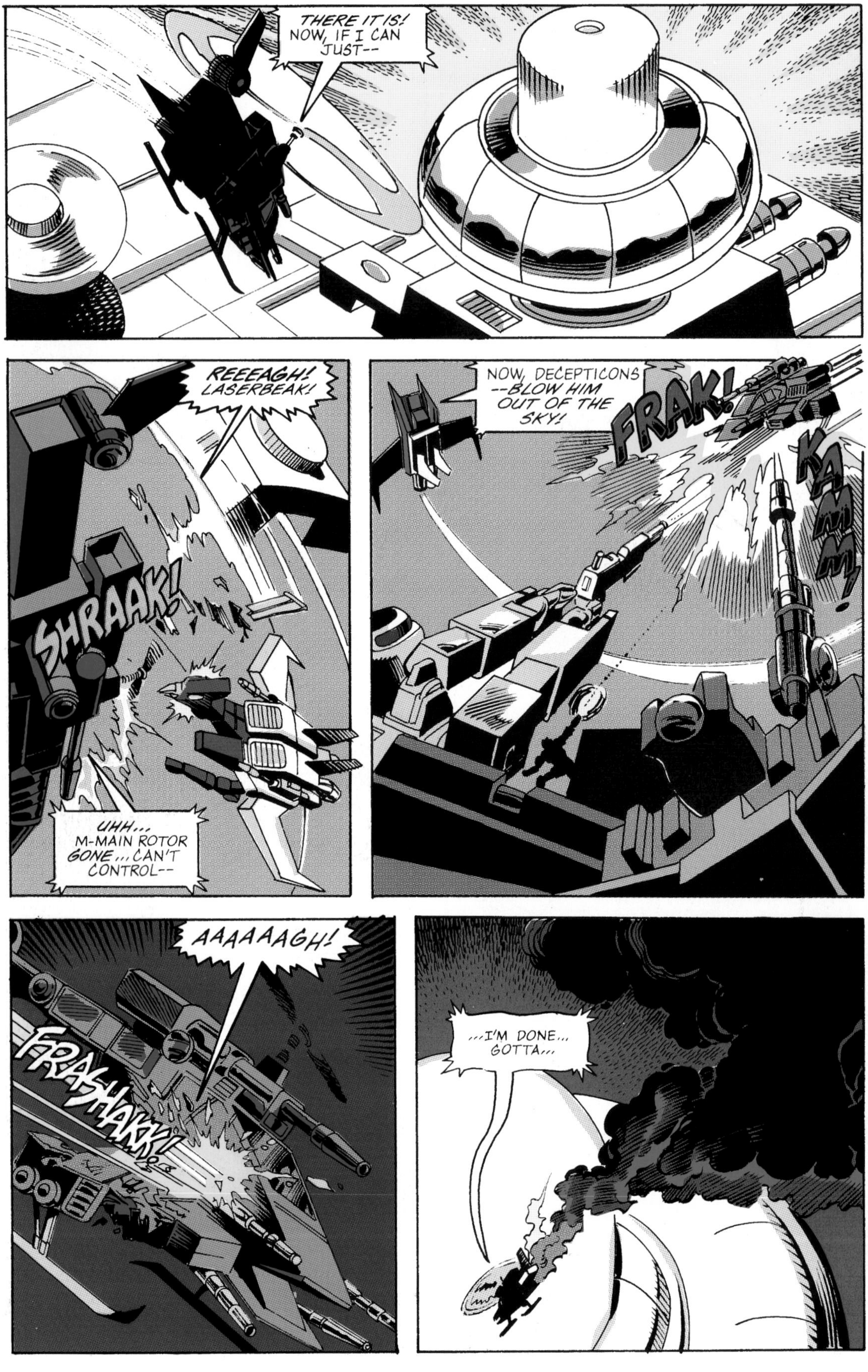
THERE IT IS! NOW, IF I CAN JUST--
REEEAGH! LASERBEAK!
SHRAAK!
UHH... M-MAIN ROTOR GONE... CAN'T CONTROL--
NOW, DECEPTICONS --BLOW HIM OUT OF THE SKY!
FRAK!
KAMM!
AAAAAAGH!
FRASHAKK!
...I'M DONE... GOTTA...

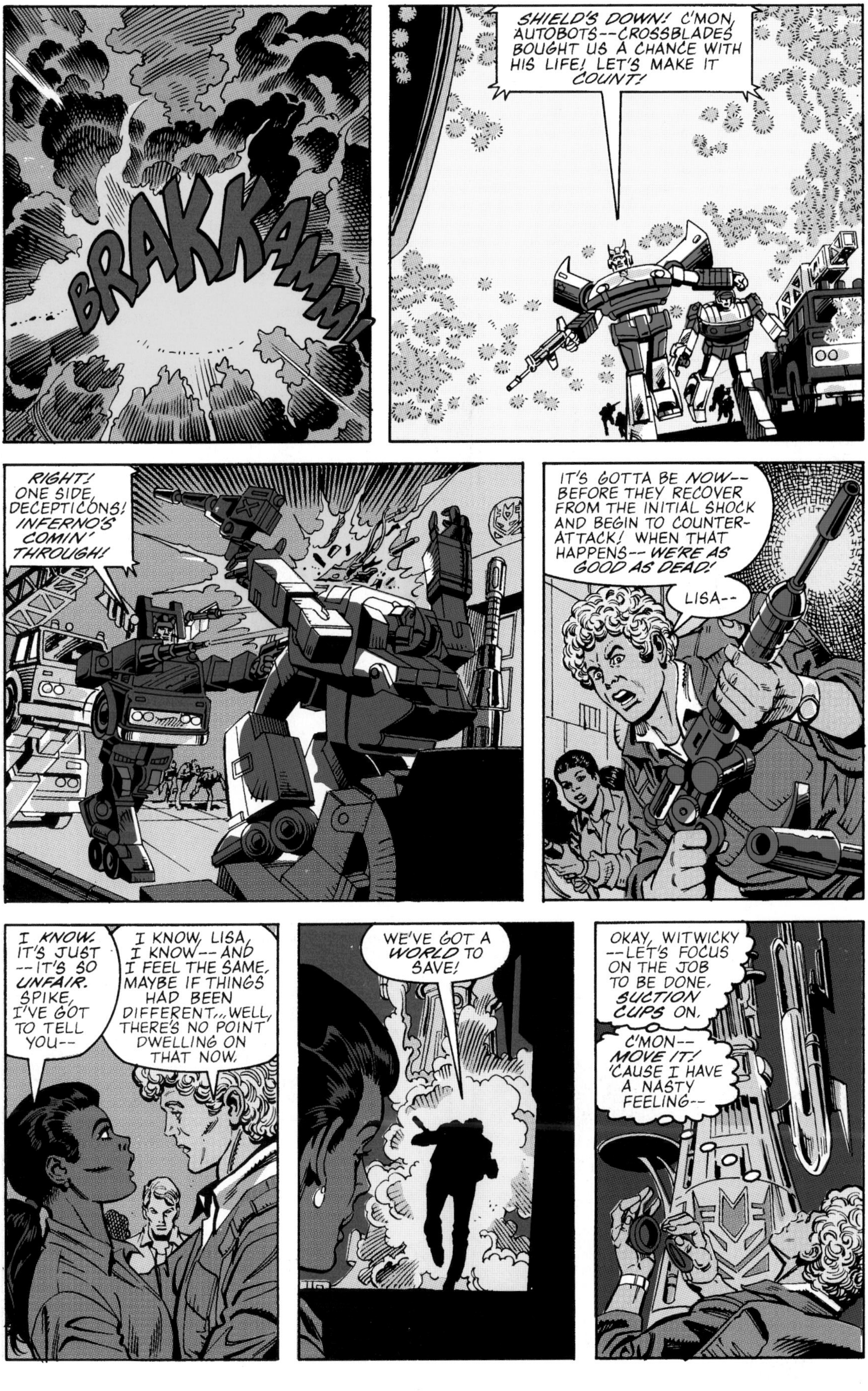
BRAKKAMM!
SHIELD'S DOWN! C'MON, AUTOBOTS--CROSSBLADES BOUGHT US A CHANCE WITH HIS LIFE! LET'S MAKE IT COUNT!
RIGHT! ONE SIDE, DECEPTICONS! INFERNO'S COMIN' THROUGH!
IT'S GOTTA BE NOW--BEFORE THEY RECOVER FROM THE INITIAL SHOCK AND BEGIN TO COUNTER-ATTACK! WHEN THAT HAPPENS--WE'RE AS GOOD AS DEAD!
LISA--
I KNOW. IT'S JUST --IT'S SO UNFAIR. SPIKE, I'VE GOT TO TELL YOU--
I KNOW, LISA, I KNOW--AND I FEEL THE SAME. MAYBE IF THINGS HAD BEEN DIFFERENT...WELL, THERE'S NO POINT DWELLING ON THAT NOW.
WE'VE GOT A WORLD TO SAVE!
OKAY, WITWICKY --LET'S FOCUS ON THE JOB TO BE DONE. SUCTION CUPS ON.
C'MON--MOVE IT! 'CAUSE I HAVE A NASTY FEELING--

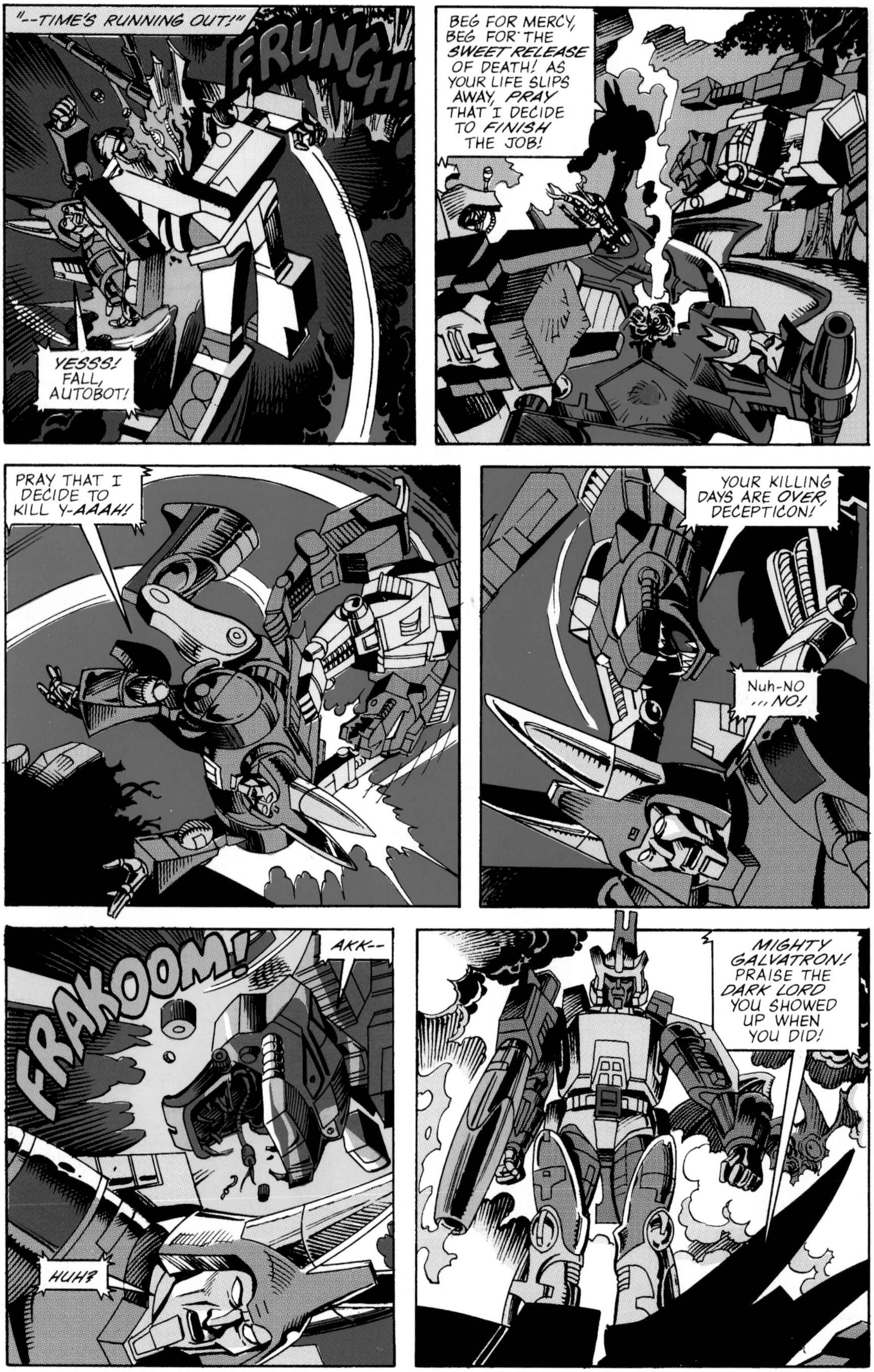

"--TIME'S RUNNING OUT!"
FRUNCH!
YESSS! FALL, AUTOBOT!
BEG FOR MERCY, BEG FOR THE SWEET RELEASE OF DEATH! AS YOUR LIFE SLIPS AWAY, PRAY THAT I DECIDE TO FINISH THE JOB!
PRAY THAT I DECIDE TO KILL Y-AAAH!
YOUR KILLING DAYS ARE OVER, DECEPTICON!
Nuh-NO ...NO!
FRAKOOM!
AKK--
HUH?
MIGHTY GALVATRON! PRAISE THE DARK LORD YOU SHOWED UP WHEN YOU DID!

I KNEW YOU WOULDN'T ALLOW YOUR LOYAL SERVANT TO PERISH! I KNEW--

MIGHTY GALVATRON?

WEAK FOOL! YOU ALLOWED YOURSELF, A BEING FORGED IN THE FIRES OF UNICRON HIMSELF, TO BE BESTED BY A MERE AUTOBOT!

I ONLY SAVED YOU--

--SO THAT I COULD DESTROY YOU MYSELF!

KUSSHA

NOW COME, PRETENDERS! WE HAVE SOMETHING OF A REBELLION TO CRUSH!

NO! THIS IS IT --THE END! WE'RE DEAD-- ALL OF US!

I GOTTA GET OUT OF HERE! GALVATRON ACCOUNTED FOR THE MOST POWERFUL AUTOBOTS AROUND, SO WHAT CHANCE DO I HAVE?

BUT IF I GO, SPIKE'LL BE SPOTTED FOR SURE! HE'LL DIE.... AND WITH HIM THE EARTH!

AUTOBOT!

I'VE STOOD HERE AND WATCHED HUMANS --FRAIL FLESH CREATURES --FIGHT AND DIE FOR THEIR WORLD. CAN I DO LESS? I CAN GIVE SPIKE THE PRECIOUS SECONDS HE NEEDS TO UNLEASH OUR SECRET WEAPON!

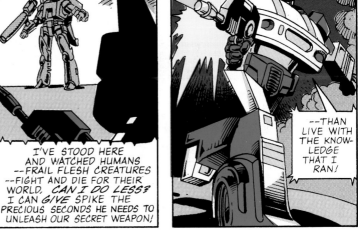

YEAH, BETTER TO FIGHT AND DIE--

--THAN LIVE WITH THE KNOWLEDGE THAT I RAN!

HIGH ABOVE THE EARTH, A SPY SATELLITE WATCHES, RELAYING THE BATTLE LIVE--

--TO HEADQUARTERS OF THE *EUROPEAN CRISIS COALITION* IN GENEVA.

IT'S NOT ENOUGH!

THE PEOPLE HAVE SEEN *ENOUGH* OF THEIR FELLOWS FIGHT AND DIE AGAINST THE DECEPTICONS! WE NEED SOMETHING *MORE* --WE NEED A *VICTORY!*

DA. THE REMAINING WORLD IS *WATCHING,* WAITING FOR A SIGN, BUT UNLESS WE GET ONE IN THE NEXT NINE MINUTES--

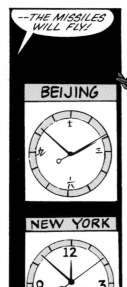

--THE MISSILES WILL FLY!

BEIJING

NEW YORK

12

*ENOUGH!* FOR YOU, AUTOBOT--*THE WAR IS OVER!*

UUUHK!

UUUH... Y-YOU'RE *RIGHT,* B-BUT THIS TIME... WE'VE WON!

WHAT ARE YOU-?

NO!

TOO LATE, *GALVATRON!* I *CLAIM* THIS STRONGHOLD--

--IN THE NAME OF THE AMERICAN PEOPLE!

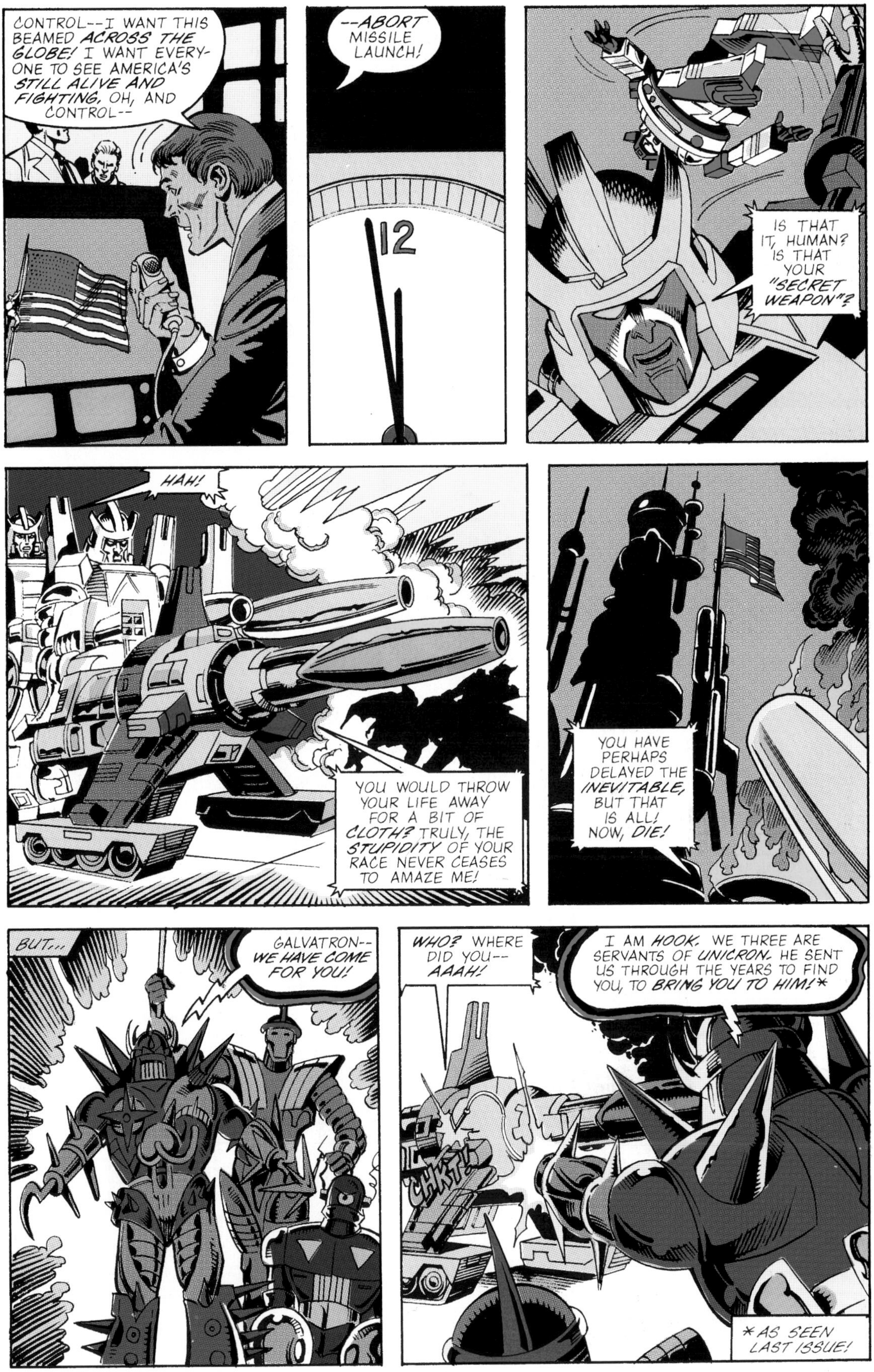
CONTROL--I WANT THIS BEAMED ACROSS THE GLOBE! I WANT EVERYONE TO SEE AMERICA'S STILL ALIVE AND FIGHTING. OH, AND CONTROL--
--ABORT MISSILE LAUNCH!
12
IS THAT IT, HUMAN? IS THAT YOUR "SECRET WEAPON"?
HAH!
YOU WOULD THROW YOUR LIFE AWAY FOR A BIT OF CLOTH? TRULY, THE STUPIDITY OF YOUR RACE NEVER CEASES TO AMAZE ME!
YOU HAVE PERHAPS DELAYED THE INEVITABLE, BUT THAT IS ALL! NOW, DIE!
BUT...
GALVATRON-- WE HAVE COME FOR YOU!
WHO? WHERE DID YOU-- AAAH!
I AM HOOK. WE THREE ARE SERVANTS OF UNICRON. HE SENT US THROUGH THE YEARS TO FIND YOU, TO BRING YOU TO HIM!*
CHKT!
*AS SEEN LAST ISSUE!

LINE-- YOURS!

UNH! GETTING *TANGLED*, CAN'T--

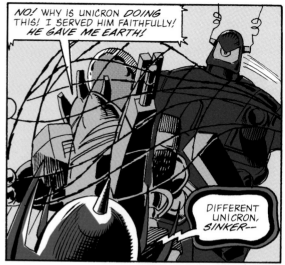

NO! WHY IS UNICRON *DOING* THIS! I SERVED HIM FAITHFULLY! *HE GAVE ME EARTH!*

DIFFERENT UNICRON, SINKER--

--FINISH IT!

NO! IT'S NOT FA-AAAGH!

BHANG!

CHANG!

Urrr...

IS DONE, WE GO, TO UNICRON,

SHUMM!

THEY- *THEY BEAT HIM! THEY BEAT GALVATRON!*

I DON'T KNOW HOW, OR WHY... BUT WE'VE BEEN GIVEN *A CHANCE!* LET'S DO IT-- LET'S FIGHT FOR THIS PLANET!

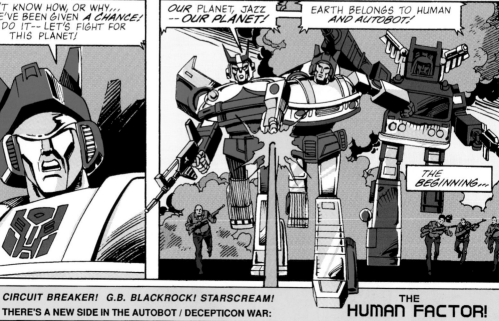

OUR PLANET, JAZZ -- *OUR PLANET!*

EARTH BELONGS TO HUMAN AND AUTOBOT!

*THE BEGINNING...*

NEXT ISSUE: *CIRCUIT BREAKER! G.B. BLACKROCK! STARSCREAM!* THERE'S A NEW SIDE IN THE AUTOBOT / DECEPTICON WAR:

THE HUMAN FACTOR!

They **were** the dream--mechanical beings able to transform their bodies into vehicles, machinery and weapons; a last line of defense against the chaos-bringer, **Unicron**! They **are** at war, heroic **Autobot** pitted against evil **Decepticon**, both on their homeworld, the metal planet called **Cybertron**, and here on our **Earth**. They **are** the galaxy's last hope, they **are**-- TRANSFORMERS

**simon furman**, writer / **dwayne turner**, artist / **rick parker**, letterer / **nel yomtov**, colorist / **don daley**, editor / **tom defalco**, mutant

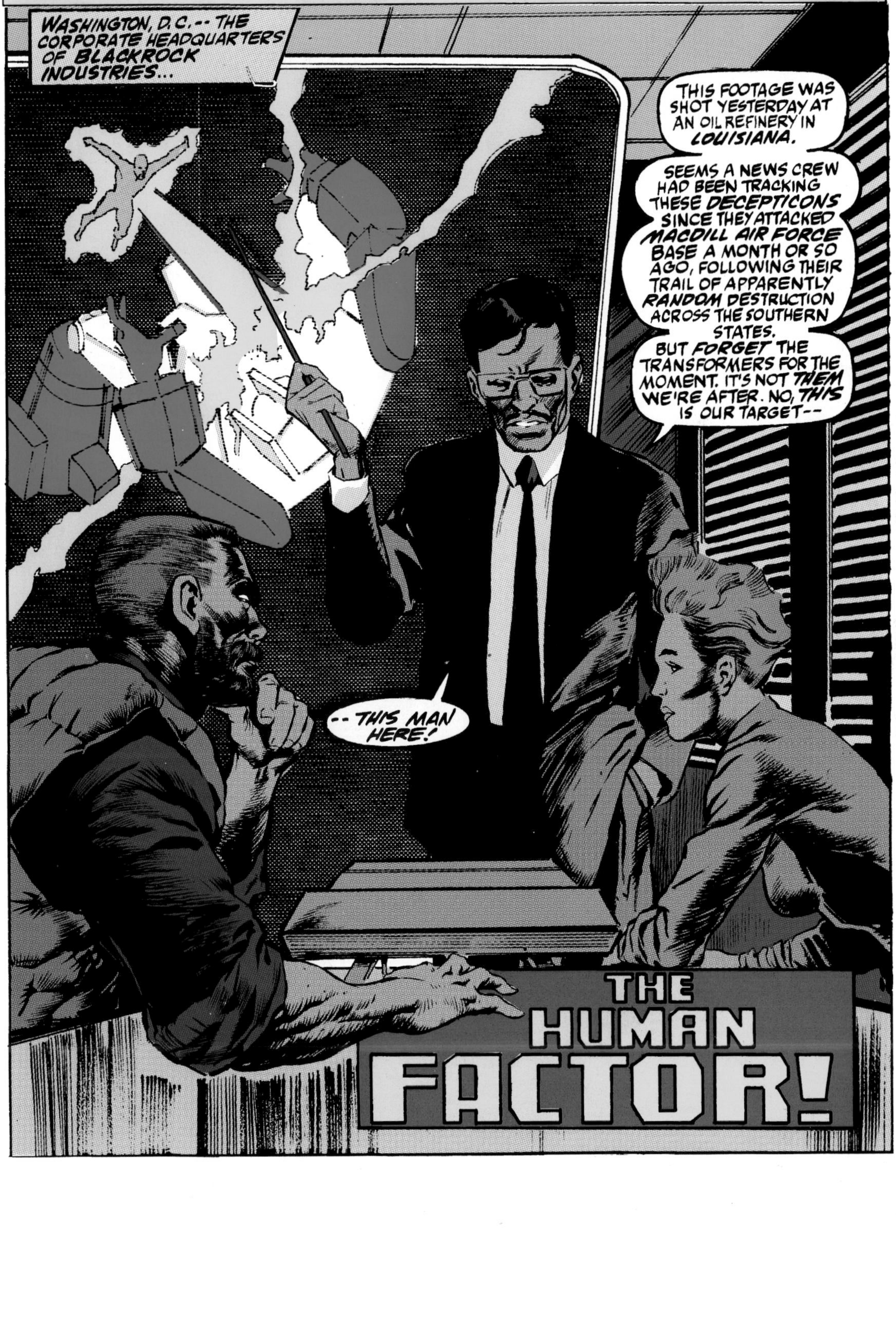

WASHINGTON, D.C.-- THE CORPORATE HEADQUARTERS OF BLACKROCK INDUSTRIES...
THIS FOOTAGE WAS SHOT YESTERDAY AT AN OIL REFINERY IN LOUISIANA.
SEEMS A NEWS CREW HAD BEEN TRACKING THESE DECEPTICONS SINCE THEY ATTACKED MACDILL AIR FORCE BASE A MONTH OR SO AGO, FOLLOWING THEIR TRAIL OF APPARENTLY RANDOM DESTRUCTION ACROSS THE SOUTHERN STATES.
BUT FORGET THE TRANSFORMERS FOR THE MOMENT. IT'S NOT THEM WE'RE AFTER. NO, THIS IS OUR TARGET--
--THIS MAN HERE!
THE HUMAN FACTOR!

APOLOGIES FOR THE LACK OF *SOUNDTRACK*. I'LL TRY AND FILL IN AS WE GO ALONG.

I'M SURE YOU GET THE BASIC IDEA -- A GROUP OF DECEPTICONS CALLING THEMSELVES THE *AIR STRIKE PATROL* HIT THE REFINERY, MAYBE TO STEAL FUEL, MAYBE JUST TO *TRASH* THE PLACE. WE'LL NEVER KNOW.

ANYWAY, THEY RUN INTO OUR *MISTER X* -- A WORKER THERE -- WHO OBJECTS. *SCRATCH ONE DECEPTICON!*

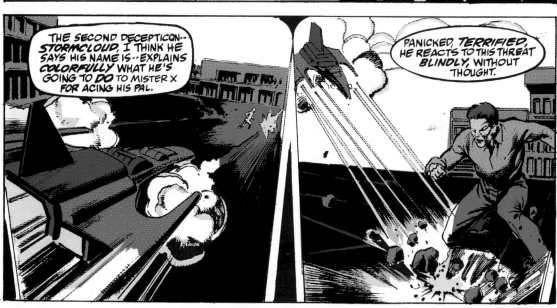

THE SECOND DECEPTICON -- *STORMCLOUD*, I THINK HE SAYS HIS NAME IS -- EXPLAINS *COLORFULLY* WHAT HE'S GOING TO *DO* TO MISTER X FOR ACING HIS PAL.

PANICKED, *TERRIFIED*, HE REACTS TO THIS THREAT *BLINDLY*, WITHOUT THOUGHT.

A *GESTURE* -- AND THE DECEPTICON IS NEARLY *SLAGGED* BY A COLUMN OF *MOLTEN ROCK* FORCED UP FROM DEEP UNDERGROUND!

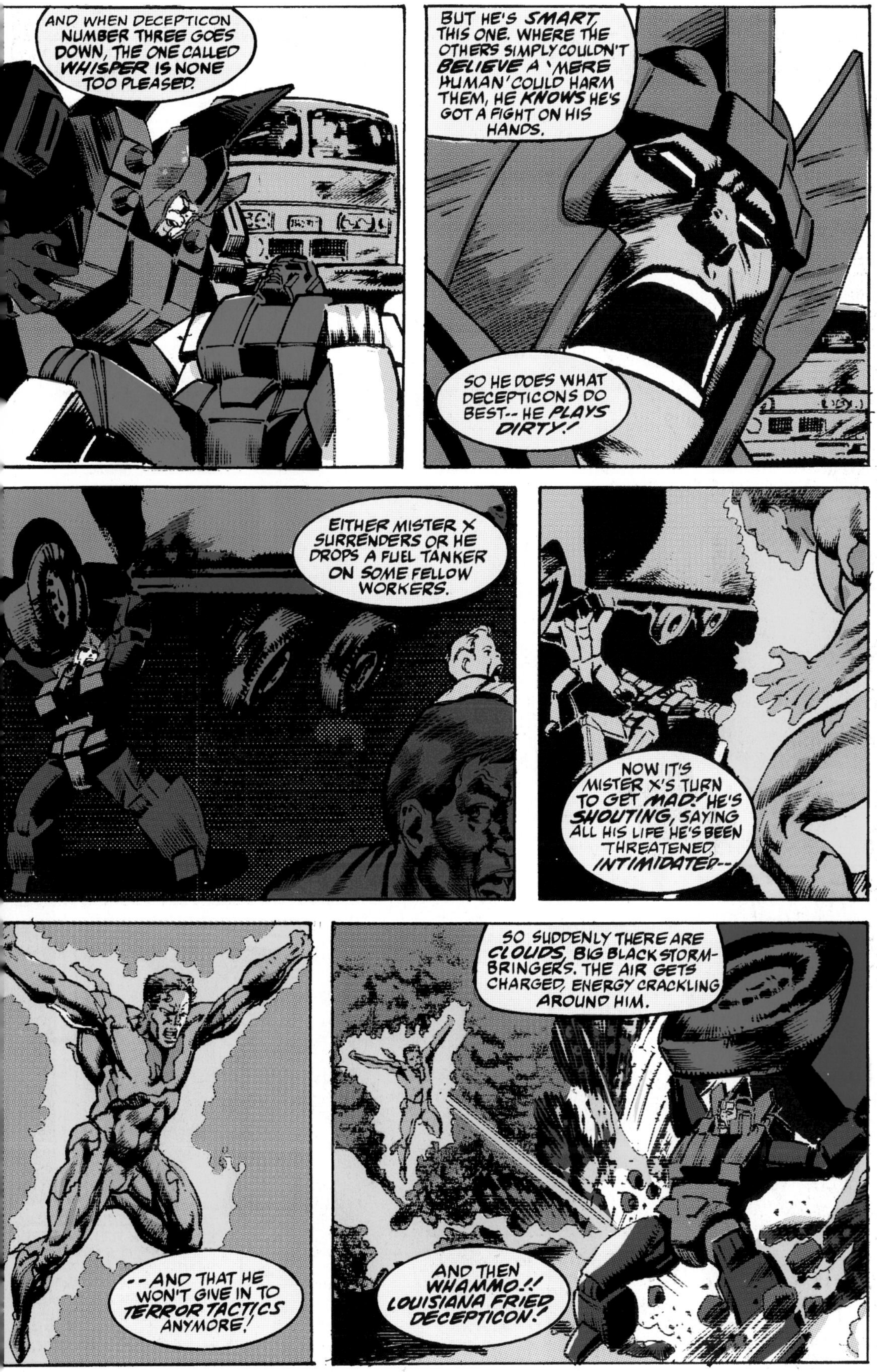
AND WHEN DECEPTICON NUMBER THREE GOES DOWN, THE ONE CALLED WHISPER IS NONE TOO PLEASED.
BUT HE'S SMART, THIS ONE. WHERE THE OTHERS SIMPLY COULDN'T BELIEVE A 'MERE HUMAN' COULD HARM THEM, HE KNOWS HE'S GOT A FIGHT ON HIS HANDS.
SO HE DOES WHAT DECEPTICONS DO BEST-- HE PLAYS DIRTY!
EITHER MISTER X SURRENDERS OR HE DROPS A FUEL TANKER ON SOME FELLOW WORKERS.
NOW IT'S MISTER X'S TURN TO GET MAD! HE'S SHOUTING, SAYING ALL HIS LIFE HE'S BEEN THREATENED, INTIMIDATED--
--AND THAT HE WON'T GIVE IN TO TERROR TACTICS ANYMORE!
SO SUDDENLY THERE ARE CLOUDS, BIG BLACK STORM-BRINGERS. THE AIR GETS CHARGED, ENERGY CRACKLING AROUND HIM.
AND THEN WHAMMO!! LOUISIANA FRIED DECEPTICON!

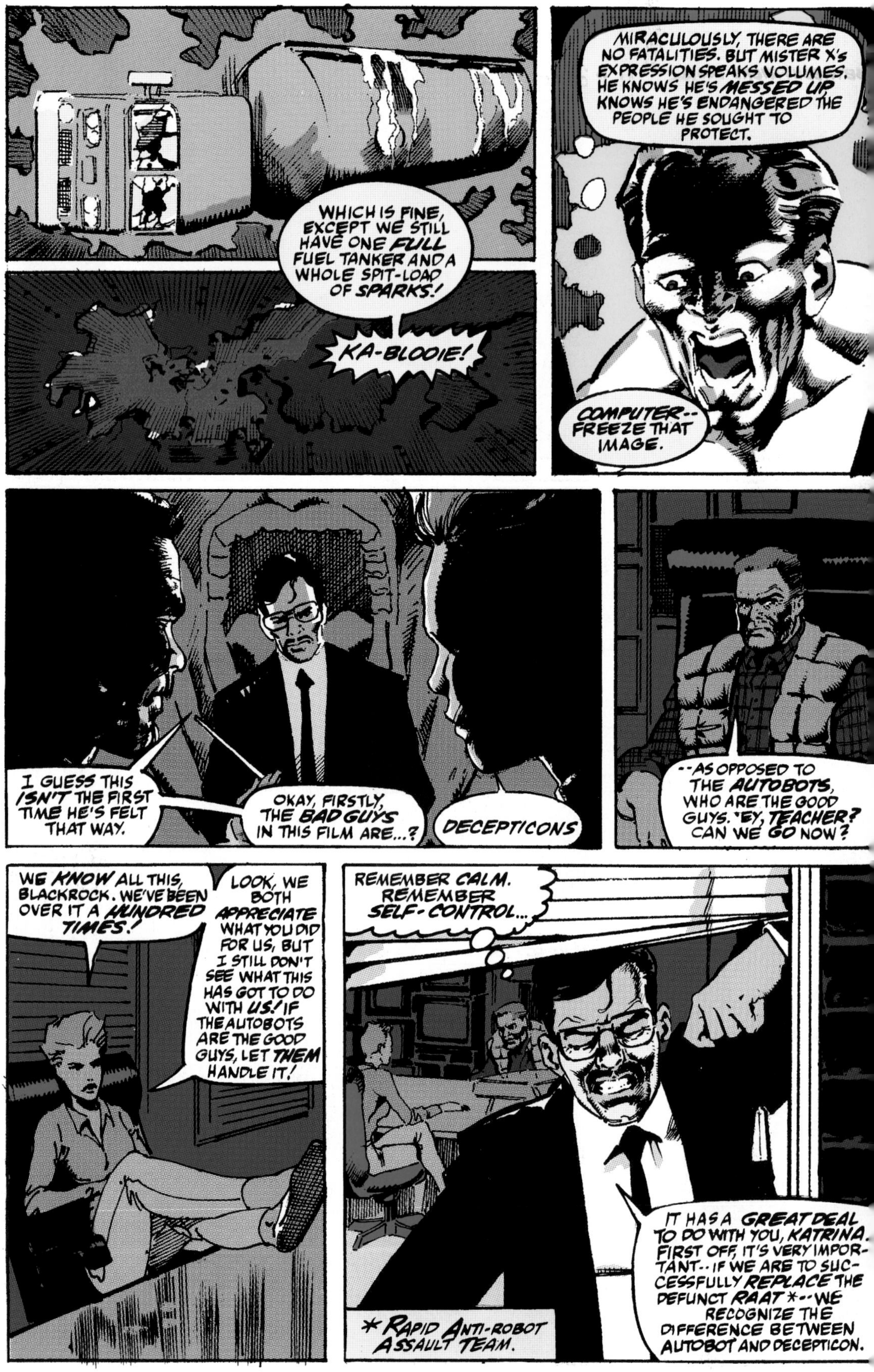
WHICH IS FINE, EXCEPT WE STILL HAVE ONE FULL FUEL TANKER AND A WHOLE SPIT-LOAD OF SPARKS!
KA-BLOOIE!
MIRACULOUSLY, THERE ARE NO FATALITIES. BUT MISTER X's EXPRESSION SPEAKS VOLUMES. HE KNOWS HE'S MESSED UP, KNOWS HE'S ENDANGERED THE PEOPLE HE SOUGHT TO PROTECT.
COMPUTER-- FREEZE THAT IMAGE.
I GUESS THIS ISN'T THE FIRST TIME HE'S FELT THAT WAY.
OKAY, FIRSTLY, THE BAD GUYS IN THIS FILM ARE...?
DECEPTICONS
--AS OPPOSED TO THE AUTOBOTS, WHO ARE THE GOOD GUYS. 'EY, TEACHER? CAN WE GO NOW?
WE KNOW ALL THIS, BLACKROCK. WE'VE BEEN OVER IT A HUNDRED TIMES!
LOOK, WE BOTH APPRECIATE WHAT YOU DID FOR US, BUT I STILL DON'T SEE WHAT THIS HAS GOT TO DO WITH US! IF THE AUTOBOTS ARE THE GOOD GUYS, LET THEM HANDLE IT!
REMEMBER CALM. REMEMBER SELF-CONTROL...
IT HAS A GREAT DEAL TO DO WITH YOU, KATRINA. FIRST OFF, IT'S VERY IMPORTANT-- IF WE ARE TO SUCCESSFULLY REPLACE THE DEFUNCT RAAT*-- WE RECOGNIZE THE DIFFERENCE BETWEEN AUTOBOT AND DECEPTICON.
*RAPID ANTI-ROBOT ASSAULT TEAM.

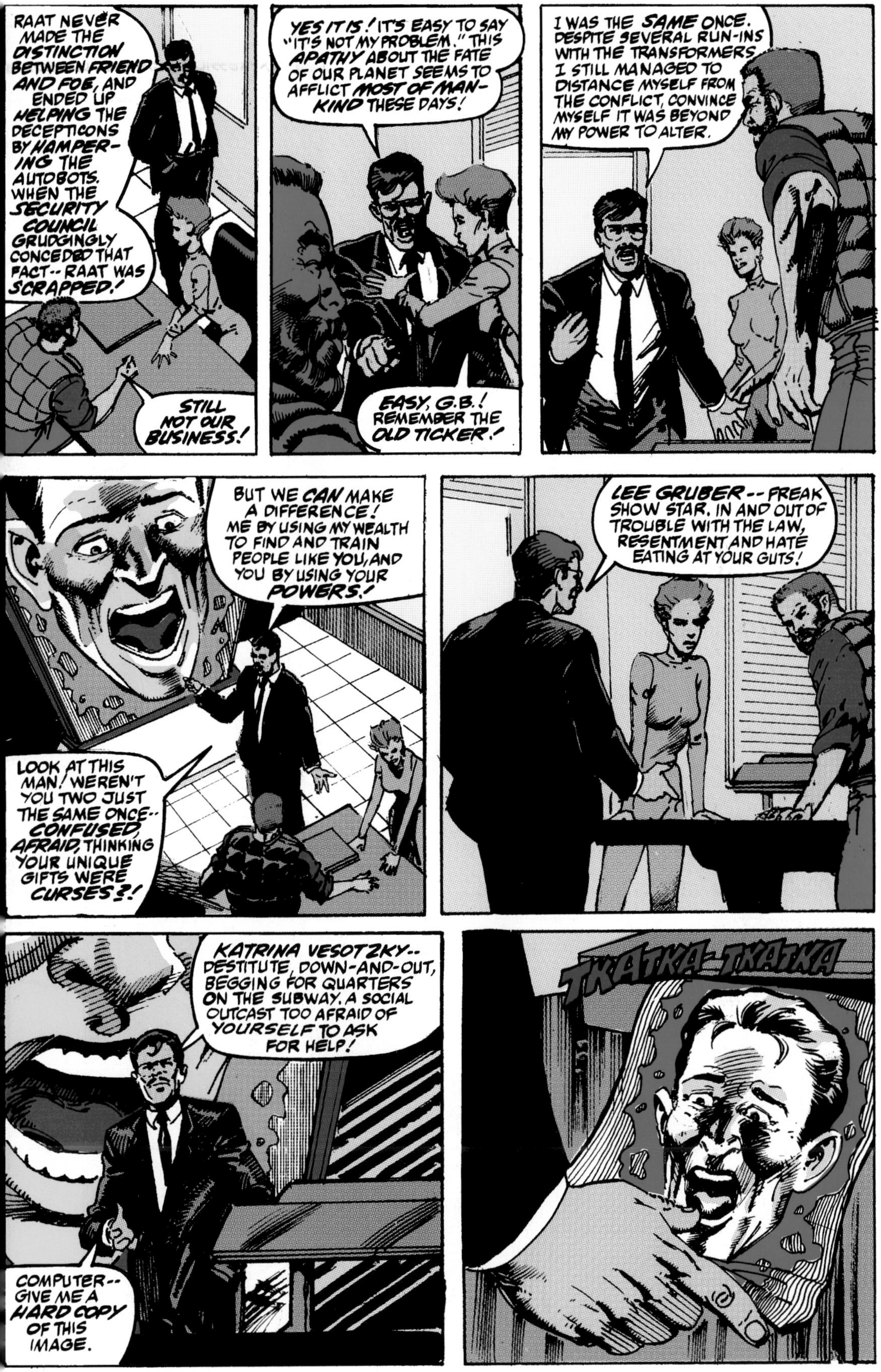
RAAT NEVER MADE THE DISTINCTION BETWEEN FRIEND AND FOE, AND ENDED UP HELPING THE DECEPTICONS BY HAMPERING THE AUTOBOTS. WHEN THE SECURITY COUNCIL GRUDGINGLY CONCEDED THAT FACT-- RAAT WAS SCRAPPED!
STILL NOT OUR BUSINESS!
YES IT IS! IT'S EASY TO SAY "IT'S NOT MY PROBLEM." THIS APATHY ABOUT THE FATE OF OUR PLANET SEEMS TO AFFLICT MOST OF MANKIND THESE DAYS!
EASY, G.B.! REMEMBER THE OLD TICKER!
I WAS THE SAME ONCE. DESPITE SEVERAL RUN-INS WITH THE TRANSFORMERS I STILL MANAGED TO DISTANCE MYSELF FROM THE CONFLICT, CONVINCE MYSELF IT WAS BEYOND MY POWER TO ALTER.
BUT WE CAN MAKE A DIFFERENCE! ME BY USING MY WEALTH TO FIND AND TRAIN PEOPLE LIKE YOU, AND YOU BY USING YOUR POWERS!
LOOK AT THIS MAN! WEREN'T YOU TWO JUST THE SAME ONCE-- CONFUSED, AFRAID, THINKING YOUR UNIQUE GIFTS WERE CURSES?!
LEE GRUBER-- FREAK SHOW STAR. IN AND OUT OF TROUBLE WITH THE LAW, RESENTMENT AND HATE EATING AT YOUR GUTS!
KATRINA VESOTZKY-- DESTITUTE, DOWN-AND-OUT, BEGGING FOR QUARTERS ON THE SUBWAY. A SOCIAL OUTCAST TOO AFRAID OF YOURSELF TO ASK FOR HELP!
COMPUTER-- GIVE ME A HARD COPY OF THIS IMAGE.
TKATKA-TKATKA

THIS MAN IS THE SAME -- *LOST, FRIGHTENED,* UNSURE OF THE *GENETIC QUIRK* HE WAS BORN WITH.

WE MUST FIND HIM, CONVINCE HIM TO JOIN US. LIKE YOU... *HE NEEDS PURPOSE.*

NOW GO AND GET READY.

*READY? 'EY, HANG ON... YOU DON'T MEAN --*

I MOST CERTAINLY *DO!*

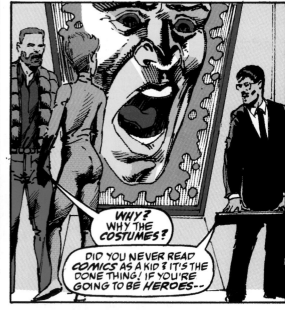

*WHY? WHY THE COSTUMES?*

DID YOU NEVER READ *COMICS* AS A KID? IT'S THE DONE THING! IF YOU'RE GOING TO BE *HEROES* --

-- YOU HAVE TO *LOOK THE PART!*

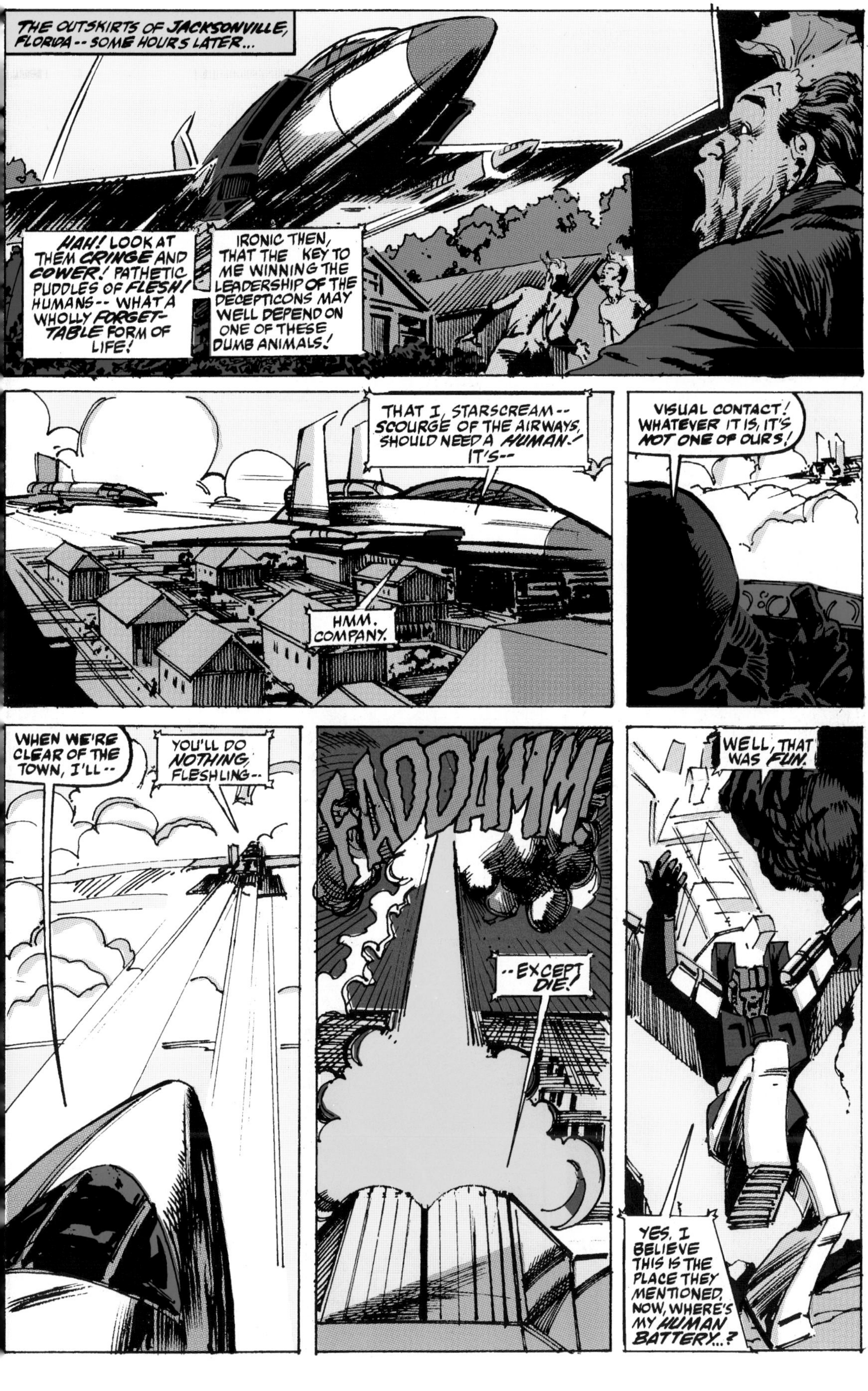
THE OUTSKIRTS OF JACKSONVILLE, FLORIDA -- SOME HOURS LATER...
HAH! LOOK AT THEM CRINGE AND COWER! PATHETIC PUDDLES OF FLESH! HUMANS-- WHAT A WHOLLY FORGETTABLE FORM OF LIFE!
IRONIC THEN, THAT THE KEY TO ME WINNING THE LEADERSHIP OF THE DECEPTICONS MAY WELL DEPEND ON ONE OF THESE DUMB ANIMALS!
THAT I, STARSCREAM -- SCOURGE OF THE AIRWAYS, SHOULD NEED A HUMAN! IT'S--
HMM. COMPANY.
VISUAL CONTACT! WHATEVER IT IS, IT'S NOT ONE OF OURS!
WHEN WE'RE CLEAR OF THE TOWN, I'LL--
YOU'LL DO NOTHING, FLESHLING--
FADDAMM!
--EXCEPT DIE!
WELL, THAT WAS FUN.
YES, I BELIEVE THIS IS THE PLACE THEY MENTIONED. NOW, WHERE'S MY HUMAN BATTERY...?

THAT'S THE *TROUBLE* WITH THIS MISERABLE MUDBALL -- YOU JUST CAN'T BOOST ENERGY LEVELS TO *MAXIMUM* ON THEIR FUEL. AND WITH *ENERGON* SCARCE, IT MEANS WE'RE *ALL* OPERATING BELOW PAR!

BUT WITH *THIS* HUMAN, WHO SEEMINGLY CREATES ENERGY *AT WILL*, IT WOULD BE LIKE HAVING YOUR OWN PERSONAL RECHARGER, THE *POWERMASTER* PROCESS BOOSTED TO THE Nth DEGREE!

FROM WHAT I SAW ON THAT NEWS BROADCAST, IT LOOKS AS THOUGH HE DRAWS POWER FROM *NATURAL SOURCES*--LIKE *THE SUN*, THE EARTH BENEATH MY FEET!

*ALL* HIS RAW MATERIALS, CONTINUALLY *ON TAP!*

WITH HIM BY MY SIDE, I WILL BE POWERFUL ENOUGH TO *DESTROY SCORPONOK* AND LEAD THE DECEPTICONS IN HIS PLACE!

ONE WAY OR ANOTHER-- THIS HUMAN *MUST* BE MADE TO SERVE ME!

*INTERROGATIVE:* WHY HAVE I FOLLOWED STARSCREAM? *ANSWER.* I DO NOT KNOW.

THIS IS WORRYING. BEFORE, EVERYTHING WAS A *LOGICAL* PROGRESSION OF TACTICS AND PLANS. AND YET HERE I AM, FOLLOWING MY *INSTINCTS*, RELYING ON *CHANCE*.

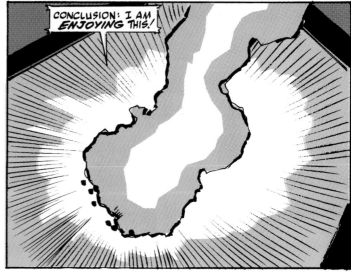

*CONCLUSION: I AM ENJOYING THIS!*

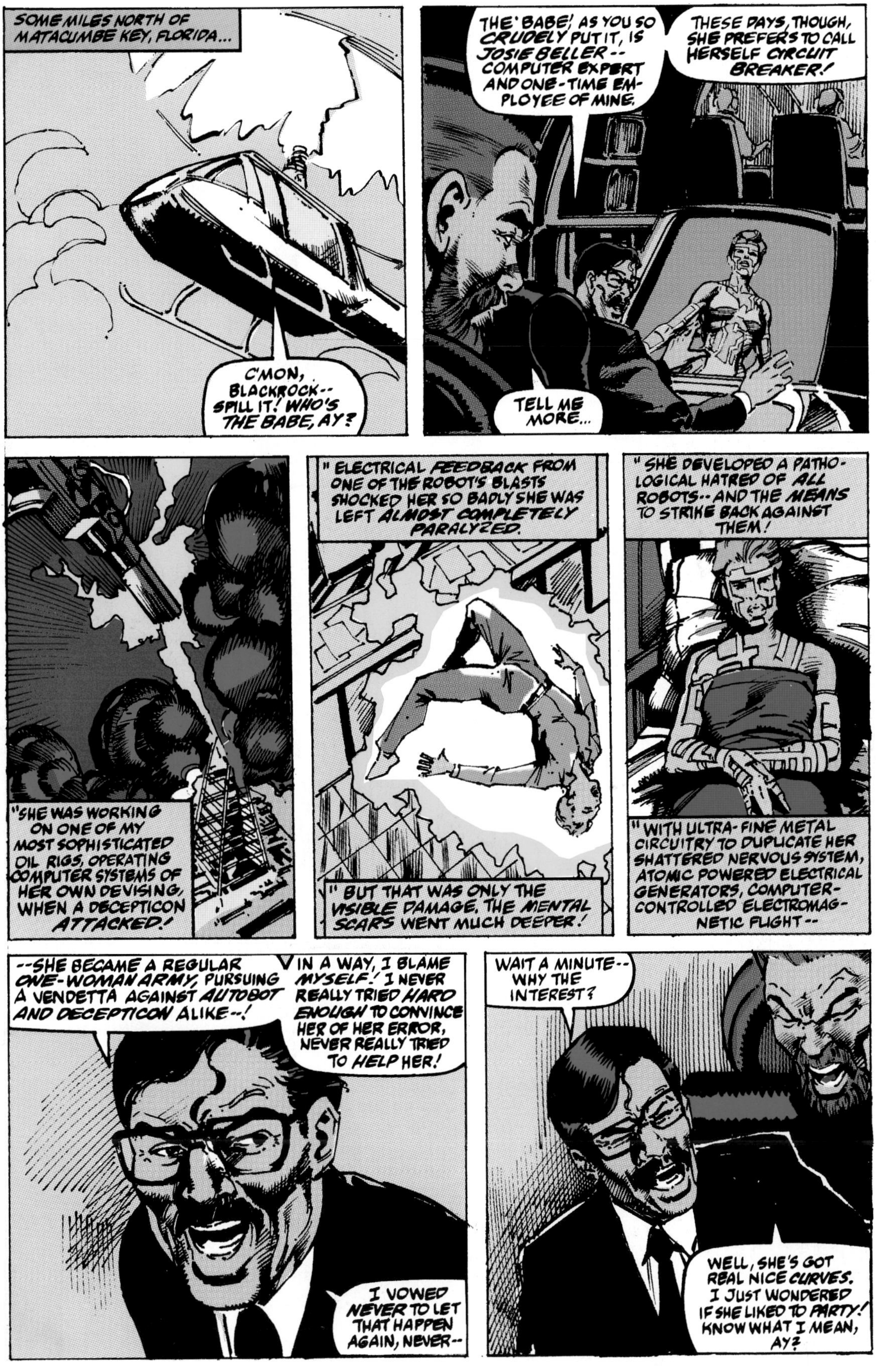
SOME MILES NORTH OF MATACUMBE KEY, FLORIDA...
C'MON, BLACKROCK-- SPILL IT! WHO'S THE BABE, AY?
THE 'BABE', AS YOU SO CRUDELY PUT IT, IS JOSIE BELLER -- COMPUTER EXPERT AND ONE-TIME EMPLOYEE OF MINE.
THESE DAYS, THOUGH, SHE PREFERS TO CALL HERSELF CIRCUIT BREAKER!
TELL ME MORE...
"SHE WAS WORKING ON ONE OF MY MOST SOPHISTICATED OIL RIGS, OPERATING COMPUTER SYSTEMS OF HER OWN DEVISING, WHEN A DECEPTICON ATTACKED!
" ELECTRICAL FEEDBACK FROM ONE OF THE ROBOT'S BLASTS SHOCKED HER SO BADLY SHE WAS LEFT ALMOST COMPLETELY PARALYZED.
" BUT THAT WAS ONLY THE VISIBLE DAMAGE. THE MENTAL SCARS WENT MUCH DEEPER!
" SHE DEVELOPED A PATHOLOGICAL HATRED OF ALL ROBOTS-- AND THE MEANS TO STRIKE BACK AGAINST THEM!
" WITH ULTRA-FINE METAL CIRCUITRY TO DUPLICATE HER SHATTERED NERVOUS SYSTEM, ATOMIC POWERED ELECTRICAL GENERATORS, COMPUTER-CONTROLLED ELECTROMAGNETIC FLIGHT --
--SHE BECAME A REGULAR ONE-WOMAN ARMY, PURSUING A VENDETTA AGAINST AUTOBOT AND DECEPTICON ALIKE--!
IN A WAY, I BLAME MYSELF! I NEVER REALLY TRIED HARD ENOUGH TO CONVINCE HER OF HER ERROR, NEVER REALLY TRIED TO HELP HER!
I VOWED NEVER TO LET THAT HAPPEN AGAIN, NEVER--
WAIT A MINUTE-- WHY THE INTEREST?
WELL, SHE'S GOT REAL NICE CURVES. I JUST WONDERED IF SHE LIKED TO PARTY! KNOW WHAT I MEAN, AY?

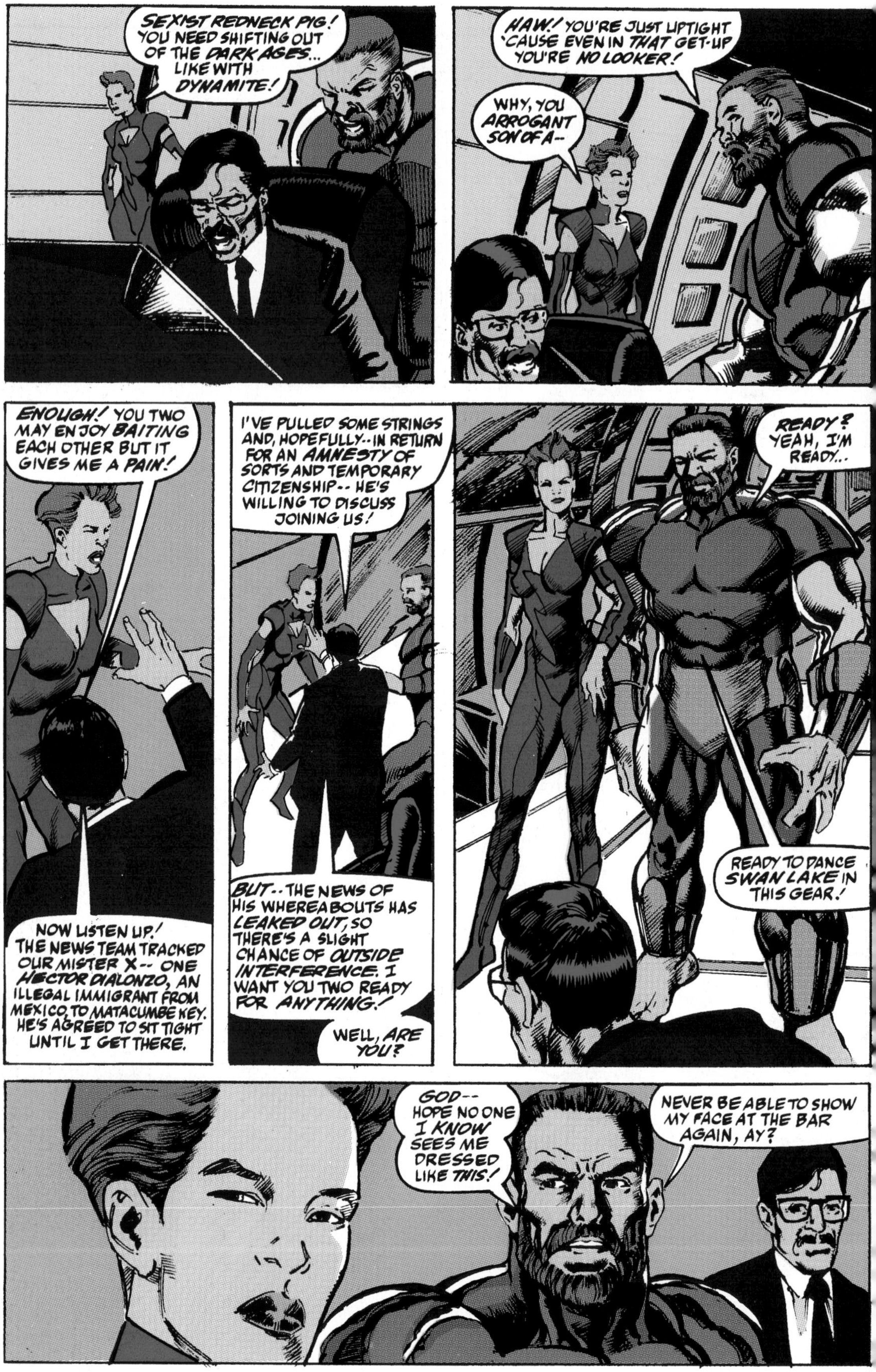
SEXIST REDNECK PIG! YOU NEED SHIFTING OUT OF THE DARK AGES... LIKE WITH DYNAMITE!
HAW! YOU'RE JUST UPTIGHT 'CAUSE EVEN IN THAT GET-UP YOU'RE NO LOOKER!
WHY, YOU ARROGANT SON OF A--
ENOUGH! YOU TWO MAY ENJOY BAITING EACH OTHER BUT IT GIVES ME A PAIN!
NOW LISTEN UP! THE NEWS TEAM TRACKED OUR MISTER X-- ONE HECTOR DIALONZO, AN ILLEGAL IMMIGRANT FROM MEXICO, TO MATACUMBE KEY. HE'S AGREED TO SIT TIGHT UNTIL I GET THERE.
I'VE PULLED SOME STRINGS AND, HOPEFULLY-- IN RETURN FOR AN AMNESTY OF SORTS AND TEMPORARY CITIZENSHIP-- HE'S WILLING TO DISCUSS JOINING US!
BUT-- THE NEWS OF HIS WHEREABOUTS HAS LEAKED OUT, SO THERE'S A SLIGHT CHANCE OF OUTSIDE INTERFERENCE. I WANT YOU TWO READY FOR ANYTHING!
WELL, ARE YOU?
READY? YEAH, I'M READY...
READY TO DANCE SWAN LAKE IN THIS GEAR!
GOD-- HOPE NO ONE I KNOW SEES ME DRESSED LIKE THIS!
NEVER BE ABLE TO SHOW MY FACE AT THE BAR AGAIN, AY?

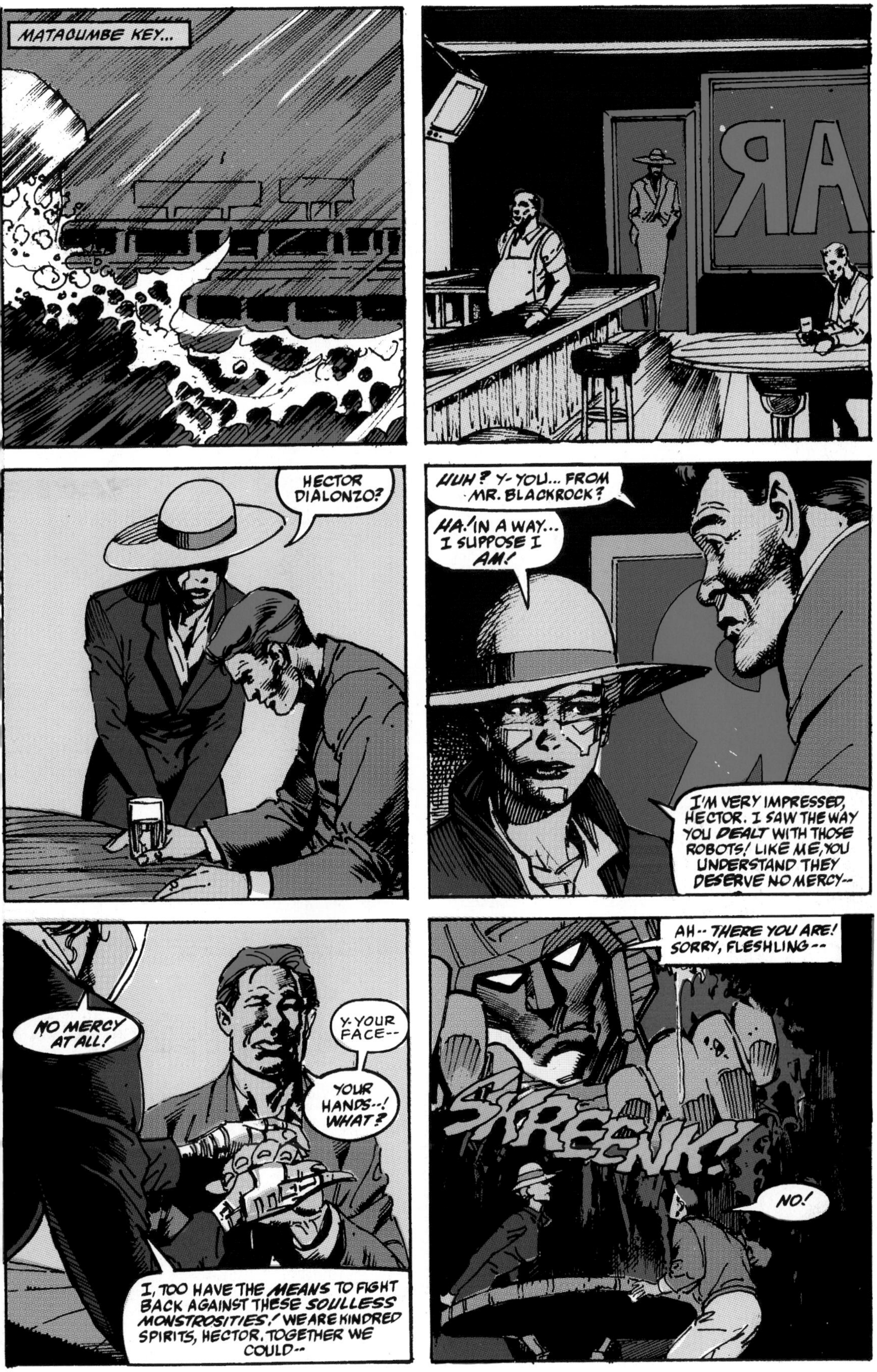
MATACUMBE KEY...
HECTOR DIALONZO?
HUH? Y-YOU... FROM MR. BLACKROCK?
HA! IN A WAY... I SUPPOSE I AM!
I'M VERY IMPRESSED, HECTOR. I SAW THE WAY YOU DEALT WITH THOSE ROBOTS! LIKE ME, YOU UNDERSTAND THEY DESERVE NO MERCY--
NO MERCY AT ALL!
Y-YOUR FACE--
YOUR HANDS--! WHAT?
I, TOO HAVE THE MEANS TO FIGHT BACK AGAINST THESE SOULLESS MONSTROSITIES! WE ARE KINDRED SPIRITS, HECTOR. TOGETHER WE COULD--
AH-- THERE YOU ARE! SORRY, FLESHLING--
SKREENK!
NO!

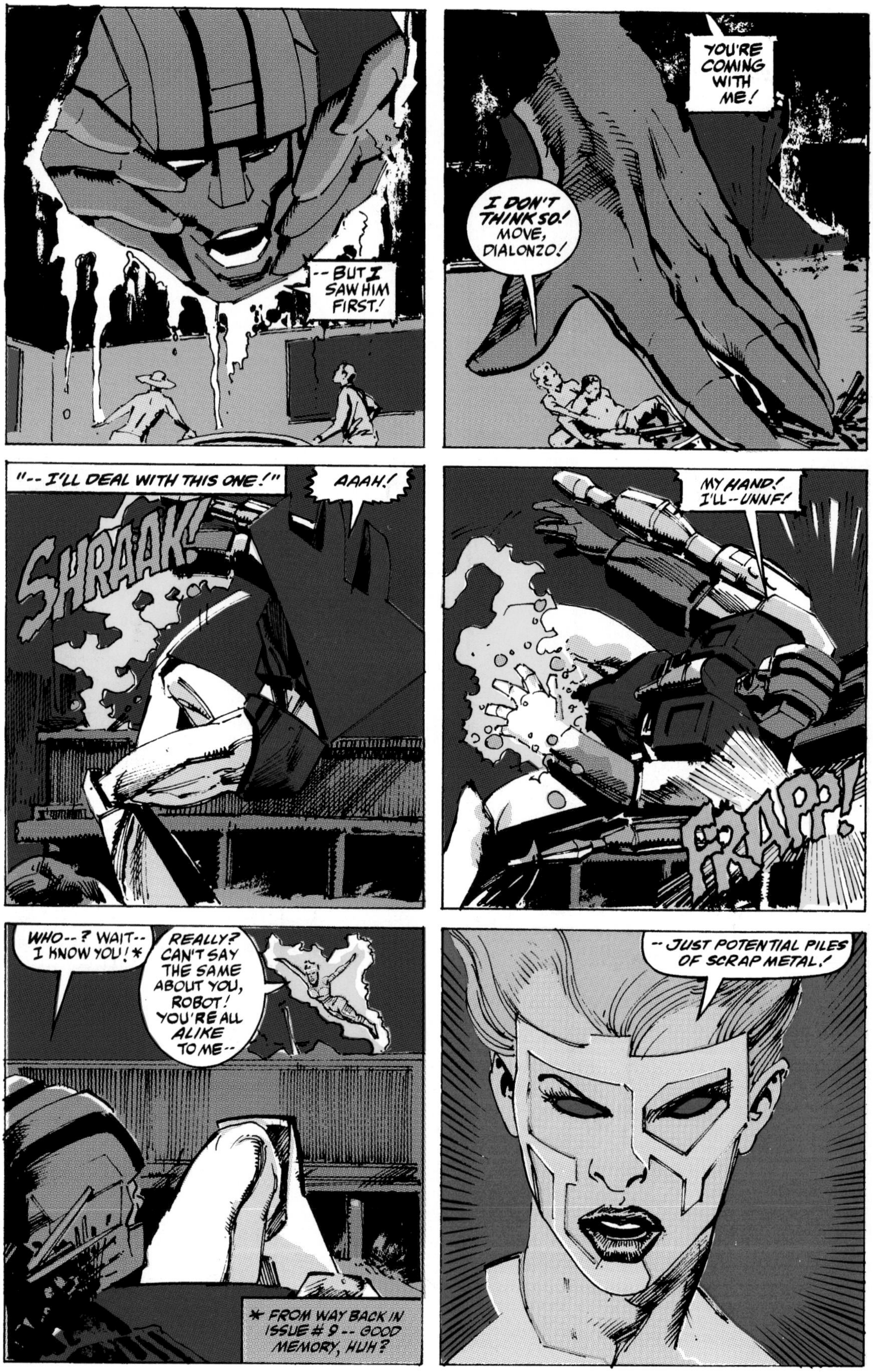
--BUT I SAW HIM FIRST!
YOU'RE COMING WITH ME!
I DON'T THINK SO! MOVE, DIALONZO!
"--I'LL DEAL WITH THIS ONE!"
AAAH!
SHRAAK!
MY HAND! I'LL--UNNF!
FRAPP!
WHO--? WAIT--I KNOW YOU!*
REALLY? CAN'T SAY THE SAME ABOUT YOU, ROBOT! YOU'RE ALL ALIKE TO ME--
* FROM WAY BACK IN ISSUE #9 -- GOOD MEMORY, HUH?
--JUST POTENTIAL PILES OF SCRAP METAL!

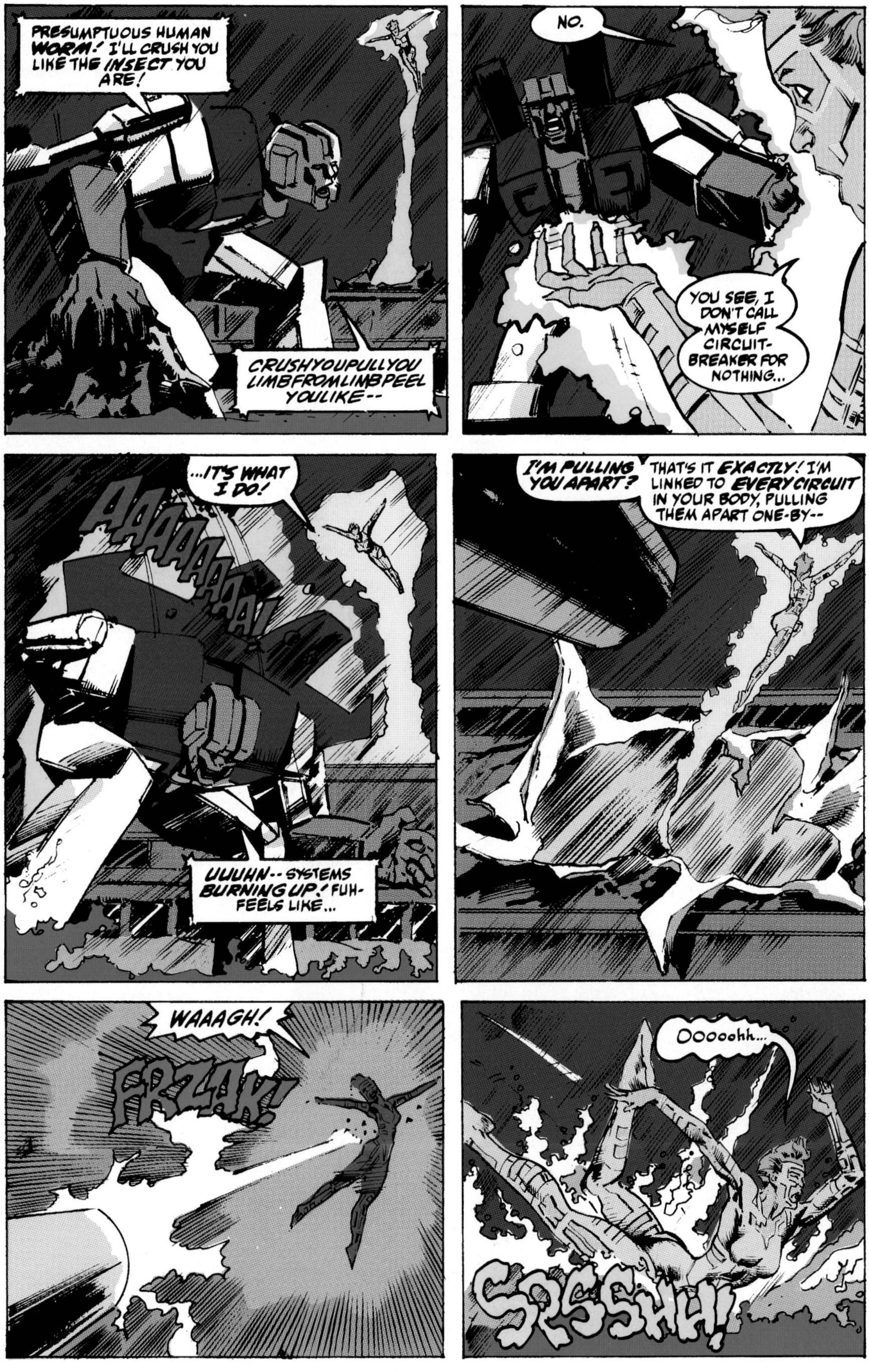
PRESUMPTUOUS HUMAN WORM! I'LL CRUSH YOU LIKE THE INSECT YOU ARE!
CRUSHYOUPULLYOU LIMBFROMLIMBPEEL YOULIKE--
NO.
YOU SEE, I DON'T CALL MYSELF CIRCUIT-BREAKER FOR NOTHING...
...IT'S WHAT I DO!
AAAAAAAAAAI!
UUUHN-- SYSTEMS BURNING UP! FUH-FEELS LIKE...
I'M PULLING YOU APART?
THAT'S IT EXACTLY! I'M LINKED TO EVERY CIRCUIT IN YOUR BODY, PULLING THEM APART ONE-BY--
WAAAGH!
FRZAK!
OOOoohh...
SSSSHH!

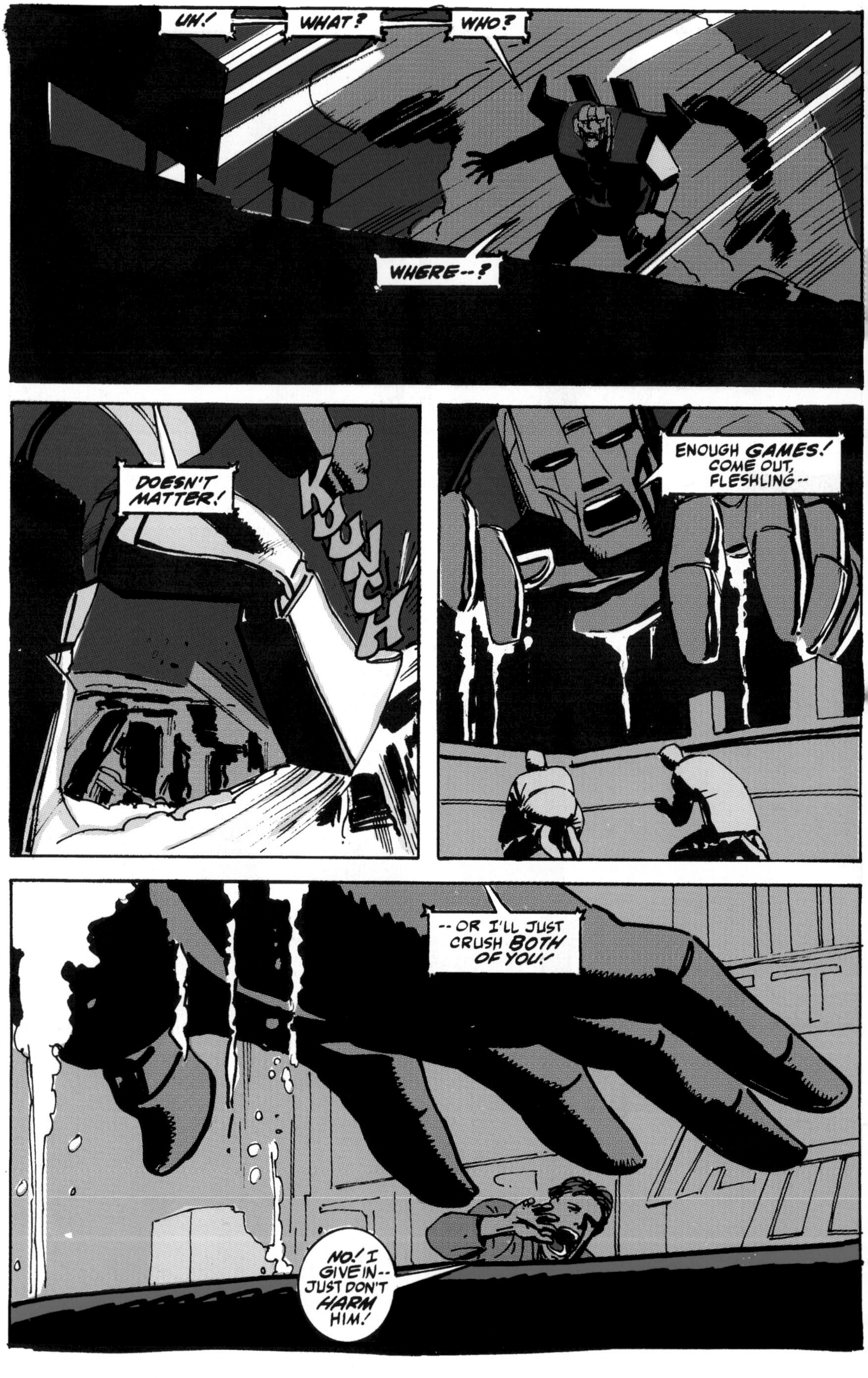
UH!
WHAT?
WHO?
WHERE--?
DOESN'T MATTER!
KRUNCH
ENOUGH GAMES! COME OUT, FLESHLING--
--OR I'LL JUST CRUSH BOTH OF YOU!
NO! I GIVE IN-- JUST DON'T HARM HIM!

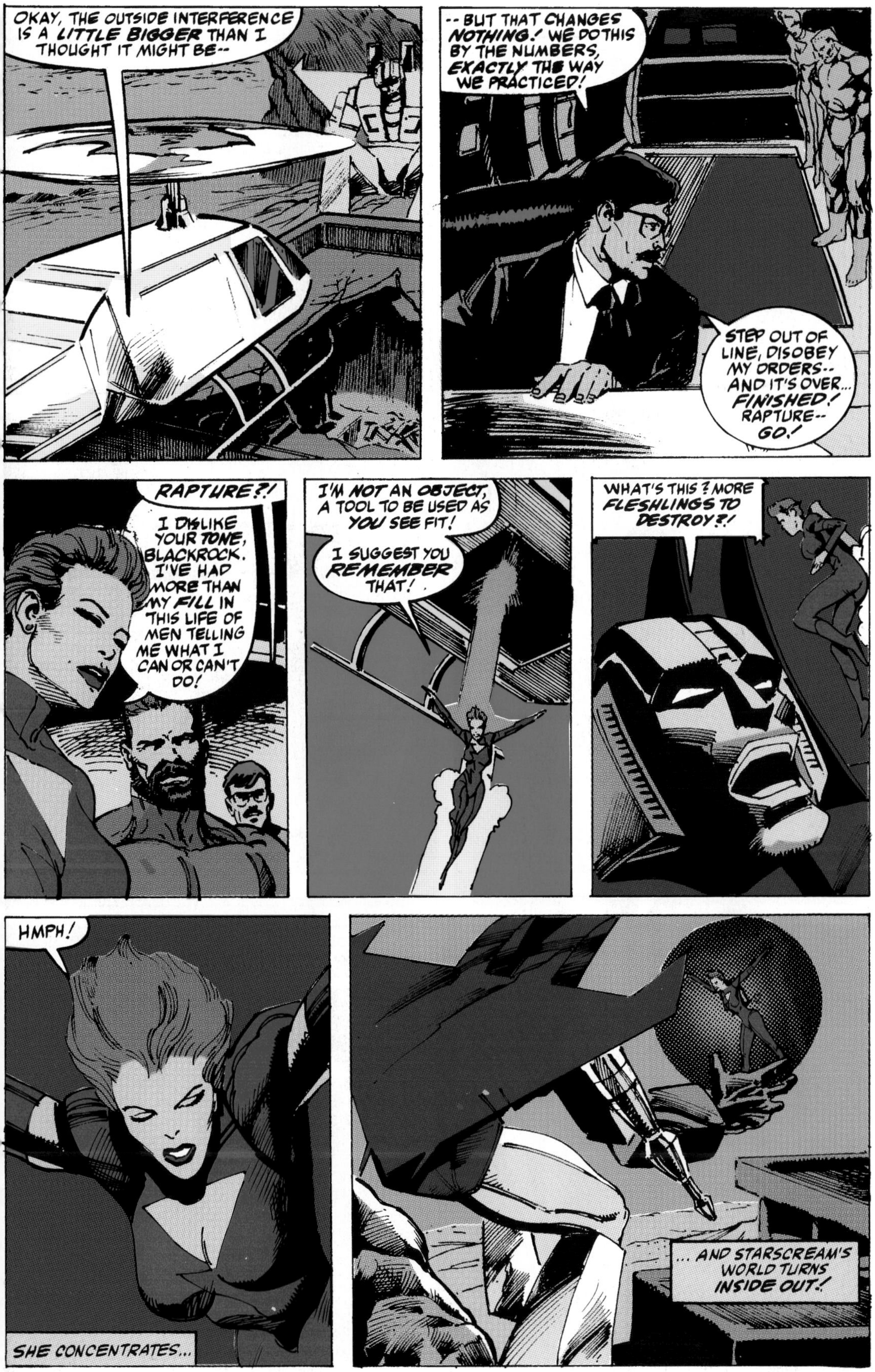
OKAY, THE OUTSIDE INTERFERENCE IS A LITTLE BIGGER THAN I THOUGHT IT MIGHT BE--
-- BUT THAT CHANGES NOTHING! WE DO THIS BY THE NUMBERS, EXACTLY THE WAY WE PRACTICED!
STEP OUT OF LINE, DISOBEY MY ORDERS-- AND IT'S OVER... FINISHED! RAPTURE-- GO!
RAPTURE?!
I DISLIKE YOUR TONE, BLACKROCK. I'VE HAD MORE THAN MY FILL IN THIS LIFE OF MEN TELLING ME WHAT I CAN OR CAN'T DO!
I'M NOT AN OBJECT, A TOOL TO BE USED AS YOU SEE FIT!
I SUGGEST YOU REMEMBER THAT!
WHAT'S THIS? MORE FLESHLINGS TO DESTROY?!
HMPH!
SHE CONCENTRATES...
... AND STARSCREAM'S WORLD TURNS INSIDE OUT!

HE HAS WON!

DEAD AUTOBOTS LIE SCATTERED AS FAR AS THE EYE CAN SEE.

THE DECEPTICONS HAIL THEIR NEW LEADER!

ONLY ONE TASK REMAINS...

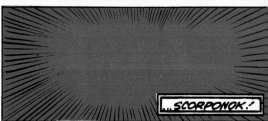

THE BEST PART...

...SCORPONOK!

SHE'S GOT HIM!

GO, THUNDER-PUNCH-- GO!!

THAMM!

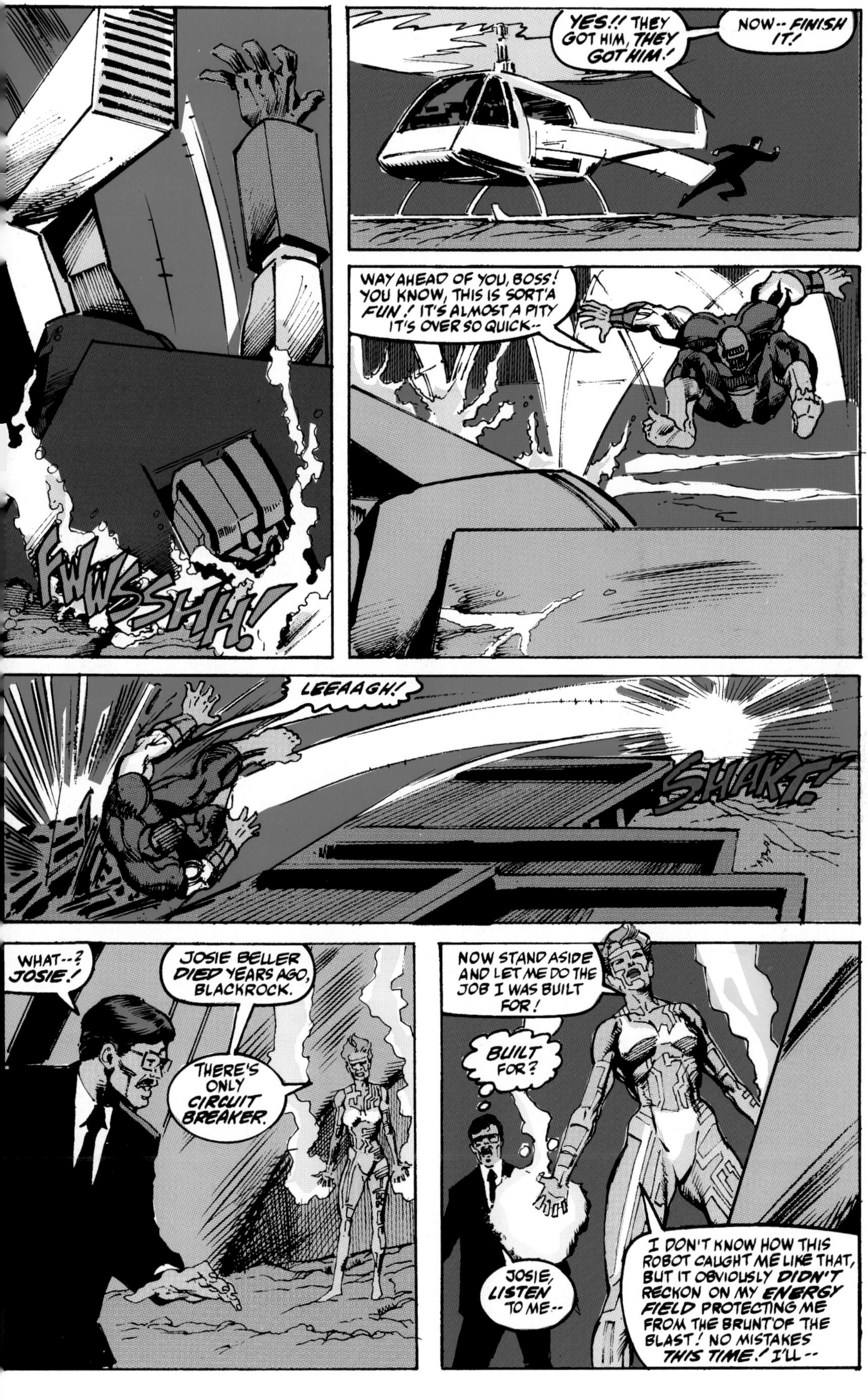

YES!! THEY GOT HIM, THEY GOT HIM!
NOW-- FINISH IT!
WAY AHEAD OF YOU, BOSS! YOU KNOW, THIS IS SORT'A FUN! IT'S ALMOST A PITY IT'S OVER SO QUICK--
KWWSSHH!
LEEAAGH!
SHAKT!
WHAT--? JOSIE!
JOSIE BELLER DIED YEARS AGO, BLACKROCK.
THERE'S ONLY CIRCUIT BREAKER.
NOW STAND ASIDE AND LET ME DO THE JOB I WAS BUILT FOR!
BUILT FOR?
JOSIE, LISTEN TO ME--
I DON'T KNOW HOW THIS ROBOT CAUGHT ME LIKE THAT, BUT IT OBVIOUSLY DIDN'T RECKON ON MY ENERGY FIELD PROTECTING ME FROM THE BRUNT OF THE BLAST! NO MISTAKES THIS TIME! I'LL--

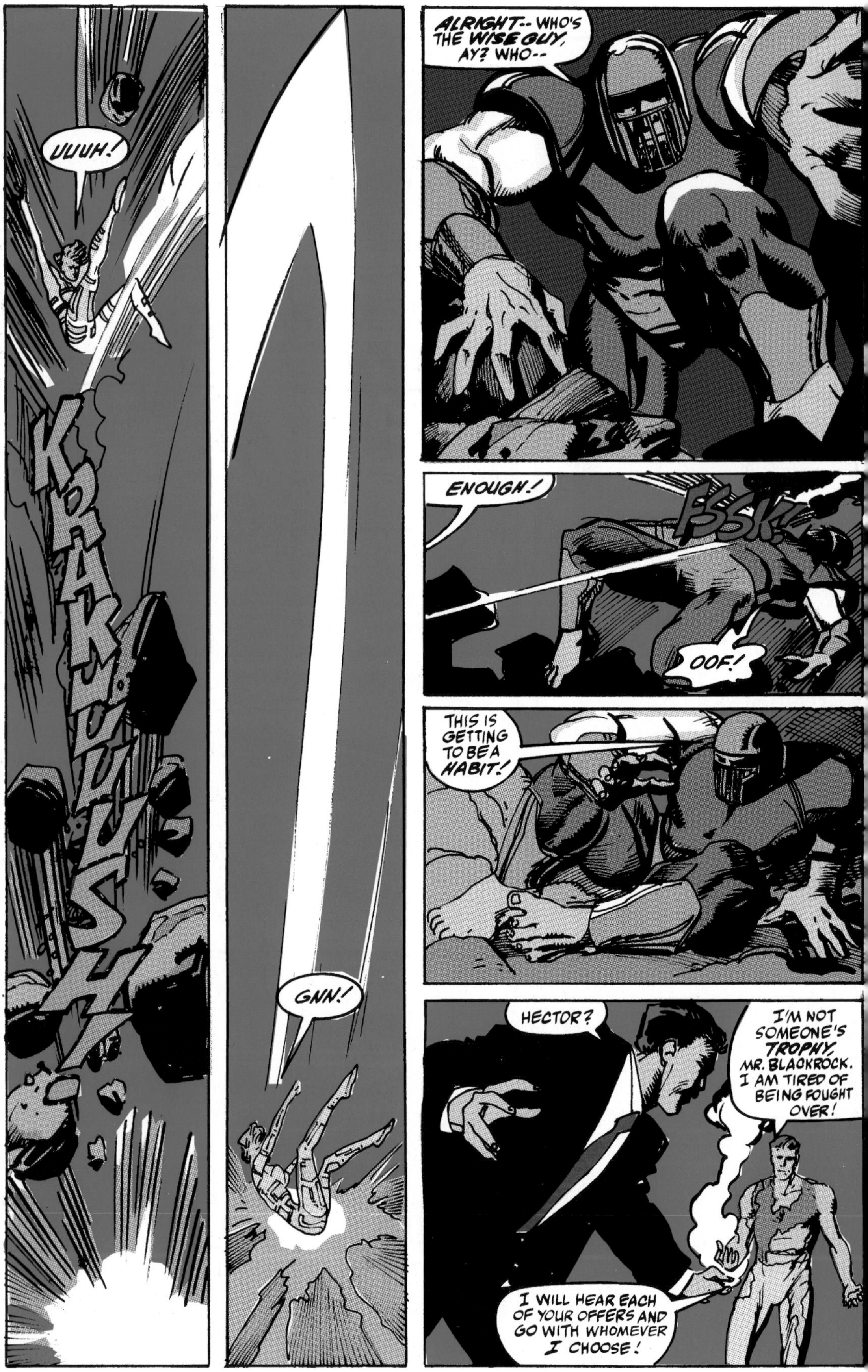
UUUH!
KRAKUUUUSH
GNN!
ALRIGHT-- WHO'S THE WISE GUY, AY? WHO--
ENOUGH!
FSSK!
OOF!
THIS IS GETTING TO BE A HABIT!
HECTOR?
I'M NOT SOMEONE'S TROPHY, MR. BLACKROCK. I AM TIRED OF BEING FOUGHT OVER!
I WILL HEAR EACH OF YOUR OFFERS AND GO WITH WHOMEVER I CHOOSE!

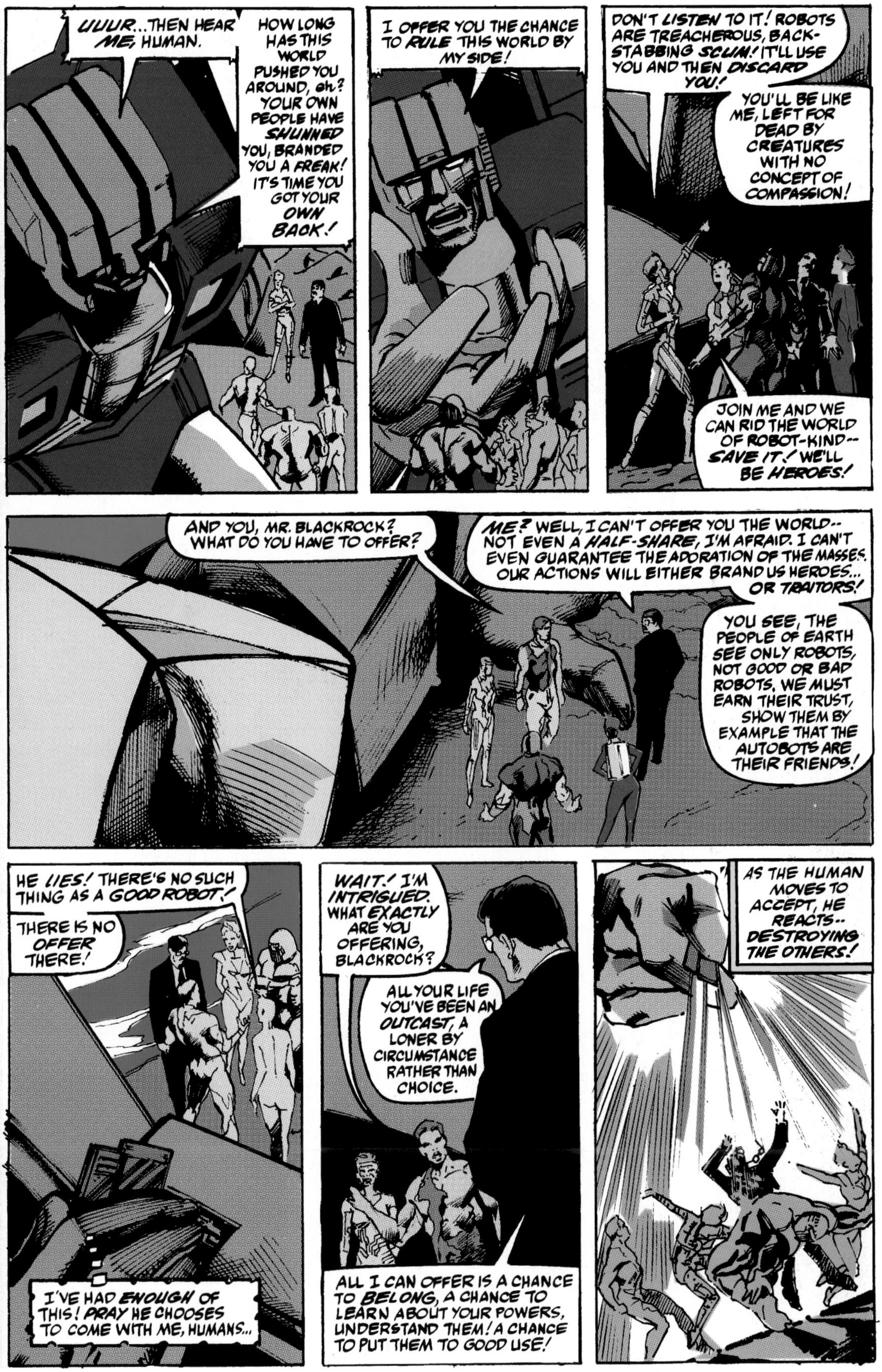
UUUR... THEN HEAR ME, HUMAN.
HOW LONG HAS THIS WORLD PUSHED YOU AROUND, eh? YOUR OWN PEOPLE HAVE SHUNNED YOU, BRANDED YOU A FREAK! IT'S TIME YOU GOT YOUR OWN BACK!
I OFFER YOU THE CHANCE TO RULE THIS WORLD BY MY SIDE!
DON'T LISTEN TO IT! ROBOTS ARE TREACHEROUS, BACK-STABBING SCUM! IT'LL USE YOU AND THEN DISCARD YOU!
YOU'LL BE LIKE ME, LEFT FOR DEAD BY CREATURES WITH NO CONCEPT OF COMPASSION!
JOIN ME AND WE CAN RID THE WORLD OF ROBOT-KIND-- SAVE IT! WE'LL BE HEROES!
AND YOU, MR. BLACKROCK? WHAT DO YOU HAVE TO OFFER?
ME? WELL, I CAN'T OFFER YOU THE WORLD-- NOT EVEN A HALF-SHARE, I'M AFRAID. I CAN'T EVEN GUARANTEE THE ADORATION OF THE MASSES. OUR ACTIONS WILL EITHER BRAND US HEROES... OR TRAITORS!
YOU SEE, THE PEOPLE OF EARTH SEE ONLY ROBOTS, NOT GOOD OR BAD ROBOTS. WE MUST EARN THEIR TRUST, SHOW THEM BY EXAMPLE THAT THE AUTOBOTS ARE THEIR FRIENDS!
HE LIES! THERE'S NO SUCH THING AS A GOOD ROBOT!
THERE IS NO OFFER THERE!
I'VE HAD ENOUGH OF THIS! PRAY HE CHOOSES TO COME WITH ME, HUMANS...
WAIT! I'M INTRIGUED. WHAT EXACTLY ARE YOU OFFERING, BLACKROCK?
ALL YOUR LIFE YOU'VE BEEN AN OUTCAST, A LONER BY CIRCUMSTANCE RATHER THAN CHOICE.
ALL I CAN OFFER IS A CHANCE TO BELONG, A CHANCE TO LEARN ABOUT YOUR POWERS, UNDERSTAND THEM! A CHANCE TO PUT THEM TO GOOD USE!
AS THE HUMAN MOVES TO ACCEPT, HE REACTS-- DESTROYING THE OTHERS!

THE HUMAN IS HIS-- HE HAS WON!

RAPTURE?

SAW THE ROBOT REACH FOR SOME KIND OF WEAPON AND *ZAPPED* HIM.

GOOD. I SUGGEST, PEOPLE--

"-- THAT WE PUT THIS ONE DOWN FOR GOOD!"

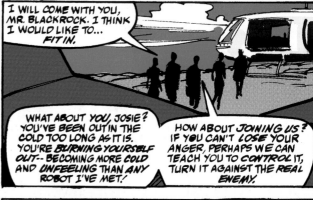

I WILL *COME* WITH YOU, MR. BLACKROCK. I THINK I WOULD LIKE TO... *FIT IN.*

WHAT ABOUT *YOU*, JOSIE? YOU'VE BEEN OUT IN THE COLD TOO LONG AS IT IS. YOU'RE *BURNING YOURSELF OUT*-- BECOMING MORE COLD AND *UNFEELING* THAN *ANY* ROBOT I'VE MET!

HOW ABOUT *JOINING US*? IF YOU CAN'T *LOSE* YOUR ANGER, PERHAPS WE CAN TEACH YOU TO *CONTROL* IT, TURN IT AGAINST THE *REAL ENEMY.*

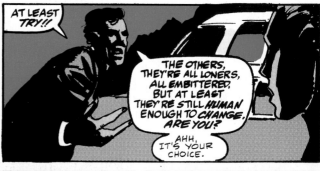

AT LEAST *TRY!!*

THE OTHERS, THEY'RE ALL LONERS, ALL EMBITTERED, BUT AT LEAST THEY'RE STILL *HUMAN* ENOUGH TO *CHANGE.* ARE YOU?

AHH, IT'S YOUR CHOICE.

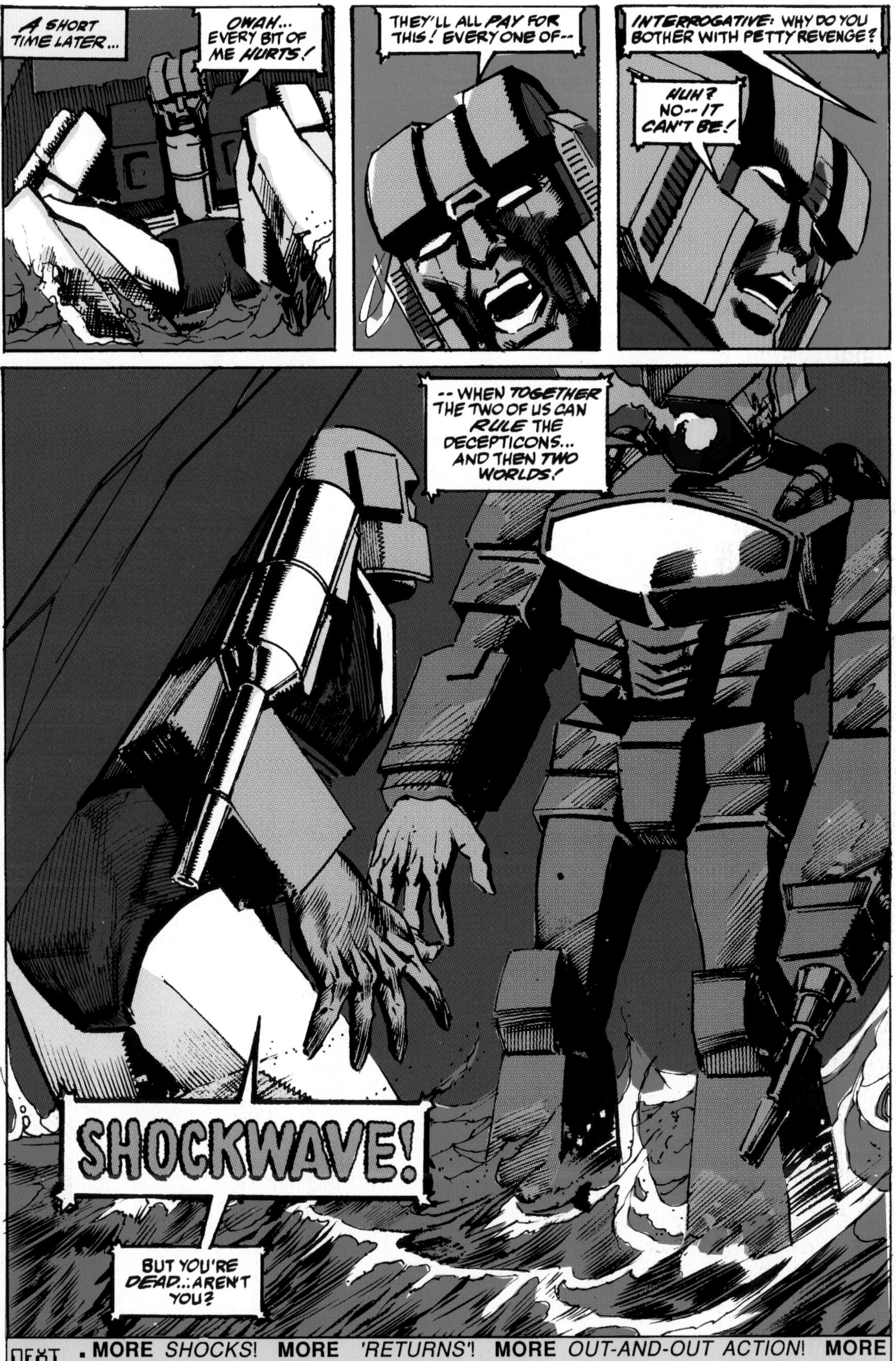

A SHORT TIME LATER...
OWAH... EVERY BIT OF ME HURTS!
THEY'LL ALL PAY FOR THIS! EVERY ONE OF--
INTERROGATIVE: WHY DO YOU BOTHER WITH PETTY REVENGE?
HUH? NO-- IT CAN'T BE!
-- WHEN TOGETHER THE TWO OF US CAN RULE THE DECEPTICONS... AND THEN TWO WORLDS!
SHOCKWAVE!
BUT YOU'RE DEAD...AREN'T YOU?


NEXT ISSUE ▪ **MORE** *SHOCKS*! **MORE** *'RETURNS'*! **MORE** *OUT-AND-OUT ACTION*! **MORE** ▪ *THRILLS*! AND **MORE** *STUPID EXCLAMATIONS*! **"The EYE of the STORM!"** in 30 days

Writer
Simon Furman

Pencillers
José Delbo, Geoff Senior & Dwayne Turner

Inkers
Dave Hunt, Geoff Senior, Al Williamson, Dan Reed &
Danny Bulanadi

Letterers
Jim Massara & Rick Parker

Colourist
Nel Yomtov

Original series editor
Don Daley

SIMON FURMAN began his long relationship with *Transformers* as of issue #13 of the UK comic. Since then, Furman's comics work has included *Transformers* (US), *Transformers: Generation 2*, *Death's Head*, *Alpha Flight* and *Turok*. Furman has also scripted episodes for animated TV series such as *Beast Wars*, *Dan Dare* and *X-Men: Evolution*. He is currently starting work on a new *Transformers* series for Dreamwave.

GEOFF SENIOR has been a Marvel UK mainstay for many years, drawing *Transformers*, *Dragon's Claws*, *Death's Head* and *Battletide* (to mention but a few). His US work has included *Transformers* and *What If?* Senior now works almost exclusively within the advertising industry.

JOSE DELBO drew no less than twenty-four of the original eighty issues of the US *Transformers* series. But that still only amounts to a small fraction of a credits list that includes *Action Comics*, *Batman*, *Conan*, *House of Secrets*, *Superman* and *Wonder Woman*.

DWAYNE TURNER has illustrated *Butcher Knight*, *Curse of the Spawn*, *Sovereign Seven* and *Witchblade/Tomb Raider: Dark Crossings*. He is also much in demand as a covers artist; his work can be seen on *Aliens vs. Predator vs. Terminator*.

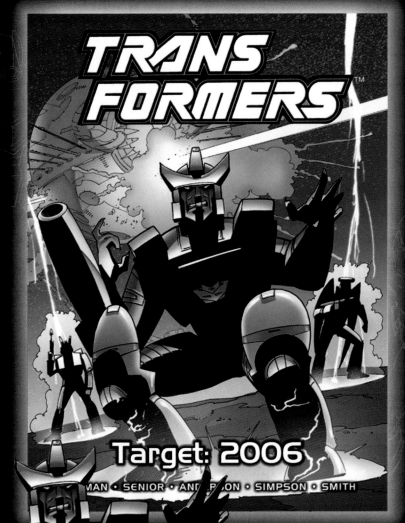

# TRANS FORMERS ™

## Target: 2006

...MAN • SENIOR • AN...R...ON • SIMPSON • SMITH

Transformers: Target 2006

ISBN: 1 84023 510 1

Spinning out from Transformers: The Movie, Galvatron travels back in time to wreak havoc on the Autobots and Decepticons and pave the way for future destruction.

Collecting the very best of the UK Transformers stories, not previously available in the US. Available through all good comic book stores. To order in the UK, telephone 01536 764 646 with your credit card details.

# #63 "KINGS OF THE WILD FRONTIER"

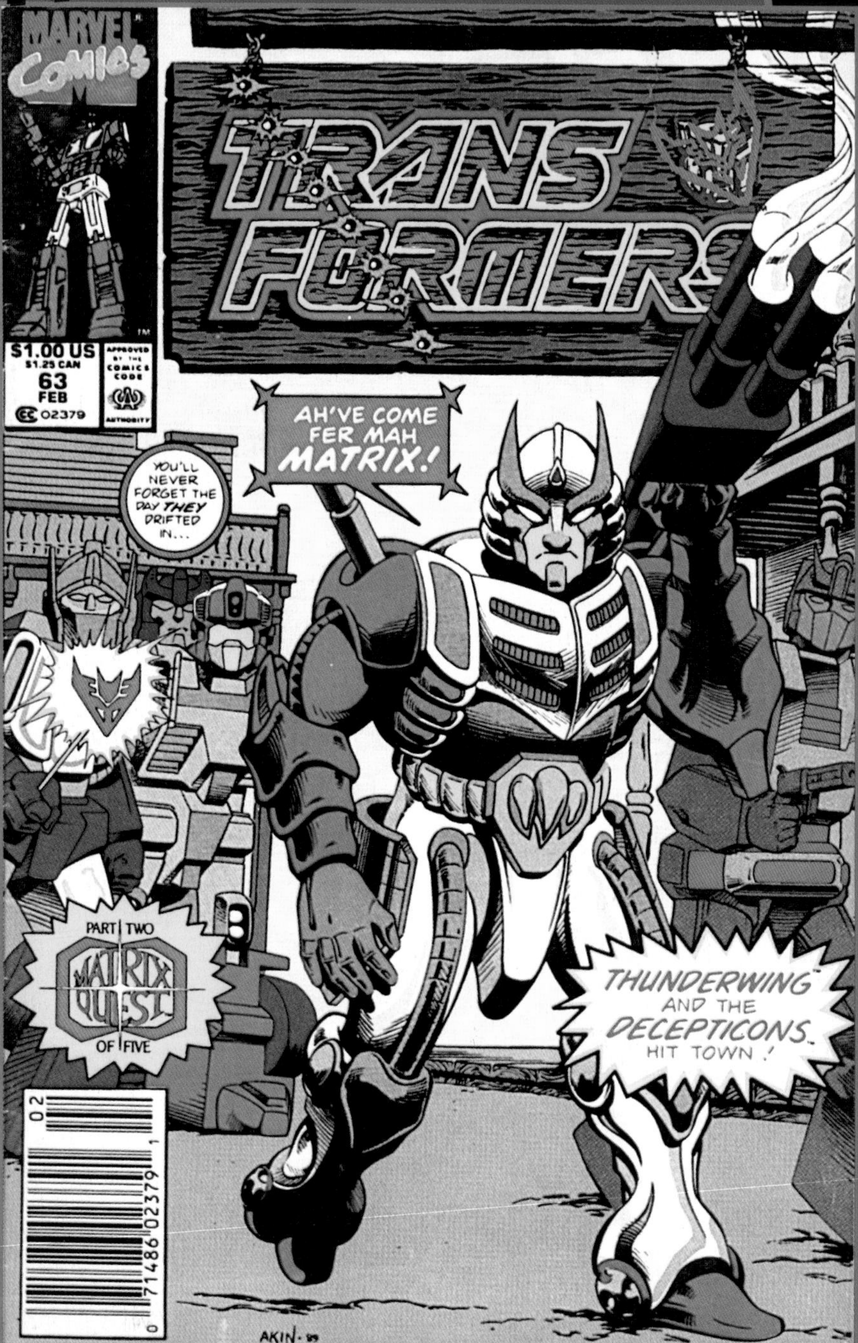
MARVEL COMICS
TRANSFORMERS
$1.00 US $1.25 CAN 63 FEB
APPROVED BY THE COMICS CODE AUTHORITY
AH'VE COME FER MAH MATRIX!
YOU'LL NEVER FORGET THE DAY THEY DRIFTED IN...
PART TWO MATRIX QUEST OF FIVE
THUNDERWING AND THE DECEPTICONS HIT TOWN!
AKIN

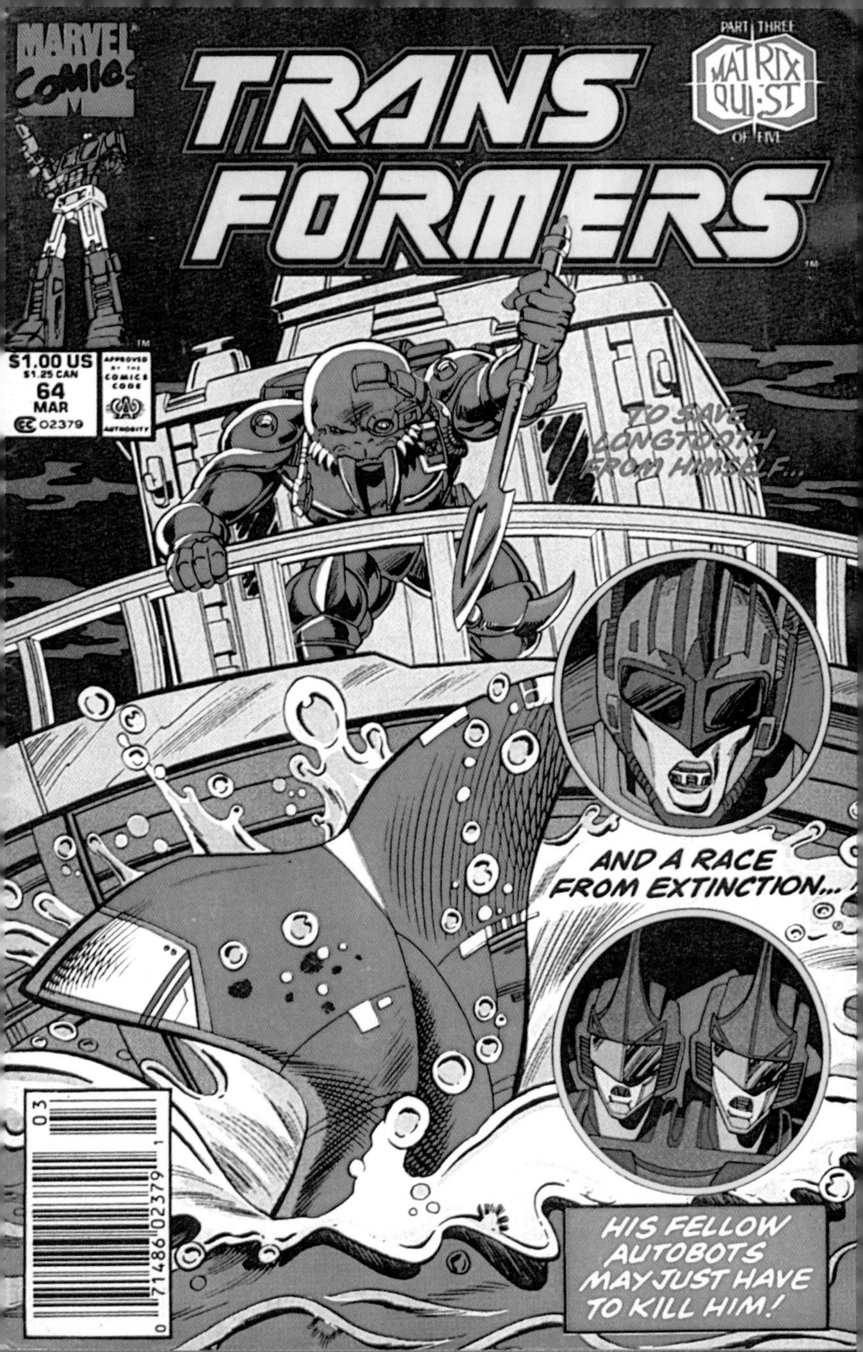
MARVEL COMICS
TRANSFORMERS
PART THREE
MATRIX QUEST
OF FIVE
$1.00 US
$1.25 CAN
64
MAR
APPROVED BY THE COMICS CODE AUTHORITY
TO SAVE LONGTOOTH FROM HIMSELF...
AND A RACE FROM EXTINCTION...
HIS FELLOW AUTOBOTS MAY JUST HAVE TO KILL HIM!

# #64 "DEADLY OBSESSION"

# #65 "DARK CREATION"

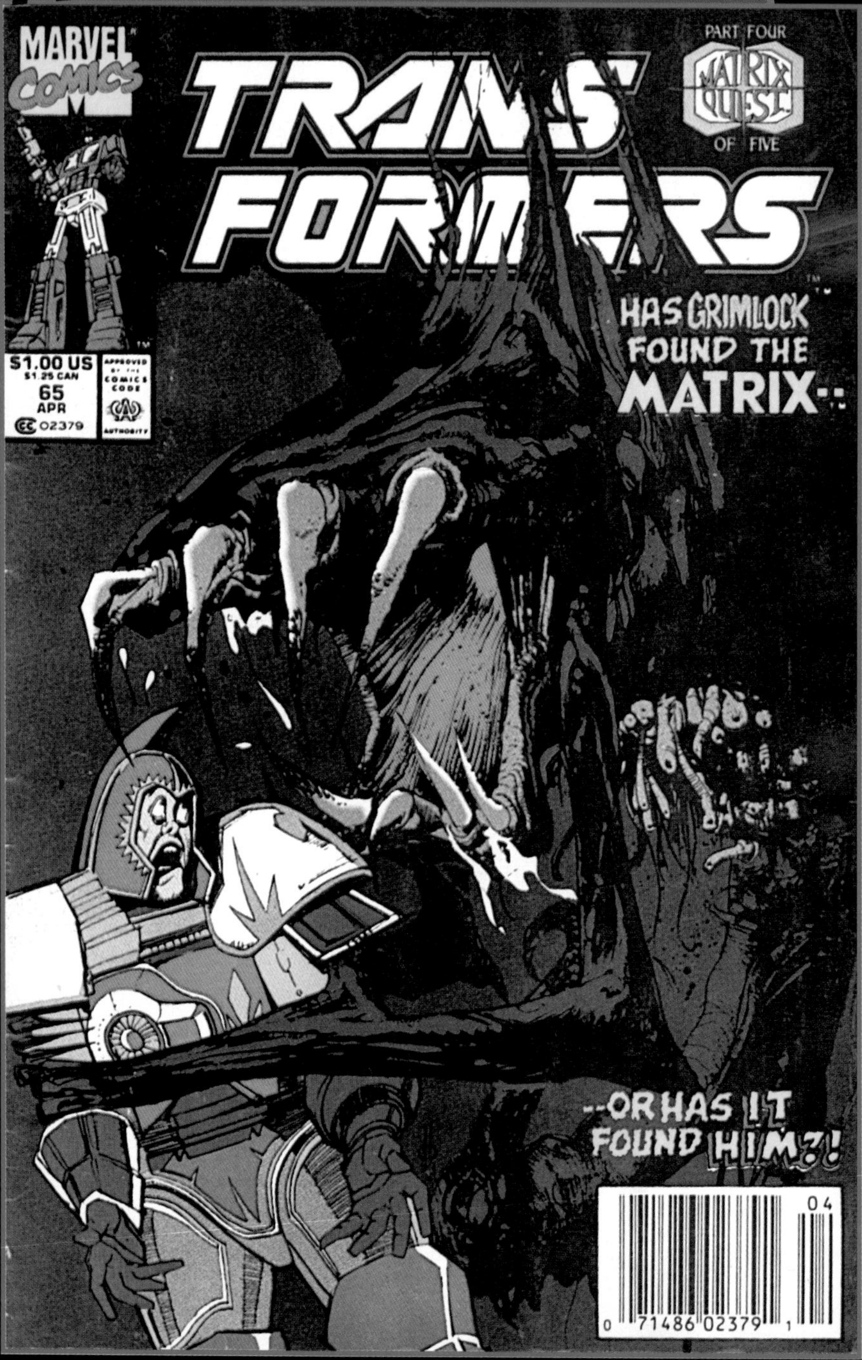
MARVEL COMICS
TRANSFORMERS
PART FOUR
MATRIX QUEST
OF FIVE
$1.00 US
$1.25 CAN
65
APR
02379
APPROVED BY THE COMICS CODE AUTHORITY
HAS GRIMLOCK FOUND THE MATRIX--
--OR HAS IT FOUND HIM?!

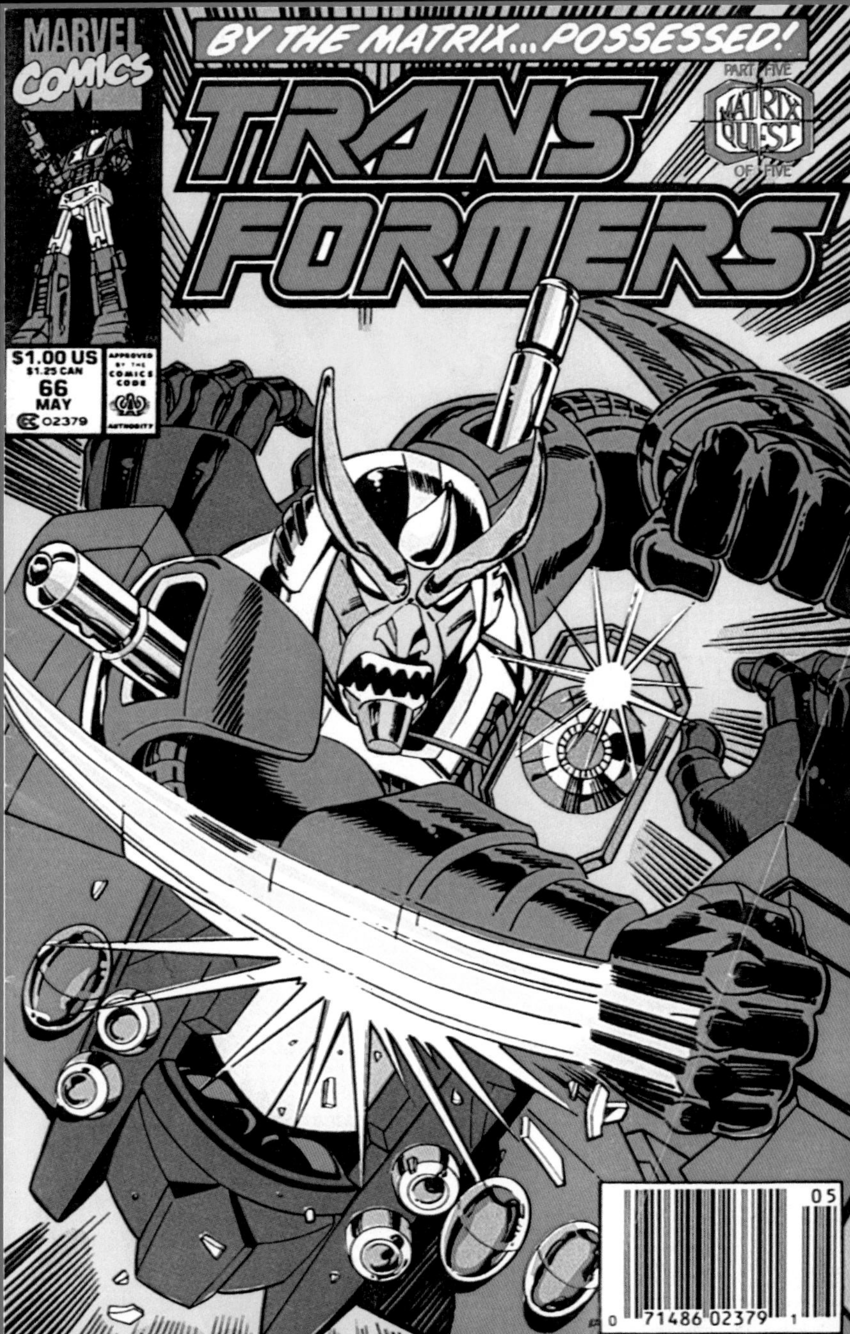
MARVEL COMICS
BY THE MATRIX... POSSESSED!
PART FIVE
MATRIX QUEST
OF FIVE
TRANS FORMERS
$1.00 US
$1.25 CAN
66
MAY
02379
APPROVED BY THE COMICS CODE AUTHORITY

# #66 "ALL FALL DOWN"

# #67 "RHYTHMS OF DARKNESS!"

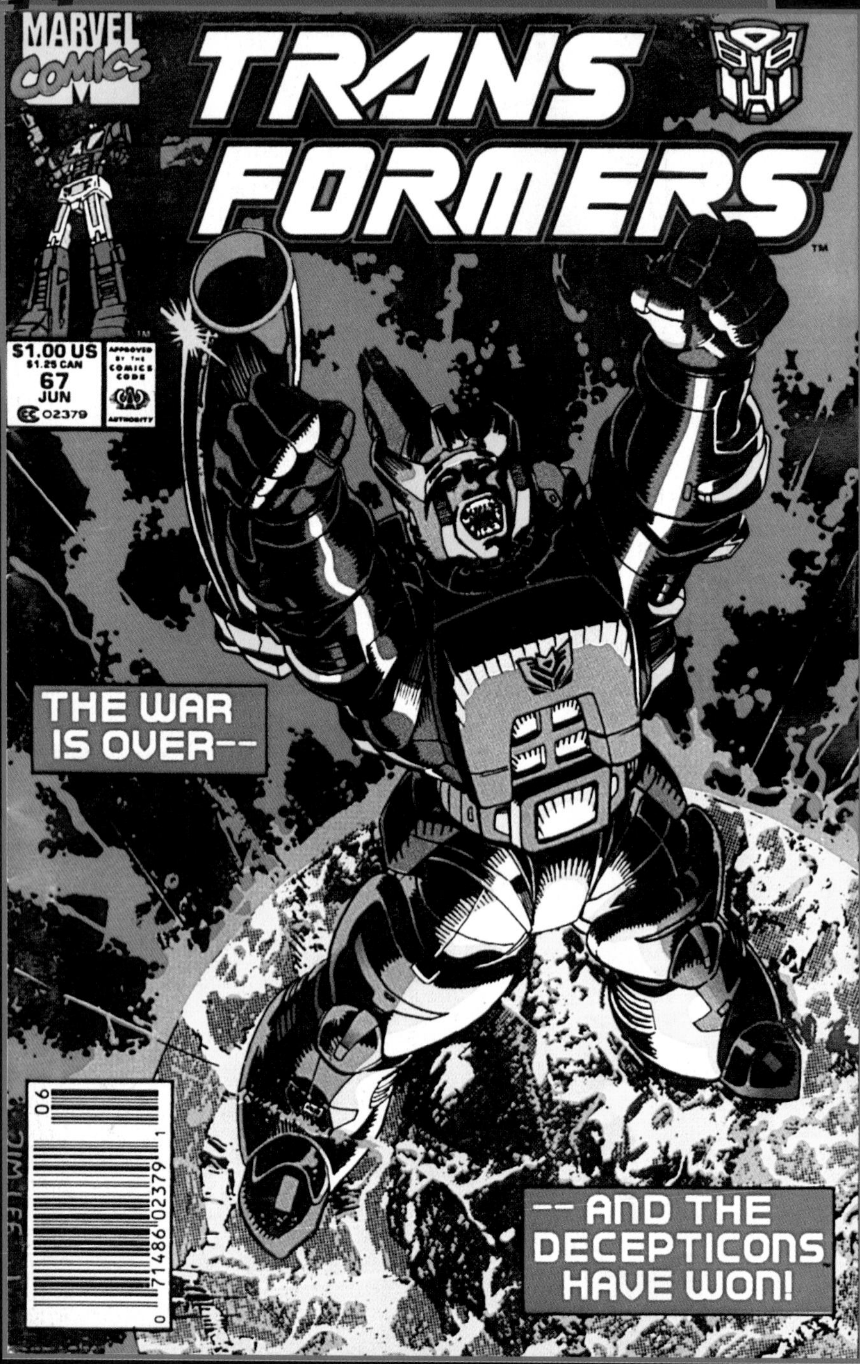
MARVEL COMICS
TRANSFORMERS
$1.00 US
$1.25 CAN
67
JUN
THE WAR IS OVER--
-- AND THE DECEPTICONS HAVE WON!

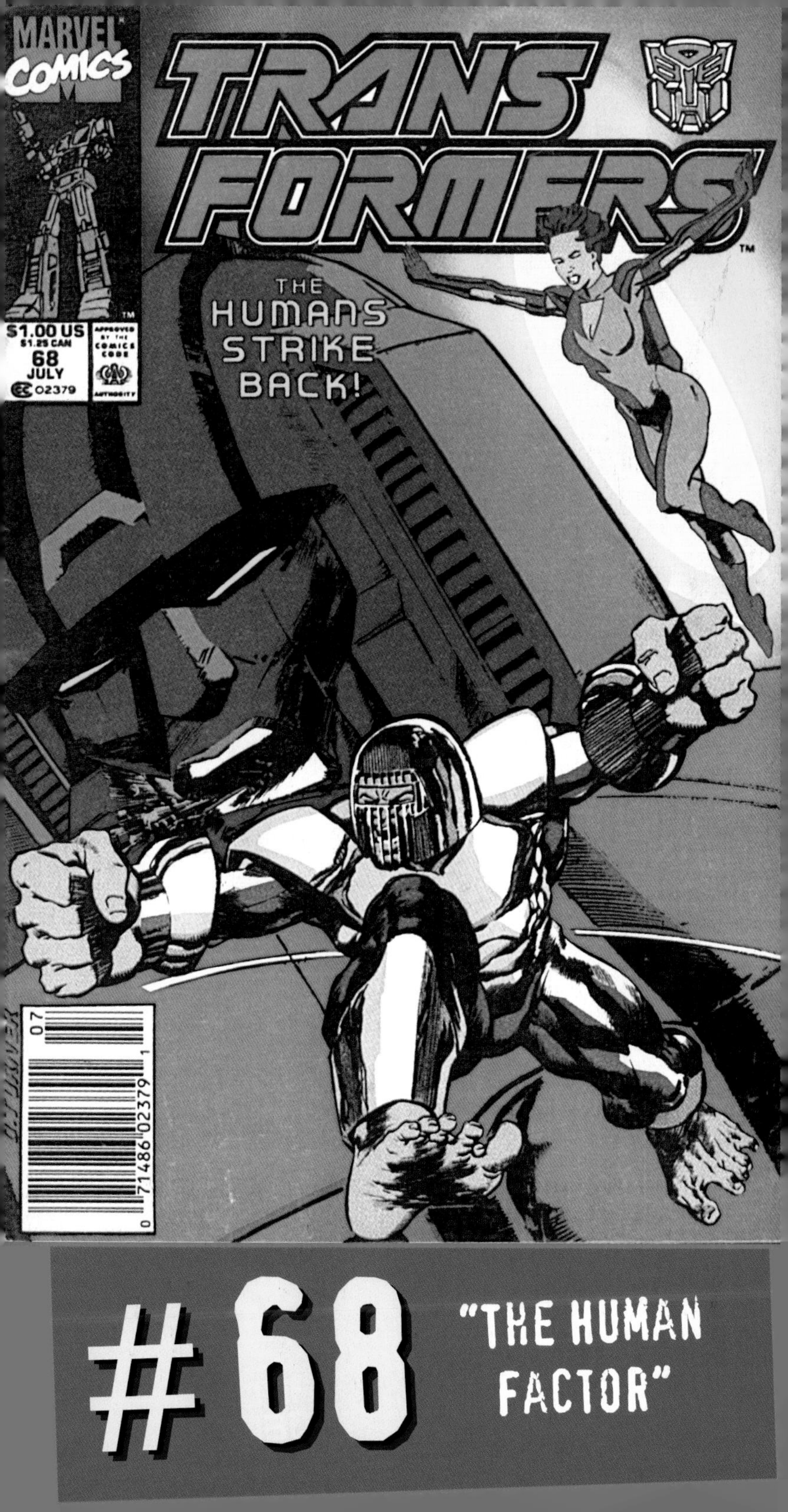
MARVEL COMICS
TRANSFORMERS
THE HUMANS STRIKE BACK!
$1.00 US
$1.25 CAN
68
JULY
02379
APPROVED BY THE COMICS CODE AUTHORITY

# #68 "THE HUMAN FACTOR"

# (MORE) SCRIPT NOTES...

As promised, and really whether or not you wanted it, more from the 'lost' script to *Transformers #56* (collected in the previous volume, *Transformers: Primal Scream*). I say 'lost', but in truth it's one of the very few of my original scripts I still have. Most are truly lost, a casualty of old, discarded computers/disks and clear-outs of paper. As I mentioned previously, this was done 'Marvel' plot-style, so the dialogue followed at a later stage, once I'd seen the artwork from José Delbo. It will, I hope, shed some light on the process behind comics scriptwriting, and while it's not essential to do so, you can probably get more out of it by comparing this script with the final printed version. And if that wasn't a cue to get yourself a copy of *Primal Scream*, I don't know what is.

## Pages 9-10:

Nevertheless... exterior view of the Ark as a shuttle streaks away from it, Earthbound. Int. Repair Bay, Ratchet still hard at work. He looks up, seeing a broadcast message from Optimus Prime on a nearby comm. screen. They are heading into battle, all Ark personnel must be on full alert. Ratchet groans. All that means is his workload goes up. How many more casualties this time? He slumps forward, and as he does catches a glimpse of something behind him, a flash (from an adjoining chamber). He turns, but there's nothing there. Prime was right, Ratchet thinks, he really does need a rest. Wide angle, as Ratchet goes back to work, we see a figure in the doorway, peering in. It's Detour. Focus on this adjoining chamber as Blackjack, Road Hugger and Hyperdrive appear, energy residue fading around them (note: all still have their fake Autobot insignias forefront). Road Hugger goes to work, removing a wall plate and tinkering with the systems behind it. Hyperdrive is antsy, unaccustomed to subterfuge, which prompts Detour to drop a disparaging remark. It almost comes to blows, but Road Hugger interrupts. It's about to begin. We cut back to Ratchet, in the Repair Bay, as (unnoticed by him) the part-dismantled body of Jazz jerks upright.

## Page 11:

Earth, and the Autobot shuttle comes in to land at MacDill Air Force base. Optimus Prime, followed by an Autobot strike force comprising GETAWAY, CLOUDBURST, LANDMINE, BLUR, SLAPDASH, HIGHBROW and HOT ROD, disembarks, utterly commanding, in control. Strangely, the gathered members of the Air Strike Patrol aren't perturbed in the least. In fact, as Tailwind whispers to, er, Whisper, we get the distinct idea this is all going exactly to plan.

## Pages 12-15:

The Ark again, int. Repair Bay. With a start, Ratchet realises it's got dark. He hears a noise, turns... and (dramatic) is shocked to see various reanimated Autobots stumbling towards him like it's the night of the living dead. Jazz, Blaster, Goldbug, Omega Supreme, Grimlock. He's hemmed in, trapped. It's like his dream, only this time for real! They close in, and Ratchet is knocked to the floor. He looks up to see the head of Blaster, on a telescoping repair arm, come face-to-face, nose-to-nose with him. Blaster tells him how he let them down, and since he couldn't reassemble them, they're going to *disassemble* him. Fast cut here to Road Hugger, speaking into a microphone (rigged up to that open panel we saw in the adjoining room). It's clear (from the dialogue link) that he's literally speaking for Blaster. Ratchet, meanwhile, is about to give up. Steely hands close around his throat. But then, he rallies, breaking free. He's no quitter... and whatever they say, he will find a way to fix them. In a mad scramble, still pursued, Ratchet makes for the emergency cut-off switch. But he pauses, if he does so, if he cuts power, that's it... game over. Their systems will degrade beyond the point he could ever fix them. Better just to let them have him. In the end, he's expendable.

This sentiment doesn't sit well with Road Hugger, who terminates the sequence. They needed Ratchet broken, but alive. Time for plan B. The Sports Car Patrol exit into the main Repair Bay, where Ratchet is struggling to free himself from under the collapsed Autobots. They claim to be Autobots, on their way back to Cybertron after consultation with Optimus Prime. They maybe have the answer to all his problems... he just has to come back to Cybertron with them. Ratchet, naturally, is suspicious, and tries to contact Optimus Prime. It's no go, the screen just a mess of static. Ratchet considers. He shouldn't abandon his post, but if there's a slightest chance... Gathering up the remains of Grimlock, Goldbug and Jazz, he joins Detour, Hyperdrive and Blackjack as they step into a shimmering Trans-time portal. As they start to fade away, Ratchet realises Road Hugger isn't with them, but it's too late. Ratchet reappears in Megatron's base on Cybertron, and is greeted by a chilling voice. He turns, horrified...

## Page 16:

... to see Megatron, full reveal. Dramatic final full page SPLASH, Megatron looming over Ratchet. Go for the full on, uplift, shock ending, as we learn that "Megatron lives again!"

To be continued.

# ROBOTS IN DISGUISE
## are back!

**Available in all good toy shops.**

DREAMWAVE PRODUCTIONS PRESENTS:
TRANSFORMERS™
the COMIC BOOK
AUTOBOTS
PROCLAIM YOUR ALLEGIANCE!
NOW AVAILABLE WHEREVER COMIC BOOKS ARE SOLD!
DECEPTICONS
o find a comic book store near you call :
888 COMIC BOOK (266-4226)
Look for Transformers Generation 1 and Armada Comic Books from Dreamwave Productions!
icensed by:
Hasbro
Consumer Products
www.Dreamwaveprod.com

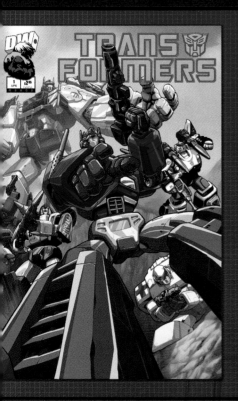

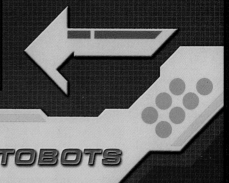

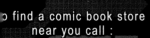

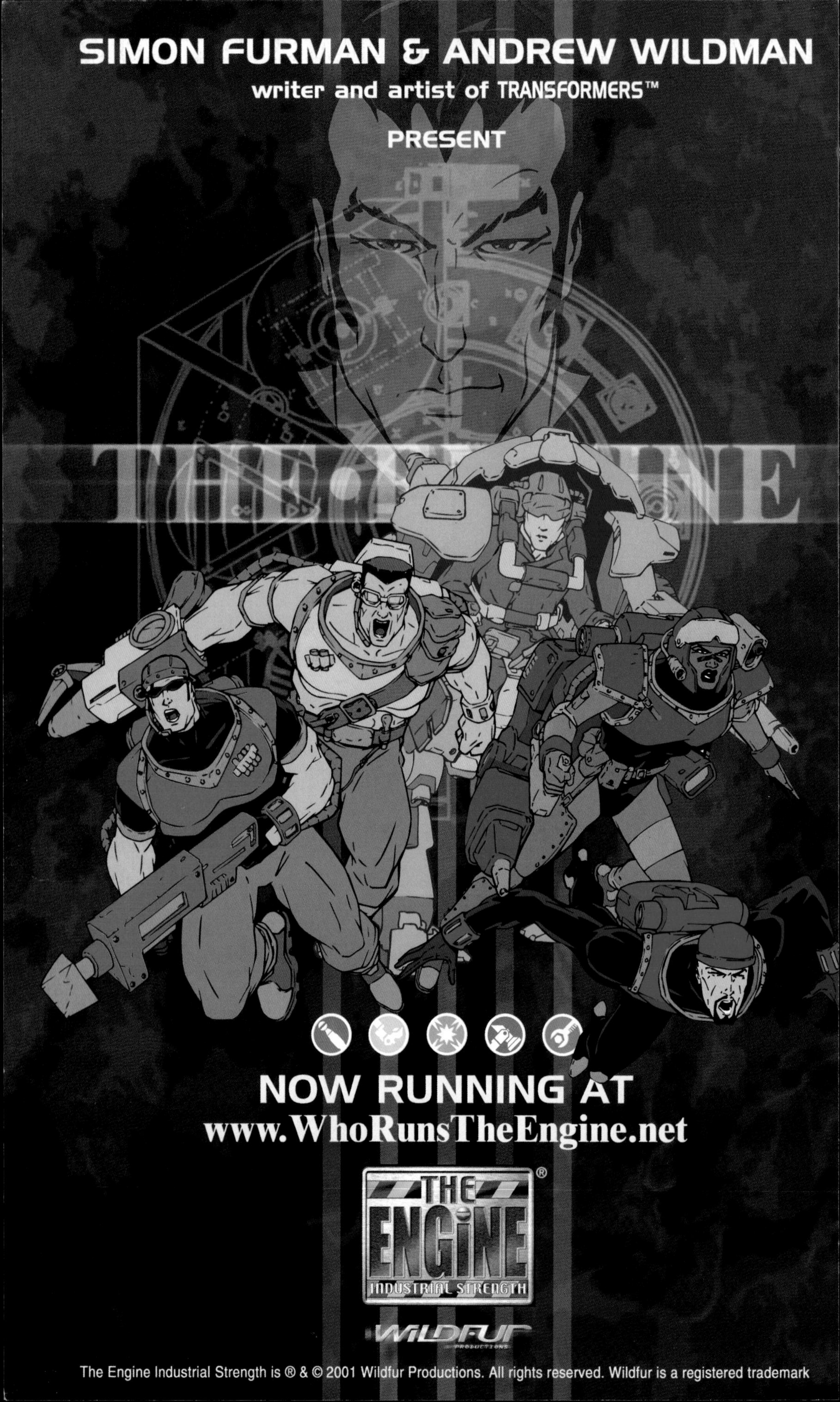

SIMON FURMAN & ANDREW WILDMAN
writer and artist of TRANSFORMERS™
PRESENT
THE ENGINE
NOW RUNNING AT
www.WhoRunsTheEngine.net
THE ENGINE
INDUSTRIAL STRENGTH
WILDFUR
The Engine Industrial Strength is ® & © 2001 Wildfur Productions. All rights reserved. Wildfur is a registered trademark